Contents

S0-BSR-401

for less guidebooks . . .

London for less is part of a revolutionary new series of guidebooks. Unlike "budget guides", these high quality guidebooks are designed to enable <u>every</u> visitor, however much they anticipate spending, to explore and to save money at the <u>best</u> places.

For less guidebooks cut your costs by providing you with specially negotiated discounts at hundreds of top attractions, hotels, tours, restaurants, shops, theaters and other venues.

These unique discounts ensure that, unlike any other guidebook, *for less* guidebooks really do "pay for themselves – in one day".

Over 100,000 people from 30 different countries have already saved money with *for less* guidebooks. If you look through this book you will quickly understand why *for less* guidebooks are becoming the natural choice for the intelligent traveler.

Customer Response Card

We want your comments so that we can continue to improve this book. On page 287 you will find a customer response card that you can mail back to us (at no postal cost) from anywhere in the world.

. . . *for less* guidebooks

For less guidebooks have been designed to make visiting a city as easy and pleasant as possible.

The simple, attractive, area-by-area format ensures that you can focus on enjoying the city and do not waste time puzzling your way through a complicated guidebook.

The substantial discounts are easy to obtain and can cut the total cost of a stay for an individual, a couple or a family by over 20%.

For example, each of the restaurants offers 25% off the total bill (including <u>all</u> food and beverage costs) at <u>any</u> time.

Uniquely, each *for less* guidebook comes with a fold-out city map, divided by neighborhood. This large map links to hundreds of mini-maps in the guidebook, enabling you to find exact locations quickly and easily.

How to Use *London for less*

London for less has been created to enable visitors to save money by obtaining discounts at the best places in London. All discounts are applicable for up to four people for up to eight consecutive days. Each page is colour coded as follows:

Attractions and Museums	Tours
Hotels	Restaurants
Shops	Performing Arts

Before you use the card, you must validate it by following the instructions printed underneath it on the inside front cover. The card should always be presented when you request the bill (check) and before payment is made.

Discounts apply whatever method of payment you choose, however, *London for less* cannot be used in conjunction with other offers or discounts.

Throughout this book, you will find the *London for less* logo. Every time it appears, it indicates that you are entitled to a discount.

Use of the card or vouchers must conform to the instructions on pages 7 and 8 and to the specific instructions set out in each entry.

All organizations offering discounts in this guidebook have a contract with the publisher to give genuine discounts to holders of valid *London for less* cards and/or vouchers.

Care has been taken to ensure that discounts are only offered at reputable establishments, however, the publisher and/or its agents cannot accept responsibility for the quality of merchandise or service provided, nor for errors or inaccuracies in this guidebook.

The publisher and/or its agents will not be responsible if any establishment breaches its contract (although it will attempt to secure compliance) or if any establishment changes ownership and the new owners refuse to honour the contract.

For post-publication updates and amendments to the discounts offered you should call ☎ 0181-964-8686. For any other information please call Metropolis International ☎ 0181-964-4242.

CREDIT CARD SYMBOLS USED

AM = AMEX
VS = VISA
MC = MASTERCARD
DC = DINERS CLUB
DS = DISCOVER

How to Obtain Discounts...

ATTRACTIONS AND MUSEUMS

To obtain discounts at attractions or museums you must either show your card or hand in a voucher which you will find at the back of the book. When you hand in the voucher you should circle the number of people in your party and also show your card.

At most attractions, discounts are available off the adult, child, senior and student prices. Children are usually defined as under 12, seniors as over 65. An index of attractions, museums and galleries that offer *London for less* discounts is on page 260.

Tower of London

HOTELS

For details of how to book hotels see page 32.

TOURS AND TRANSPORTATION

London for less offers you discounts on transfers into London from Heathrow, Gatwick and Stansted Airports (see pages 18-19). *London for less* also offers large savings on coach tours (pages 238-244), car rental (page 221), open-top bus tours (page 236), walking tours (page 237) and river trips (page 237).

To obtain the discounts, you must book as instructed in each tour's entry. You cannot book through a travel agent, hotel concierge or other intermediary.

Open-top bus tours

RESTAURANTS

London for less entitles you to a flat 25% off the total bill (check), including food and beverages, at 90 restaurants in London, listed on pages 263-264. The vouchers on page 285 entitle you to discounts at any Bella Pasta, Pizza Piazza or Pizzaland restaurant.

The price indicated is not a fixed or minimum price. It is only a guide to the average cost of a meal. It is based on a typical two-course meal for one person without an alcoholic drink. You are entitled to the discount however much you spend.

So that the service (tip) is not reduced by the discount, it is recommended that you tip on the total amount of the bill, before the discount is applied. A standard tip in London is 10-15% of the bill.

The Pavilion restaurant

SHOPS

London for less offers a 20% discount at 50 shops, listed on page 262. To obtain the discount, simply show the card before you pay for the goods. Discounts on goods already reduced in price or on sale are at the discretion of the shop's management.

Carlyle & Forge

. . . How to Obtain Discounts

PERFORMING ARTS

London for less offers you discounts on tickets for West End theater productions (see page 202). Unfortunately, we cannot guarantee that you will be able to obtain discounts for particular performances, as certain shows are frequently sold out.

Royal Shakespeare Company

FOREIGN CURRENCY EXCHANGE

With the voucher on page 283, you can change money commission-free at branches of Travelex / Mutual of Omaha listed on page 253. Their rates are competitive and you will save 100% on the transaction charge.

TELEPHONE CALLING CARD

Your *London for less* card acts as a calling card. Best of all, you receive £5 ($8) worth of free calls when you activate it. You can use it for all international or domestic calls. Calls are billed to your credit card and there are no connection charges.

To activate your *London for less* card as a discount calling card:

Dial freephone (toll free) 0800-0181800 and wait approximately 20 seconds for an operator (ignore the instruction to enter your card number and PIN).

Give the operator the last 8 digits of your *London for less* card and your credit card details. You will then be given a secret Personal Identification Number (PIN).

West End shows

To make a telephone call using your *London for less* card:

1. Dial 0800-0181716
2. Enter the last 8 digits of your *London for less* card followed by your PIN
3. At the second message, dial the country code + area code + telephone number you require (do not dial the international connection prefix "00")
4. If you have any problems dial * 0 and an operator will assist you at no charge.

You can continue to use your card to make phone calls anywhere in the world, forever. Ask the operator for a user guide with access numbers in 50 countries.

Some hotels even charge you for making toll-free calls. To avoid this, use your calling card at any public telephone.

Public telephone box

This calling card service is operated by Interglobe Telecommunications (International) PLC (☎ 44-(0)171-972-0800).

Introduction

Introduction to London . . .

'When a man is tired of London, he is tired of life; for there is in London all that life can afford.'
– Dr. Samuel Johnson

Each of the world's great cities has breathtaking monuments from its heyday: Istanbul has its Blue Mosque, New York its skyscrapers, Rome its classical and renaissance architecture. But only London has emerged from each era in its 2,000 years of history more magnificent, more varied and more richly endowed with the treasures of a long and proud civilization.

The Royal Household Cavalry

REFLECTIONS

'London: a nation, not a city.' – Benjamin Disraeli, Prime Minister (1874-80)

The unique appeal of London includes the splendid collections of the **British Museum** and the **National Gallery**, famous department stores like **Harrods** and **Liberty**, and 'must-see' attractions such as **Madame Tussaud's** and the **Tower of London**.

With its multiplicity of traditions and customs – from the pomp and ceremony of the **Changing of the Guard** at Buckingham Palace to the youthful vigour of the **Notting Hill Carnival** – London is a multicoloured tapestry of living history.

This happy marriage of old and new is most striking in the City, London's financial district and the site of the original Roman town. Gleaming office blocks surround the 1,000-year-old Tower of London.

The Tower of London

The City is Europe's financial centre, with many billions of pounds traded each day on the various exchanges: London has more Japanese banks than Tokyo and more American banks than New York.

On most maps, it is impossible to see the seams of London's patchwork of urban 'villages'. Yet many of these areas retain a good deal of the

The City from the Thames

. . . Introduction to London . . .

distinctive character they enjoyed before they were engulfed by the city's growth. **Chelsea**, with its chic boutiques and bars, as well as its streets of elegant terraced homes, is a world apart from the exotic cafés and shops of **Notting Hill's** ethnic melting pot. To help you make sense of London's vastness, the eight most important areas have each been given their own chapter in this guide and their boundaries are shown on the fold-out map.

Tower Bridge

London is an extraordinarily cosmopolitan city, with large Asian, Afro-Caribbean, Arab, Jewish and Chinese communities. It has a knack of adopting the best of each culture, with restaurants and shops from more than one hundred different countries.

Pigeons in Trafalgar Square

While various ethnic groups have settled in different areas – Afro-Caribbeans in Notting Hill, Arabs in Bayswater and Jews in Golders Green – no place has become the exclusive preserve of one culture. London, by and large, enjoys broad-minded racial harmony.

REFLECTIONS

'Oh, London is a fine town,
A very famous city,
Where all the streets are
paved with gold,
And all the maidens
pretty.' – George Colman
(1797)

Although Greater London stretches over more than 600 square miles, nearly all the major sights are within a compact area. The 100-year-old **Tube** network, which is constantly being overhauled, makes travel across the traffic-snarled city fast and simple. None of the main attractions is more than a ten-minute walk from a tube station.

London may have seven million inhabitants (not to mention 28 million visitors each year), but it is still possible to find, and enjoy, peaceful solitude. After fighting through the army of shoppers on **Oxford Street** or braving the British Museum's huge summer crowds, you can soothe jangled nerves with a stroll through one of London's many parks and gardens. Apart from the vast expanses of **Hyde Park/Kensington Gardens** and **Regent's Park**,

An aerial view of Westminster

. . . Introduction to London . . .

there are dozens of smaller gardens and grassy squares.

Britain's **royal family**, which has in the past decade become a daily soap opera, is perhaps the country's top tourist attraction.

Charles and Diana in happier days

Though they have a string of sumptuous palaces across the land, the royals spend much of their time in London. Some of their homes are open to visitors. **Buckingham Palace** (pages 50-51) can be visited during August and September, when the Queen holidays in Scotland. From May to December, you can tour **Kensington Palace** (page 191), home of Diana, Princess of Wales.

Di, as she is affectionately known in Britain's tabloid newspapers, is often to be seen around the exclusive streets of west London, flitting between her favourite Italian café off Kensington High Street and the top fashion store **Harvey Nichols** on Knightsbridge. At other times, she can be seen walking or roller-blading in Kensington Gardens.

Big Ben

There are several other former royal residences scattered across London. They include the mighty Tower of London (pages 138-139) on the river at the eastern edge of the City and Henry VIII's **Hampton Court Palace** (pages 212-213) several miles upstream to the west. **Windsor Castle** (pages 214-215), which was ravaged by fire in 1992 but is now being restored, requires a day trip.

Many visitors feel bound, like pilgrims, to visit London's world-renowned religious and cultural monuments such as **St. Paul's Cathedral** (pages 136-137), **Westminster Abbey** (pages 52-53) and the British Museum (pages 166-167). While these are undeniably impressive, the city abounds with beautiful churches and fine museums. One of the great pleasures of London is straying off the crowded tourist trail to find 'secret' treasures tucked away, like the tiny **Sir John Soane's Museum** (page 142), with its wonderfully eclectic art collection, or the picturesque tranquillity of **Little Venice** (page 184).

. . . Introduction to London

You will quickly learn that the cliché about English reserve is unfounded. Most Londoners have busy working and social lives, but, in general, they are friendly and helpful if you can get them to stop for a moment. It's true that no one talks on the Tube, but few will cold-shoulder your efforts to strike up conversation.

Another myth about London, or rather England, is that it rains all the time. This is not true, indeed, London has less rainfall than either

Parliament from the Thames

Paris or New York. It enjoys warm summers, which are rarely unpleasantly hot. The winters are mild, and even in the coldest month, January, the average temperature is over 6°C (43°F).

From the visitor's point of view, London enjoys another great advantage: personal safety. It has one of the

A young Londoner!

lowest violent crime rates of any capital city in the world.

Anyone visiting London in the late 1990s will be struck by the number of young tourists. They are drawn from around the world by the hundreds of fascinating micro-cultures, each with its own music, clothes and clubs. The rise of **'Britpop'**, spear-headed by the London-based bands Oasis and Blur, has created a new mood reminiscent of the Swinging Sixties and the heyday of the Beatles. In fact, London has become so trendy that the American magazine *Newsweek* recently dubbed London "the coolest city on the planet". By comparison, youth culture in other European cities can seem dull and uniform.

Whenever you visit London, in addition to the perennial attractions, special events will be taking place. The **Boat Show** in January, the **Chelsea Flower Show** in May, the **Wimbledon Lawn Tennis Championships** in June/July, the Notting Hill Carnival in August and the Lord Mayor's Show in November are just some of the highlights (see pages 246-247 for the calendar of events).

(see pages 246-247 for the calendar of events).

REFLECTIONS

'Cause in sleepy London town / There's just no place for a street fighting man!' – The Rolling Stones

Britpop phenomenon 'Oasis'

London: Area by Area . . .

WESTMINSTER

For centuries, this historic area has been the centre of political and royal power. Dozens of London's grandest buildings and monuments, including the Houses of Parliament, Nelson's Column, Westminster Abbey, 10 Downing Street and the Queen's London home, Buckingham Palace, are found in this area. It is the most popular tourist area but is also a working part of London with dozens of government offices.

WEST END

Always bustling with people, the West End is London's entertainment and theatre district. There are dozens of pavement cafés, lively pubs and trendy clubs drawing in massive evening crowds. Covent Garden offers daytime street entertainment, while Soho's bars and sex shops ply their trade into the small hours. Hundreds of restaurants serve every kind of cuisine. In Chinatown, centred on Gerrard Street, you will find a wide choice of Chinese food. Oxford Street and Regent Street form London's busiest shopping district.

MAYFAIR AND ST. JAMES'S

Once the home of Britain's aristocracy, this exclusive area now contains many of London's up-market clubs, art galleries and luxury hotels. Designer stores can be found on Bond Street. It is bordered by three royal parks, Hyde Park, Green Park and St. James's Park.

SOUTH KENSINGTON AND CHELSEA

Three magnificent museums – the Victoria and Albert, the Natural History and the Science – are the principal attractions in South Kensington. Harrods, the famous department store, and other luxury shops line Knightsbridge. Chelsea's King's Road, on the cutting edge of fashion since the 1960s, has many popular shops, bars and restaurants.

... London: Area by Area

CITY OF LONDON

London's financial district boasts some of the capital's finest historic buildings, including St. Paul's Cathedral, the Tower of London and Tower Bridge. The medieval street pattern remains though the skyline is now dominated by office blocks like the NatWest Tower and futuristic new buildings like Lloyd's of London. The City becomes a ghost town in the evening and at weekends when the 300,000 office workers have gone home.

SOUTH OF THE RIVER

The once dilapidated southern river frontage has sprung to life in recent years, with impressive developments such as London Bridge City and Butler's Wharf. Shakespeare's reconstructed Globe Theatre has recently joined the South Bank arts centre in attracting both tourists and Londoners across the river.

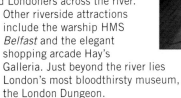

Other riverside attractions include the warship HMS *Belfast* and the elegant shopping arcade Hay's Galleria. Just beyond the river lies London's most bloodthirsty museum, the London Dungeon.

BLOOMSBURY AND MARYLEBONE

The British Museum sets the tone for Bloomsbury, a neighbourhood replete with cultural and literary associations. Its leafy squares and the smart 18th-century streets around Portland Place are full of architectural gems. Further west, there are two hugely popular attractions: Madame Tussaud's and the London Planetarium.

BAYSWATER AND NOTTING HILL

Bayswater contains many of London's tourist hotels, with Queensway and Whiteley's shopping mall staying open until late in the evening. Portobello Market is the star attraction of Notting Hill, a trendy residential area packed with interesting little restaurants, modern art galleries and seriously hip bars.

Before You Go . . .

WHEN TO GO

Tourists visit London all year round, but the high season is from June to September. Attractions are most crowded in July and August, during the school summer holidays.

There are special events nearly every weekend and on holidays throughout the year (see pages 246-247).

London's climate is generally mild, with average daytime temperatures ranging from a low of 10°C (50°F) in winter to a high of 20°C (70°F) in the summer. Summer and winter extremes are rare, as is air-conditioning in London buildings.

VISAS AND ENTRY REQUIREMENTS

Virgin Atlantic Airways

All visitors require a valid passport to enter the United Kingdom, except European Union (EU) citizens who can show their identity card instead. Visas are not needed by visitors from the EU, the United States, Canada, New Zealand or Australia. Citizens of all other countries should check visa requirements with the local British embassy before they leave home.

For import restrictions on duty-free goods, see page 250. Pets cannot be brought into Britain without a six month quarantine period, because of the danger of rabies.

MONEY

The currency is Sterling: 100 pence (p) equals one pound (£). Most major credit cards, especially MasterCard and Visa, are widely accepted in London. Many of the automatic teller machines offer cash advances on credit and debit cards. Only a few major stores accept Sterling traveller's cheques as a cash alternative. For

Travelex foreign currency exchange

commission free (i.e. no transaction charge) currency and travellers cheque exchange at Travelex/Mutual of Omaha see page 253 and the vouchers on page 283.

London is an expensive city, and the average daily tourist budget, excluding accommodation but

. . . Before You Go

including entrance prices, meals, transportation and entertainment, is approximately £50 per person.

HEALTH AND INSURANCE

There is little risk of contracting an infectious disease in Britain. Citizens of EU countries are entitled to free National Health Service (NHS) treatment, though they

must provide the appropriate form showing that their country has a reciprocal arrangement.

Citizens of other countries get free on-the-spot treatment at accident and emergency units at NHS hospitals, but must pay for all other medical services. Health insurance is, therefore, advisable for visitors. Pharmacists can only

A West End theatre

dispense a limited range of drugs without a doctor's prescription.

PACKING FOR LONDON

A warm coat is needed in winter and a jacket is advisable in summer, when there are occasional cold, wet days. An umbrella is useful throughout the year.

Electricity is 240 volts (at 50 hz) with unique, square, three-pin plugs. Most travellers will need an adaptor and sometimes an electric current converter. Shaver sockets in hotels conform to the international standard.

BOOKING A HOTEL ROOM IN ADVANCE

London hotels tend to be fairly expensive and fill up quickly in high season. You should therefore book as far ahead as possible. With *London for less* you can

A bedroom at the Dorchester Hotel

obtain specially discounted rates at 42 hotels listed on pages 33 to 46. For information on how to book these see page 32.

BOOKING THEATRE TICKETS IN ADVANCE

It is a good idea to book seats well in advance for the more popular London shows. The *London for less* ticket line (page 202), which is operated by Ticketmaster, takes 24-hour credit card bookings for all West End shows. Remember to ask which shows offer *London for less* discounts and check if there is a booking fee.

Arriving in London . . .

CHANGING MONEY AT THE AIRPORT

Although credit cards are widely accepted in London you will need cash for transportation, entrance prices and food. You can change money at Travelex branches at Heathrow and Gatwick when you arrive (see page 253 for a listing of branches and 283 for vouchers).

GETTING FROM THE AIRPORT

HEATHROW AIRPORT

 Airbus Express is a frequent, walk on/ walk off scheduled bus service between all **Heathrow** terminals and the centre of London.

Airbus bus service - Heathrow

When you arrive at the airport simply follow the signs marked "Airbus". There are two services: the A1 Express goes to Victoria via Earl's Court, Cromwell Road and Knightsbridge; the A2 Express goes to Kings Cross via Bayswater, Marble Arch, Russell Square and Euston. Both services run approximately every 30 minutes from 5am to 9pm every day and take 1½ hours. Tickets cost £6 single (reduced to £5 with the voucher on page 275) and £10 return (reduced to £8 with the voucher on page 275).

Alternatively, the **Piccadilly Line tube** to central London runs approximately every 15 minutes, takes one hour and costs £3.20 single, £6.40 return. A **taxi** to central London takes 45 minutes and costs £30-40. A new overland train link to central London (Paddington Station) is due to open in the summer of 1998. From autumn 1997 until then, a coach service will operate the "Paddington Shuttle" route.

Flightline coach service - Gatwick and Stansted

GATWICK AIRPORT

Flightline coach service from **Gatwick** to Marble Arch and Victoria runs once an hour from 5am to 8pm and takes 1½ hours. Tickets cost £7.50 single (reduced to £5.50 with voucher on page 273) and £11 return (reduced to £7 with voucher on page 273). Children travel at half the adult price.

Alternatively, the **Gatwick Express** train to Victoria leaves every 15 minutes and takes 30 minutes: £8.90 single, £17.80 return. A **taxi** to central London will cost up to £60.

. . . Arriving in London

Flightline coach service from **Stansted** to Marble Arch or Victoria runs once an hour from 8am to 10pm and takes 1½ hours. Tickets cost £8 single (reduced to £6 with voucher on page 273) and £12 return (reduced to £8 with voucher on page 273). Children travel at half the adult price.

Alternatively, the **train** to London Liverpool Street leaves every 30 minutes, takes 45 minutes and costs £10 single, £20 return. If you take a **taxi**, it will cost close to £100!

GETTING AROUND LONDON

If time is at a premium, you can avoid time-consuming travel and concentrate your sightseeing each day on a particular area. To help you do this, *London for less* is organized into areas.

Bus and coach tours - Taking a guided tour on an open-top double-decker bus is the best way to orient yourself and see most of the capital's major sites. Several companies operate bus tours, including London Pride, which offers a 50% discount to *London for less* card holders (page 236). If you would prefer a

more luxurious overview of the city you can take a Frames Rickards guided coach tour (pages 238-244).

A London double-decker bus

The Underground (tube) - The tube is the easiest way to get around London. Trains run every three to ten minutes, depending on the time of day. Travelcards, either for a single day, for a weekend or for a whole week, offer unlimited travel on tubes, buses and trains within central London, and can be bought at any tube station (see page 258).

Double-decker buses - The ordinary red double-decker buses, which operate hundreds of routes around London, can be complicated for visitors to understand. The Travelcard works on the buses too.

Taxis - A ride in one of London's famous black cabs is a unique experience.

A London black cab

However, even short journeys will usually cost you at least £5. You are most likely to need a cab after midnight, when the tube stops running. Unfortunately, at this time it can be hard to find one that is available.

Planning Your Trip . . .

IF YOU HAVE ONE DAY

This itinerary will give you a flavour of London life and afford a glimpse of the riches of English culture.

Sightseeing - Head for Trafalgar Square, from where you can walk down Whitehall to the Houses of Parliament (pages 54-55) and Westminster Abbey (pages 52-53). A stroll through St. James's Park (page 194) brings you to the Queen's London residence, Buckingham Palace (pages

St. Paul's Cathedral

50-51). Unless you are a dedicated royal watcher, it's not worth queuing to go inside when it is open in August and September. After lunch head east – preferably on an open top double-decker bus (see below and page 236) – to the Tower of London (pages 138-139) and St. Paul's Cathedral (pages 136-137). From there, head down to the River Thames and walk along Victoria Embankment, back towards Westminster. Waterloo Bridge, on a curve in the river, offers the finest views of London.

A river trip

Double-decker bus tour - Starting and finishing at Piccadilly Circus, the 90-minute tours usually cover two huge loops around the west and east of the city. Tickets are valid for 24 hours and allow you to hop on and off to visit attractions (see page 236 for discount).

Lunch in a pub - Most pubs in central London serve food at lunchtime and usually offer traditional English dishes, like shepherd's pie and rhubarb crumble.

Afternoon tea - Several of the up-market hotels and shops offer special afternoon teas (sandwiches, cakes, scones and

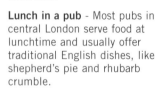

A typical London pub

different varieties of tea), usually available from lunchtime until early evening. The crème de la crème is tea at the Ritz or the Dorchester (pages 256-257), costing over £20.

West End show - Many of Broadway's biggest hits start life in London, the world's theatre capital. Andrew Lloyd Webber has a string of long-running hit musicals

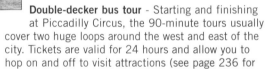

. . . Planning Your Trip

but there are also dozens of other theatres showing new plays or inventive revivals. For discounts on tickets for West End shows see page 202.

IF YOU HAVE TWO DAYS

Spreading the previous itinerary over two days will be far more relaxing. The extra day should allow you to spend an afternoon exploring a major museum or historical site, such as the British Museum (pages 166-167). A late afternoon walk through the peaceful tree-lined paths of Hyde Park will help recharge your batteries.

The British Museum

IF YOU HAVE THREE OR FOUR DAYS

Harrods

A trip to the South Kensington museums (pages 114-116) will take up most of a day, but can be combined with shopping at nearby Harrods (page 117) and walking in the gardens beside Kensington Palace (pages 190-191).

London's renowned street markets (page 252) offer bargains galore and the chance to buy exotic and quirky goods.

DON'T MISS

On Fridays and Saturdays Portobello market in West London has antiques, jewellery, trendy clothing and stores that sell food from around the world (page 252)

IF YOU HAVE ONE WEEK

A week allows you to go in search of hidden London: the hundreds of smaller museums, historic buildings and characterful streets that are glossed over by tourist brochures. Here are some ideas:

1. Highgate Cemetery (page 207), which inspired Bram Stoker's *Dracula*, contains the tombs of hundreds of intellectuals and artists, including Karl Marx, Michael Faraday and George Eliot.

2. The City of London, which has 36 churches (many built by Wren) and a number of ancient guild and livery company buildings (Apothecaries' Hall is the most impressive, inquire at the tourist office beside St. Paul's).

Hampton Court Palace

3. A guided walk around one of London's many historic neighbourhoods, such as the Bloomsbury literary walk, the East End Jack the Ripper walk or the London of Sherlock Holmes (see page 237).

4. A day-trip by river boat from Westminster Pier to Greenwich (page 237) or Hampton Court Palace.

If You Do One Thing . . .

These ten ideas may not be the most famous
or popular destinations, but they are an
honest selection of personal
favourites.

If you visit one attraction:

Tower of London
(page 138)

If you go to one art gallery:

Wallace Collection
(page 171)

If you walk in one park:

Holland Park
(page 121)

If you go to one nightclub:

Ronnie Scott's
(page 201)

If you dine at one traditional
English restaurant:

Veronica's
(page 185)

If you take one tour:

London Pride open-top bus
(page 236)

If you go to one store:

Liberty
(page 69)

If you visit one museum
(apart from the British):

Victoria & Albert (V & A)
(page 114)

If you make one excursion:

Boat trip to Greenwich
(page 212 & 237)

If you visit one church:

St. Paul's Cathedral
(page 136)

History . . .

London began life in 43AD, when the **Emperor Claudius** decided to establish a far-flung outpost of the Roman empire beside the River Thames. Roman Londinium stood in the vicinity of the present day financial district known as the City.

The Romans stayed for almost 400 years and, during their occupation, London became a thriving port.

In the 5th century, the Teutonic Saxons took control of the settlement, which was attacked repeatedly over the next few centuries by marauding Vikings. **King Alfred the Great** built up London's fortifications in the 9th century, but governed his kingdom from Winchester, 50 miles to the south.

It was not until **William the Conqueror** invaded Britain in 1066 that London gained a great ruler. William was the first monarch to be crowned at Westminster Abbey, where most subsequent coronations have taken place. He made London his capital and strengthened its defences, building the White Tower, a key riverside fortress, which remains the centrepiece of the Tower of London to this day.

Head recovered from Temple of Mithras (Museum of London)

REFLECTIONS

'London, thou art the flower of cities all!/ Gemme of all joy, jasper of jocunditie.' – William Dunbar (1501)

'This blessed plot, this earth, this realm, this England.' – *Richard II*, William Shakespeare (1595)

The city's merchants thrived during the Middle Ages, developing a trading empire that stretched across Europe. Unfortunately, many of the fine religious buildings erected with the profits were destroyed during **Henry VIII's** Protestant Reformation of the 1530s. In recompense, his turbulent reign saw the construction of Hampton Court Palace a few miles up river.

It was during the reign of **Elizabeth I** (1558-1603) that London first emerged

Queen Elizabeth I (National Portrait Gallery)

as a great cultural capital. Several theatres, such as the Rose and the Globe, were built to show new plays by Shakespeare and others.

. . . History . . .

London experienced massive population growth in the 16th century and, by 1600, it had more than

16th-century view of London with the Globe and Rose theatres, old London Bridge and old St. Paul's

200,000 inhabitants. As a result, the densely packed streets along the main thoroughfare of the Thames became overcrowded and filthy.

The physical decay of London was mirrored by the moral decay of the monarchy under **Charles I** (1625-1649). When the English Civil War broke out, ordinary Londoners – who detested the extravagance of the royal court – supported **Oliver Cromwell** instead. The war culminated in the beheading of **Charles I** in Whitehall in 1649.

However, the city's merchants rapidly became disillusioned with Cromwell, who reneged on promises of democratic reform and assumed the quasi-royal title of Lord Protector. As a result, two years after Cromwell's death in 1658, **Charles II** was welcomed back to the throne. Cromwell's body was disinterred and his head spiked on the roof of Westminster Hall.

REFLECTIONS

'Pish! A woman might pisse it out.' – Lord Mayor of London on seeing the beginning of the Great Fire of 1666

The Great Fire of London

In 1665, the Great Plague blighted the city's slums, claiming 75,000 lives. The following year, the Great Fire broke out, destroying two-thirds of the city, including 87 churches.

The fire allowed planners and architects like Sir Christopher Wren to redesign much of the city, and dozens of beautiful churches were built as the cornerstones of blossoming London neighbourhoods. Wren's masterpiece, St. Paul's Cathedral, rose majestically above the revitalised city.

. . . History . . .

During the 18th century, London grew rapidly as the nobility moved out of the cramped city to spacious, elegant mansions further west. London's intellectual life flourished in the Georgian era, with the opening of the British Museum (1759) and the establishment of learned societies, such as the Royal Academy (1768).

Crystal Palace built in Hyde Park for the Great Exhibition (1851)

With the construction of the West India Dock to the east of the city in 1802, London became the largest port in the world. 19th-century London saw unprecedented development, with a dozen bridges built across the Thames and a complex railway network laid out with termini ringing the city.

During the reign of **Queen Victoria**, who ruled for 63 years from 1837 to her death in 1901, a quarter of the world's land mass was governed from London. The imperial pride of Victorian London was expressed in Hyde Park's hugely successful Great Exhibition (1851), the profits from which left an enduring legacy of museums and cultural institutions in South Kensington.

REFLECTIONS

'The capital [London] is become an overgrown monster.'
– Scottish novelist Tobias Smollett (1771)

By 1901, London's population had topped 6.5 million and its suburbs stretched ten miles in each direction from the city centre.

St. Paul's during the Blitz

During the First World War (1914-18), London suffered its first aerial bombardment, but it was nothing to compare with the catastrophic destruction wrought by the Blitz in the Second World War (1939-45). More than 30,000 people were killed by bombs and many historic buildings, including the Houses of Parliament and Westminster Abbey, were either damaged or destroyed. Miraculously, St. Paul's Cathedral survived almost unscathed, while the surrounding streets were levelled to the ground.

. . . History

In the 45 years since the coronation of **Queen Elizabeth II**, London has grown upwards, with thousands of new office blocks and high-rise flats. Fortunately, much of the capital's distinctive architecture has been spared and a few striking buildings, such as Canary Wharf Tower and the Lloyd's Building, have been added.

In the 1950s, mass immigration from Britain's former colonies helped give London its fascinating ethnic

mix. Some areas, such as Notting Hill and parts of Camden, became ghettos, but in recent years they have been transformed into lively, colourful areas.

Margaret Thatcher and a young Londoner

Despite the steady erosion of the British Empire throughout the 20th century, London has retained its importance. It is, for example, one of the world's leading financial centres.

During the twelve years Margaret Thatcher was Prime Minister (1979-1992), London experienced an economic boom, but lost its governing authority, when she abolished the socialist Greater London Council in 1986.

The problems that have beset the Royal Family, with all three of the Queen's married children getting divorced, were symbolized by the terrible fire at Windsor Castle in 1992. However, the Queen has striven to maintain royal dignity and continues to represent the nation at historic ceremonies, such as the opening of the Channel Tunnel in 1994. Once worlds apart, London and Paris are now connected by a three-hour express train.

Windsor Castle

The launch of the National Lottery in 1994 has raised hundreds of millions of pounds for charitable causes, including London's great arts institutions, such as the Royal Opera House and the Tate Gallery. A gigantic millennium exhibition, to rival the Great Exhibition of 1851, is planned for Greenwich in 1999.

Timeline . . .

ROMAN

43 AD Roman Emperor Claudius invades Britain and establishes Londinium as a key port and garrison. He builds the first London Bridge across the Thames, 50 metres east of today's London Bridge.

61 The Iceni people, led by their queen Boadicea, massacre the Romans and burn down the town.

200 The Romans construct massive fortifications around a rebuilt London.

410 Emperor Honorius withdraws the last Roman troops, leaving London at the mercy of Saxon pirates. London is abandoned for the next two centuries.

SAXON

604 The Saxons control most of England and develop the area immediately to the west of the Roman walls, known as Ludenwic. The chronicler Bede records the building of the first St. Paul's Cathedral.

VIKING

871 After decades of raiding, the Vikings establish London as their winter base.

886 Alfred the Great, the Saxon Christian King of Wessex, defeats the Vikings. He rebuilds London's walls and turns the city into a major trading centre.

984 The Vikings start trying to re-conquer London, finally succeeding in 1013.

1016 The Viking leader Canute becomes King of all-England and pronounces London the national capital, in place of Winchester.

1042 London expands westwards after Edward the Confessor becomes king. He moves his court and church upstream to Thorney Island and builds a magnificent palace so he can oversee construction of his 'West Minster', later Westminster Abbey.

NORMAN

1066 William the Conqueror defeats King Harold at the Battle of Hastings. He crowns himself William I at Westminster Abbey, a tradition followed ever since. He grants the city a charter guaranteeing its semi-autonomy.

1290 The Jews are expelled from London and are not allowed to return for 400 years.

1348-50 The Black Death, or bubonic plague, wipes out half the capital's 50,000 population.

1381 The Peasants' Revolt, in which hundreds of clerics and merchants are lynched, is only quelled when the peasants' leader, Wat Tyler, is stabbed to death by Mayor William Walworth at Smithfield.

... Timeline ...

1300-1400 English culture continues to blossom, with Geoffrey Chaucer (1340-1400) producing the first truly great work of literature in English with the publication of *The Canterbury Tales*.

1477 William Caxton, working in Westminster, publishes the first printed book in England.

1485 Henry VII initiates 120 years of Tudor rule, during which London enjoys rapid growth, more than doubling in population to 200,000 by 1600.

1533 Henry VIII breaks with the Catholic church and commences the dissolution of the monasteries.

1566 The Royal Exchange is founded, establishing London as a leading market for world trade.

1574 The City of London bans theatres, forcing companies to decamp to the south bank of the Thames. In 1599, the Burbages build the Globe, where Shakespeare premières many of his plays.

1605 Guy Fawkes's Gunpowder Plot to blow up Parliament is thwarted.

1643 The power struggle between Charles I and Parliament erupts into Civil War. Londoners successfully defend the capital against royalists.

1649 Charles is beheaded. Oliver Cromwell rules Britain as a Commonwealth.

1660 The monarchy is restored, Charles II is crowned.

1665 The Great Plague kills over 75,000.

1666 The Great Fire destroys two-thirds of the City, including 87 churches, 13,200 houses and St. Paul's Cathedral.

1675 The foundation stone of Sir Christopher Wren's new St. Paul's Cathedral is laid.

1710 London has a population of 575,000 and is the largest city in western Europe.

1751 An Act of Parliament restricts gin retailing which had led to alcoholism of epidemic proportions in London's overcrowded slums.

1759 The British Museum opens.

1801 First census reveals a population of 959,000.

1802 West India Dock opens in marshes to the east of the City; the huge docks serve ships from the rapidly expanding British Empire.

. . . Timeline

1816 Architect John Nash begins laying out grand terraces and circuses. Much of London as we know it today is built during the 19th century.

1833 Construction of London's rail network begins.

VICTORIAN

1837 Queen Victoria is crowned, aged 18, and rules for 63 years until her death in 1901.

1851 The Great Exhibition, held in Hyde Park, attracts six million visitors and funds the construction of South Kensington's museums, as well as the Royal Albert Hall.

1890 The first electric 'tube' line (part of the present Northern Line) opens in tunnels excavated far below ground level.

EDWARDIAN

1914 Outbreak of World War I, during which London experiences its first aerial attacks from Zeppelin airships.

INTER-WAR YEARS

1936 Edward VIII abdicates to marry American divorcée Wallis Simpson.

1939 Outbreak of the Second World War. Aerial bombardment, known as the Blitz, destroys 130,000 houses and kills 30,000.

POST-WAR LONDON

1950s The post-war demand for manpower leads to mass immigration from Britain's colonies.

1956 The Clean Air Act is passed to rid London of its infamous smog.

1965 The Greater London Council is established.

1977 The tube is extended to Heathrow Airport, making London the world's first capital city to have such a link.

1981 The 600-foot (180-metre) NatWest Tower, then Britain's tallest building, opens.

1986 Prime Minister Margaret Thatcher abolishes the Greater London Council.

1990 Worst riots in many decades as thousands gather in Trafalgar Square to protest over the new Poll Tax. London's population stands at seven million, with an additional 28 million annual visitors.

1995 Huge public celebrations outside Buckingham Palace and in Hyde Park mark the 50th anniversary of the Allies' Victory in Europe.

1997 British General election, London seen as key to victory.

Hotels

Booking a Hotel Room

BHRC desk at Heathrow Airport

London hotels are expensive by international standards. In association with the British Hotel Reservation Centre (BHRC), *London for less* offers you up to 50% off the published room rates at over 40 hotels.

In order to obtain the published discount, you must book your rooms through the BHRC, either by fax on +44-(0)171-828-6439 or by telephone on +44-(0)171-828-0601. Bookings made directly with hotels or through other booking agents (such as tour operators, tourist authorities or travel agents) will not be eligible for the *London for less* discount.

Because London is extremely busy at particular times of the year, and hotel accommodation can be difficult to find, it is recommended that you book well in advance.

The £ symbols by each hotel's entry indicate the standard double room rates, before the *London for less* discount. £=under £60, ££=£61-90, £££=£91-120, ££££=£121-150, £££££=over £150. To find out what rate you can obtain with *London for less*, you must contact the BHRC. Breakfast is included where mentioned.

After you have decided how much you would like to spend, you should choose the area in which you would like to stay. Most hotels are located either in Bayswater or South Kensington. For a summary of London's areas see pages 14-15.

As long as your card is valid on the first night that you intend to stay in the hotel you can stay as long as you like at the discounted rate (subject to room availability).

BHRC desk at Victoria Station

The number of stars under each hotel's name indicate its quality:

★★ : At least half the bedrooms have en suite bath/ shower rooms and may also have phones and TVs.

★★★ : Full reception services, more formal restaurant and bar arrangements, bedrooms all have en suite facilities, mostly with baths.

★★★★ : More spacious accommodation offering high standards of comfort and food. The range of services should include porterage, room service, formal reception and often a selection of restaurants.

HOTEL FACILITIES

 Shower

 Bath

 Minibar

 Tea / coffee making

 Room service

 24-hour room service

 Radio

 TV

 Satellite / cable TV

 Direct dial telephone

 Wake-up call

 Hairdryer

 Trouser press

 Room safe

 Non-smoking rooms

Air conditioned rooms

Laundry service

Babysitting service

 Elevator / lift

 Disabled facilities

 Secretarial services

 Fitness centre

Swimming pool

Airways Hotel

★★

29-31 St. George's Drive
Westminster

Airways Hotel is housed in an elegant 19th-century building within walking distance of Victoria train and coach stations. The bedrooms are well-equipped and the tariff includes a traditional English breakfast. *(40 rooms)*

PRICE CATEGORY

££

The Rochester Hotel

★★★★

69 Vincent Square
Westminster

The Rochester is housed in a handsome Victorian building overlooking a quiet square. All bedrooms boast hand-carved rosewood furniture and marble finished bathrooms. The rate includes breakfast. *(70 rooms)*

PRICE CATEGORY

£££££

Rubens Hotel

★★★

Buckingham Palace Road
Westminster

Situated opposite the Royal Mews at Buckingham Palace, the Rubens Hotel has one of the best locations in London. The rooms are attractive and well-appointed. There is an excellent restaurant and bar. *(180 rooms)*

PRICE CATEGORY

££££

PRICE CATEGORY

££

PRICE CATEGORY

££££

PRICE CATEGORY

£££

Flora Hotel International

★★

**11-13 Penywern Road
South Kensington**

The Flora Hotel International is conveniently located close to Earl's Court tube station. Its rooms have all recently been modernized and refurbished. The room rate includes breakfast. *(53 rooms)*

The Strathmore Hotel

★★★

**41 Queen's Gate Gardens
South Kensington**

Once the London residence of the Earl of Strathmore, this hotel blends Victorian grandeur with contemporary luxury. It is located close to Knightsbridge tube station. Breakfast is included in the rate. *(77 rooms)*

The Albany Hotel

★★★

**4-12 Barkston Gardens
South Kensington**

Located close to Earl's Court tube station, The Albany Hotel has been elegantly fitted with Chinese furniture. It has a quiet lounge, a lively bar, a coffee shop and a Chinese restaurant. *(38 rooms)*

 Kensington Plaza Hotel

★★★

Gloucester Road
South Kensington

Renovated in 1992, this Victorian hotel has bedrooms furnished and equipped to a high standard. The Mongolian Barbecue restaurant offers interesting good value meals. The room rate includes breakfast. *(60 rooms)*

PRICE CATEGORY

£££

Bailey's Hotel

★★★★

140 Gloucester Road
South Kensington

Established in 1876, Bailey's has recently been restored to its original glory. The bedrooms are decorated in soft colours and have excellent facilities. It has a popular bar and bistro. *(211 rooms)*

PRICE CATEGORY

£££££

The Adelphi Hotel

★★★

127-129 Cromwell Road
South Kensington

Each of the Adelphi's bedrooms is decorated to a high standard with elegant rosewood furnishings. The hotel has a conservatory restaurant, a coffee shop and a lounge bar. *(70 rooms)*

PRICE CATEGORY

£££

The Amber Hotel

★★

**101 Lexham Gardens
South Kensington**

The Amber has a quiet location in the heart of Kensington. It boasts a private garden and room service. The rate includes a buffet-style breakfast with a complimentary newspaper. *(40 rooms)*

Barkston Gardens Hotel

★★★

**34-44 Barkston Gardens
South Kensington**

Built at the turn-of-the-century and still retaining much of its original splendour, this hotel is located in a quiet street close to Earl's Court tube station. It has a restaurant, lounge and well-appointed rooms. *(82 rooms)*

Harrington Hall Hotel

★★★

**Harrington Gardens
South Kensington**

This luxurious air-conditioned hotel has tastefully furnished and well-equipped bedrooms, a spacious restaurant and an elegant lounge bar. In addition, there is a fitness centre and a business centre. *(200 rooms)*

The Burns Park Hotel

★★★

**18-26 Barkston Gardens
South Kensington**

Situated in a quiet, attractive square in South Kensington, the Burns Park features elegant bedrooms designed and furnished to a high standard. It has an intimate bar and a pleasant restaurant. *(106 rooms)*

PRICE CATEGORY

£££

The Paragon Hotel

★★★

**47 Lillie Road
South Kensington**

This large, imposing, modern hotel is located close to the Earl's Court tube station. Its rooms are well-furnished, with excellent facilities. There is an all-day coffee shop (with evening carvery) and a pub. *(501 rooms)*

PRICE CATEGORY

£££

Henley House Hotel

★★★

**30 Barkston Gardens
South Kensington**

Henley House is a small and friendly hotel located close to Earl's Court tube station. It has elegant rooms, some of which overlook the garden square. Breakfast is included in the tariff. *(20 rooms)*

PRICE CATEGORY

£££

The Gloucester

★★★★

**Harrington Gardens
South Kensington**

The Gloucester is a luxurious hotel in the heart of fashionable South Kensington. It is elegantly furnished and has an excellent restaurant, a fashionable café, 24-hour room service and a business centre. *(548 rooms)*

PRICE CATEGORY

££££££

Holiday Inn Kensington

★★★★

**100 Cromwell Road
South Kensington**

The luxurious Holiday Inn Kensington is located close to Gloucester Road tube station. It has a whirlpool spa, steam room, sauna, fitness room and a private garden. Its duplex suites have spiral staircases. *(162 rooms)*

PRICE CATEGORY

££££££

London Tourist Hotel

★★

**15 Penywern Road
South Kensington**

The newly refurbished London Tourist Hotel is located close to Earl's Court tube station. The bedrooms are modern and well-equipped. Breakfast is included in the room rate. *(32 rooms)*

PRICE CATEGORY

££

Beaver Hotel

★★

57-59 Philbeach Gardens
South Kensington

Located close to Earl's Court, the Beaver is a small hotel situated in a quiet tree-lined crescent of charming late-Victorian townhouses. A full English breakfast is included in the tariff. *(37 rooms)*

PRICE CATEGORY

££

Park International Hotel

★★★

117-125 Cromwell Road
South Kensington

Park International is comprised of five adjoining Victorian houses. The larger executive rooms have the luxury of their own jacuzzi. The Park Grill restaurant and the Tulip Bar are pleasant places to relax. *(117 rooms)*

PRICE CATEGORY

£££

The Cranley

★★★

10-12 Bina Gardens
South Kensington

Located in the heart of South Kensington, close to the museums and to Harrods, the Cranley is a small, exclusive hotel. Each bedroom is unique, with luxurious antique furnishings and exquisite décor. *(37 rooms)*

PRICE CATEGORY

££££

The Town House

★★★

**44-48 West Cromwell Road
South Kensington**

PRICE CATEGORY

££

A five-minute walk from Earl's Court tube station, the Town House Hotel is a family-run hotel with a restaurant and a cocktail bar. Continental breakfast is included in the tariff. *(46 rooms)*

Hotel Plaza Continental

★★★

**9 Knaresborough Place
South Kensington**

PRICE CATEGORY

££

Located between Earl's Court and Gloucester Road tube stations, the Plaza Continental has well-appointed bedrooms and, for the working visitor, a fully-equipped business centre. The rate includes breakfast. *(25 rooms)*

The Bonnington

★★★

**92 Southampton Row
Bloomsbury**

PRICE CATEGORY

£££

Established in 1911, The Bonnington is owned by the same family that opened it. Close to the British Museum, it is within walking distance of the West End. The rate includes a full English breakfast. *(215 rooms)*

Euston Plaza Hotel

★★★★

**17-18 Upper Woburn Place
Bloomsbury**

This modern hotel is designed in a Swedish style, with attractive light wood décor. Among the excellent facilities are a health centre, a pleasant bar and a popular restaurant. *(150 rooms)*

 ## The Generator

Hostel

**Compton Place
Bloomsbury**

**Facilities
off-suite**

The Generator offers hostel accommodation for young travellers at amazingly low prices. The building is futuristic with hard-edged decoration. Rooms are compact and bathrooms are shared. *(207 rooms)*

 ## Holiday Inn Garden Court

★★★

**57-59 Welbeck Street
Marylebone**

Located in a quiet Edwardian terrace, the Holiday Inn Garden Court is ideally suited for West End shopping and entertainment. The rooms are modern and there is a popular restaurant and bar. *(138 rooms)*

PRICE CATEGORY

££££

PRICE CATEGORY

££££

PRICE CATEGORY

£££££

The Langham Court Hotel

★★★★

31-35 Langham Street
Marylebone

This historic, protected building is now a luxurious hotel with elegantly decorated bedrooms in traditional English style. Located in a quiet street close to the West End, breakfast is included in the tariff. *(60 rooms)*

Mandeville Hotel

★★★

Mandeville Place
Marylebone

Located in a quiet area just north of Oxford Street, the Mandeville is within walking distance of the West End. It has a studio lounge, a bar and a coffee shop. Breakfast is included in the room rate. *(165 rooms)*

White Hall Hotel

★★★

2-5 Montague Street
Marylebone

This is one of the best-appointed small luxury hotels in London. Located beside the British Museum, it has a landscaped garden. Rooms have hand-carved furniture and marble bathrooms. Rates include breakfast. *(60 rooms)*

New Linden Hotel

★★

59 Leinster Square
Bayswater

The New Linden Hotel is a five-minute walk from Queensway and Bayswater tube stations. It has friendly service and well-appointed rooms. Breakfast is included in the tariff. *(51 rooms)*

PRICE CATEGORY

£££

Pavilion Hotel

★★★

37 Leinster Gardens
Bayswater

The Pavilion Hotel has a bar, a restaurant and a leisure area with a splash pool, a sauna and jacuzzi. It is conveniently located in Bayswater, close to Queensway and Bayswater tubes. Rates include breakfast. *(94 rooms)*

PRICE CATEGORY

£££

Henry VIII Hotel

★★★

19 Leinster Gardens
Bayswater

Centrally located in cosmopolitan Bayswater, the Henry VIII Hotel has well-appointed rooms, a bar, a restaurant and, unusually for London, a heated indoor swimming-pool. Breakfast is included in the room rate. *(107 rooms)*

PRICE CATEGORY

£££

Prince William Hotel

★★

**42-44 Gloucester Terrace
Bayswater**

££

This budget hotel is located close to Lancaster Gate tube station, within easy reach of the West End. It has a quiet restaurant and a popular bar. Breakfast is included in the tariff. *(43 rooms)*

Queen's Park

★★★

**48 Queensborough Terrace
Bayswater**

PRICE CATEGORY

£££

Situated in a peaceful Victorian terrace, close to Hyde Park, in the lively centre of Bayswater, Queen's Park has tastefully decorated and well-equipped bedrooms. It also has a pleasant restaurant. *(86 rooms)*

Queensway Hotel

★★

**147-149 Sussex Gardens
Bayswater**

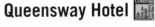

PRICE CATEGORY

££

This budget hotel is situated close to Hyde Park. It is a small hotel offering a more personal service. Some of the bedrooms, which are all well-appointed, have private jacuzzis. Rates include breakfast. *(43 rooms)*

Westminster Hotel

★★★

16 Leinster Square
Bayswater

Located in the heart of busy Bayswater, the Westminster overlooks a pretty garden square. The bedrooms are equipped with modern facilities. The hotel has a fashionable bar and rates include breakfast. *(114 rooms)*

PRICE CATEGORY

£££

Hillgate Hotel

★★★

6-14 Pembridge Gardens
Bayswater

Recently converted by linking five impressive Victorian houses, the Hillgate is situated close to Kensington Gardens. Bedrooms are well-furnished, there is a lounge and bar and breakfast is included. *(70 rooms)*

PRICE CATEGORY

£££

Eden Park Hotel

★★★

35-39 Inverness Terrace
Bayswater

Located in a tree-lined terrace, the Eden Park recalls the elegance and charm of early Victorian England. All bedrooms are appointed to a high standard. The Tulip Bar and King's Restaurant are both popular. *(137 rooms)*

PRICE CATEGORY

£££

Blakemore Hotel

★★★

**30 Leinster Gardens
Bayswater**

PRICE CATEGORY

£££

Located on a quiet street close to Bayswater tube station, the Blakemore's bedrooms have recently been refurbished to a high standard. It now offers a blend of modern facilities and Victorian grandeur. *(164 rooms)*

Norfolk Towers Hotel

★★★

**34 Norfolk Place
Bayswater**

PRICE CATEGORY

£££

Located close to Paddington station, Norfolk Towers has good transportation links to the West End. It has a popular lounge bar and, in the basement, a café/bar where you can relax. *(85 rooms)*

Quality Hotel Heathrow

★★★

**London Road
Greater London**

PRICE CATEGORY

£££

Located out of the centre of London, close to Heathrow Airport, the Quality Hotel is ideal for travellers starting their trip outside central London. It is also convenient if you have an early morning flight home. *(112 rooms)*

Westminster

Introduction . . .

From Trafalgar Square, you can see both **Buckingham Palace** (pages 50-51) and **Big Ben** (page 54), the clock tower of the **Houses of Parliament** (pages 54-55) – the twin seats of regal and political power in the United Kingdom's unique royal democracy.

For a thousand years, first monarchs and then parliamentarians have wielded their power from within the area known as Westminster.

Houses of Parliament and the River Thames

The royal court moved to Westminster in 1060, a few years before the Norman conquest of England. No buildings survive from this pre-Norman period but Westminster Hall, built by William the Conqueror's son in 1097, still stands as the vestibule of the House of Commons. In the Middle Ages, the area around Westminster Abbey deteriorated into a plague-ridden slum that was only fully cleared in the 19th century with the construction of Parliament Square and Victoria Street.

Big Ben

INSIDER'S TIP

The best view of the Houses of Parliament is from Westminster Bridge, from where you can see Members of Parliament having tea on the terraces.

Westminster was once separated by farmland from the old Roman and medieval heart of London which is a couple of miles to the east and now forms the business district known as the 'City'. Urban expansion has long since closed the gap between the two centres.

The best introduction to the area is a tour past the many grand institutions and landmarks lining the wide, triumphal avenues of Whitehall and the Mall.

You can see nearly all the major sites of Westminster by strolling a one-and-a-half-mile circuit beginning and ending in Trafalgar Square, passing along Whitehall, through Parliament Square and then on to Birdcage Walk and the Mall.

Admiralty Arch

. . . Introduction

The highlights include **Nelson's Column** on Trafalgar Square (built in 1843 to commemorate Lord Nelson's victory at the Battle of Trafalgar), 10 Downing Street (where the Prime Minister resides), **Westminster Abbey** (pages 52-53 – where Britain's kings and queens are crowned), the Houses of Parliament (with its famous clock tower Big Ben), and Queen Elizabeth II's London home, Buckingham Palace. (See pages 60-63 for details about this circuit.)

The massed bands of the Grenadier Guards

A half-mile detour along Millbank beside the Thames, brings you to the **Tate Gallery** (pages 56-57), Britain's premier collection of British and modern art.

The imposing buildings lining Whitehall are mainly occupied by government departments. Indeed, 'Whitehall' is the term used to describe the Civil Service, the public administrators who run the nation, supposedly under the direction of politicians. In the heyday of the British Empire, under Queen Victoria (who reigned from 1837-1901), a quarter of the world's land mass was governed from Whitehall.

Westminster Abbey

There are two large residential areas close to Westminster: Belgravia to the west is one of London's most exclusive neighbourhoods, while Pimlico to the south has a mix of smart townhouses and ugly public housing.

The stuccoed terraces of Belgravia were developed from the 1820s to the 1850s by the immensely rich Grosvenor family, with Belgrave Square as the centrepiece. Gerald Grosvenor, the present Duke of Westminster, owns most of Belgravia and much of Mayfair. He is one of the world's richest men, with an estimated £2 billion fortune. Unlike Mayfair, Belgravia is still home to hundreds of the wealthiest British families and many prominent individuals, including former Prime Minister Margaret Thatcher.

Genteel Belgravia

Buckingham Palace . . .

The Palace and the Victoria Monument

ADDRESS

At the end of The Mall
☎ 0171-930-4832

GETTING THERE

Green Park, St. James's
Park or Victoria tube
stations

HOURS

Changing of the Guard
Apr 1-Aug 7:
Mon-Sun: 11.30am
Aug 8-Mar 31:
11.30am every other day

State Apartments
Aug-Sep: 9.30am-4.30pm

PRICES

Adult £9
Child (under 17) £5
(under 4 free)
Senior £6.50
Student £9

The main daily attraction at Buckingham Palace is the Changing of the Guard ceremony. It lasts forty minutes, starting at 11.27am, when the Queen's Guard, accompanied by a band, leaves Wellington Barracks. The soldiers march via Birdcage Walk to Buckingham Palace.

The public have only been able to visit the state rooms of Buckingham Palace since August 1993, when the Queen decided to open up her London home to raise money for the restoration of Windsor Castle, which had been badly damaged by fire a year earlier.

The palace itself can only be visited from early August to the end of September, when the royal family spends time in Scotland.

It will open every summer until at least the year 2000,

The State Dining Room

when officials will decide whether the building can continue to cope with 7,000 pairs of feet tramping around it daily.

Same-day tickets are sold on a first-come first-served basis from a booth at the edge of Green Park, facing the piazza outside the palace. The booth opens at 9am and, at peak times, queuing can take up to two hours, with a further delay until your allocated visiting time.

Changing of the Guard

Built in 1702 on the site of a notorious brothel, Buckingham House was originally the London home of the Duke of Buckingham. Sixty years later, George III bought it as a family home to house his many children.

The architect John Nash began rebuilding the house as a palace for

. . . Buckingham Palace

George IV in the early 19th century. His flamboyant redesign went way over budget and was so widely ridiculed, that the Prime Minister, the Duke of Wellington, told the Chancellor of the Exchequer to

'make a hash of Nash'. A short time later, Nash was indeed hashed and Edward Blore finished the building.

Queen Victoria grew very attached to the new palace, remarking in her diary in 1843, "I have been so happy there".

The Grand Staircase

In 1913 the front of the palace was replaced with a Portland stone façade and the famous balcony was added. The only major changes since have been the addition of a swimming pool, a cinema and the rebuilding of the bomb-damaged chapel after the Second World War.

Only 18 of the palace's 661 rooms are on show, but they include the grand halls used for state occasions.

The tour starts in the huge **Quadrangle** and then leads to the back of the palace. The **Grand Staircase**, a curled, ornamental structure built by Nash with a floral gilt balustrade, leads up to the **Green Drawing Room**. The first room entered by guests at royal functions, it contains a fine Regency chandelier featuring three weeping women.

Next is the **Throne Room**, which – disappointingly – contains only a pair of pink chairs initialled E II R for Elizabeth and P for Philip. It is here that the Queen invests those who are knighted.

The highlight of the tour is the vaulted **Picture Gallery**, which is over 150 feet (45 metres) long and contains part of the royal collection of 10,000 paintings (several times larger than that of the National Gallery).

Two Canova sculptures are among the fine art treasures in Buckingham Palace: *Fountain Nymph* at the bottom of the Ministers' staircase and *Mars and Venus* in the 200-foot (60-metre) **Marble Hall**.

The Picture Gallery

Royal memorabilia of all kinds, from paperweights to Buckingham Palace chocolates, can be bought from the souvenir shop in the garden.

INSIDERS' TIP

Avoid the inevitable queues by going on a Frames Rickards tour (page 240) or by booking in advance early in the year. Send a self-addressed envelope to The Visitor Office, Buckingham Palace, London SW1A 1AZ and ask for an application form.

REFLECTIONS

'If you expect me to put my hand to any additional expense, I'll be damned if I will' – Prime Minister, the Duke of Wellington, on being asked by architect John Nash for more money to re-build the Palace (1828)

ADDRESS

Westminster Abbey
Broad Sanctuary
☎ 0171-222-5152

GETTING THERE

Westminster or St.
James's Park tube stations

HOURS

Mon-Fri: 9am-3.45pm
Sat: 9am-2pm,
3.45pm-5pm.

PRICES

Entrance to the nave
and cloisters is free.

Admission to Royal
Chapels and Poet's Corner:
Adult £4
Child £1
Senior £2
Student £2

Super Tours, conducted by
Abbey Vergers, take place
at intervals throughout
the day. Inclusive tickets
cost £7 and can be booked
in advance by calling
0171-222-7110.

Westminster Abbey . . .

The setting for coronations for nearly 1,000 years and the final resting place of many of Britain's kings and queens, Westminster Abbey is one of the nation's pre-eminent national monuments.

The majesty of the place is immediately apparent, with its beautifully restored Gothic twin towers by Nicholas Hawksmoor, 100-foot-high nave, easily the tallest in the country, and the graceful vaulted ceilings of the royal chapels.

Westminster Abbey

The Abbey embodies more English history than any other building, from William the Conqueror's journey up the aisle on horseback in 1066 to the coronation of Queen Elizabeth II in 1953. More than 3,000 of the nation's most revered figures are buried in the Abbey.

In the centre of the aisle is the **Tomb of the Unknown Soldier,** garlanded with red poppies. It commemorates the one million British soldiers who died in the First World War. Near to it, there is a slab remembering **Sir Winston Churchill**, though he is buried in a family plot in the village of Bladon. Richard II is depicted on the first pillar on the right. It is the oldest portrait of an English monarch painted from life.

The **Musicians'** and **Statesmen's Aisles** contain dozens of monuments to famous British composers and politicians. The former includes a statue of **Henry Purcell**, who was once the Abbey's organist; the latter contains the tomb of four-time Liberal Prime Minister in the Victorian period, **William Gladstone**.

Elizabeth I and her half-sister "Bloody Mary" – bitterly opposed to each other in life – are buried in the same chapel, the first in the tour of the Royal Chapels.

The **Henry VII Chapel**, built from 1503 to 1521, has a glorious vaulted ceiling. High above stand 100 saints' statues, while below lie Henry VII and James I, in black marble tombs partially hidden by a grille.

St. Edward's Chapel houses the Coronation Chair and the tombs of several medieval monarchs grouped around Edward the Confessor's shrine, which is the most sacred part of the Abbey.

. . . Westminster Abbey

Edward I's **Coronation Chair** stands beyond the tomb. This well-worn oak throne has been used for every coronation since 1300. Until 1996, it held the **Stone of Scone**, a great slab of sandstone that was used as early as the 4th century to crown kings in Ireland and later became Scotland's coronation stone. In 1296, Edward I took the stone to England. A group of Scottish nationalists stole it back on Christmas Eve, 1950. However, it was quickly recovered and returned to the Abbey. In 1996 the stone was returned to Scotland. It is now on display in Edinburgh Castle.

St. Margaret's Church and Westminster Abbey

Shakespeare's statue is the best known memorial in **Poets' Corner** – a section of the Abbey commemorating Britain's greatest writers. Geoffrey Chaucer, Jane Austen, Charles Dickens and the actor Lawrence Olivier are among those honoured. Henry Longfellow is the only American.

The **Great Cloister** can be reached via a door in the south aisle. Souvenirs can be purchased from the shop at the front of the Abbey. For a more unusual memento, visit the brass-rubbing centre in the cloisters.

Leading off the eastern end is the octagonal **Chapter House**, where the House of Commons met from 1257 until the reign of Henry VIII in the early 16th century. Faithfully restored in the 19th century, the Chapter House contains some of the finest examples of medieval English sculpture.

The Abbey's Chapter House

Chapter House tickets include entry to the 11th-century Pyx Chamber, containing the Abbey treasures, and the Abbey Museum, with its collection of medieval royal effigies. *(Westminster Abbey, entry through Dean's Yard and Cloister. ☎ 0171-222-5897. Apr-Sep: Mon-Sun: 10am-5.30pm. Oct-Mar: Mon-Sun: 10am-4pm. Adult £2.50, child £1.30, senior £1.90, student £1.90. 2 admissions for the price of 1 with your London for less card.)*

DON'T MISS

Churchill's memorial,
Poets' Corner,
Elizabeth I's tomb,
the Coronation Chair.

INSIDER'S TIP

Visit on a midweek afternoon when it is quieter.

ADDRESS

Bridge Street and
Parliament Square

House of Commons
☎ 0171-219-4272
House of Lords
☎ 0171-219-3107

GETTING THERE

Westminster or St. James's
tube stations

HOURS

The Strangers' Gallery is
open while the house sits
(usually Mon-Thu: 2.30pm-
10pm. Fri: 9.30am-3pm).
The public is allowed in
Mon-Thu from 4.30pm and
Fri from 10am .

PRICES

Admission is free

Houses of Parliament . . .

The United Kingdom's seat of power, this fine
Victorian Gothic building contains the House of

The Palace of Westminster

Commons (to which
Members of
Parliament are
democratically
elected) and the
House of Lords
(where peers either
inherit their seats or
gain them for life by
appointment).

The building is known as the Palace of Westminster,
because kings and queens lived here from Edward the
Confessor's reign in the early 11th century until
Parliament took control in the 17th century.

The old palace burnt down
in 1834. The present
building is the product of
an inspired collaboration
between Augustus Welby
Pugin and Charles Barry. A
huge clock tower, known by
the name of its largest bell,
Big Ben, dominates the
northern end of the
building. Londoners set
their watches by the chimes
of Big Ben, which are
broadcast around the globe
by the BBC World Service.

The Queen opening Parliament

The only substantial
remnant of the medieval palace is the huge
Westminster Hall, with its grand oak hammerbeam
roof. It is where deceased members of the royal family
and senior statesmen traditionally lie in state, prior to
being buried.

State Opening of Parliament

Guy Fawkes, who tried to blow up the
Houses of Parliament in 1605, was tried in
Westminster Hall before being hanged,
drawn and quartered. It is also where **Oliver
Cromwell** was appointed Lord Protector in
1653, during Britain's 11 years without a
king. After the restoration of the monarchy
in 1660, Cromwell's body was disinterred
and his head placed on the roof where it
stayed for 25 years before his skull blew down. A
statue of Cromwell stands outside the hall.

. . . Houses of Parliament

The **House of Commons**, with its lines of green leather-upholstered benches, is surprisingly small. The party of government and the opposition party sit facing each other. Two red lines run along the floor between them.

Members of Parliament (MPs) are not allowed to cross these lines, which were installed to stop violent brawls and are, therefore, two swords' lengths apart. It is these lines that have inspired the English saying, "to toe the line".

No monarch since Charles I (beheaded in 1649) has been permitted to enter the House of Commons. At the State Opening of Parliament, which

The House of Commons in session

takes place annually in October or November, the Queen sits in the **House of Lords**, with the door of the Commons symbolically slammed shut. The House of Lords, decorated in gold and scarlet and dominated by the gold throne, is grander than the Commons.

Proceedings in the House of Commons and the House of Lords can be watched from the **Strangers' Gallery**, but queuing up and getting through the security

checks can take an hour or more. The queue starts outside St. Stephen's Gate, off Parliament Square to the rear of Westminster Abbey. On Tuesdays and Thursdays it is easier to gain entry after 4.30pm as most of the seats for Prime Minister's Question Time are booked in advance by MPs for their constituents.

Central Lobby

Past the entrance hall, a few steps from the House of Commons chamber, you reach the **Central Lobby**, where constituents are permitted to gather to petition MPs, hence the term 'to lobby' an MP.

The patch of grass opposite St. Stephen's Gate has become the unofficial TV studio of Westminster, with MPs sometimes queuing up to be interviewed with Big Ben in the background.

REFLECTIONS

'It is not at all uncommon to see a member lying stretched out on one of the benches while others are debating. Some crack nuts, others eat oranges.'
– Pastor Carl Moritz on the House of Lords (1782)

A television interview outside Parliament

ADDRESS

Millbank
☎ 0171-887-8008

GETTING THERE

Pimlico tube station

HOURS

Mon-Sun: 10am-5.50pm

PRICES

Admission is free

DISCOUNT

10% off posters, greeting cards and postcards and £2 off the Tate's colour companion in the gift shop with your *London for less* card.

 # Tate Gallery . . .

The two great attractions of the Tate are its magnificent collection of post-1550 British art and its often controversial displays of international modern art.

There are 300 paintings and some 20,000 drawings in the collection, but only a selection of these is on

Exterior of the Tate

display at any one time. Pick up a free plan of the gallery at the information desk just inside the main entrance.

Founded in the late 19th century by the sugar millionaire Henry Tate, the gallery has satellites in Liverpool and St. Ives, Cornwall.

Britain's most famous painter, **JMW Turner** (1775-1851), has a special permanent exhibition all to himself. The **Clore Gallery** contains by far the world's largest collection of Turner oil paintings, watercolours and drawings, including the celebrated *Snow Storm*.

Begin a tour with the sculpture collection in the Central Corridor, where you will find **Rodin's** much-copied *The Kiss*. The works in the rest of the gallery are displayed in broadly chronological order.

In the 18th-century section, **William Hogarth** has a room almost all to himself, including his anti-French satire *Roast Beef of England*. The next room is full of portraits by **Sir Joshua Reynolds** and his great rival **Thomas Gainsborough**. There are several sketches and cloud studies by landscape artist **John Constable**. His *Flatford Mill* brought landscape painting closer to nature than ever before.

The visionary watercolours of poet/prophet **William Blake** include 10 of his 12 works on the myth of the Creation.

The mid-Victorian painters known as the Pre-Raphaelites, whose work is

'Ophelia' by Sir John Everett Millais

. . . Tate Gallery

characteristically full of emotion and colour, are well-represented at the Tate. Life almost imitated art when **Millais** was painting his famous *Ophelia*, for his model almost died from lying too long in a bath of cold water. For his *Proserpine*, **Dante Gabriel Rossetti** used his mistress Jane Morris (wife of Willam Morris, the designer and poet) as a model. Being herself trapped in a loveless marriage, Morris captures Proserpine's forlorn expression.

'The Kiss' by Auguste Rodin

The dozen or so rooms filled with modern art tend to either outrage or enrapture visitors. The Tate features works by the best-known surrealist, **Salvador Dali**, along with works by **Magritte**, **Matisse** and **Picasso**.

Humorous works by **Roy Lichtenstein** and **Andy Warhol** are included in the exhibition of 1960s Pop Art. Warhol's famous *Marilyn Diptych* seems to represent Marilyn Monroe's gloriously colourful life fading into the bleak and colourless final years before her tragic drug overdose. **David Hockney's** *A Bigger Splash* is one the artist's series of 1960s paintings based on his fixation with Californian 'swimming-pool culture'.

The contemporary art section has works by **Lucian Freud** and **Georg Baselitz** as well as frequently-changing and often obscure 'installations'.

The Tate's modern art collection is being moved to Bankside Power Station, downriver on the opposite side of the Thames. It is due to open in the year 2000.

There are free guided tours given by Tate Gallery Guides. The general tour starts from the Rotunda at 3pm each day. Ask at the information desk for start times for tours covering particular periods and collections.

The Tate's uncluttered collection

The Tate restaurant has an à la carte lunch menu, though it is closed on Sundays. The Tate Café and Espresso Bar serve lighter refreshments.

NEW: A personal audio guide to the collection is available in the Rotunda beyond the main entrance (£2).

ADDRESS

Whitehall
☎ 0171-839-8919

GETTING THERE

Charing Cross or
Westminster tube stations

HOURS

Mon-Sat: 10am-4.30pm
Sun: closed

The main banqueting hall

PRICES

Adult £3.25
Child £2.15
Senior £2.15
Student £2.15

DISCOUNT

10% off admission with
voucher on page 277.

Banqueting House

This exquisite building is the only part of the old
Palace of Whitehall to survive a fire in 1698.

Until its
destruction, this
palace was the
sovereign's main
London residence.
Banqueting House,
designed by Inigo
Jones in 1619,
was the first purely
Renaissance

Banqueting House viewed from Whitehall

building in London. It affords a glimpse of the 17th-
century opulence of the court of Charles I.

The main banqueting hall was originally used for royal
banquets, masques and balls, which were a regular
feature of Stuart court life. The highlight of the
building is the stunning painted ceiling, which
remains in perfect condition. Painted by Peter Paul
Rubens between 1635 and 1636 under the
instructions of Charles I, the ceiling glorifies the
Stuart royal dynasty. The nine allegorical panels
celebrate the unification of England and Scotland
under James I's rule. It is one of the
largest-scale paintings in London, with
each cherub more than nine feet tall.

It is ironic that the ceiling panels depict
the benefits of good kingship, for it was
outside this building that the first and
only execution of an English monarch took
place.

On January 30, 1649, little more than a
decade after he unveiled Rubens' glorious
paintings, Charles I walked through this
room and stepped out of one of the
windows to the executioner's scaffold. He
made a brief speech declaring himself
'the Martyr of the People' and was then promptly
beheaded. The Civil War Society still holds a special
parade here on the last Sunday in January to
commemorate the execution.

Oliver Cromwell, who as self-styled Lord Protector was
the nearest Britain has ever come to having a dictator,
moved into Banqueting House in 1654.

Eleven years after Charles I's execution, Charles II
used Banqueting House to celebrate the restoration of
the monarchy.

Cabinet War Rooms

Prime Minister Winston Churchill directed operations from this underground bunker during the Second World War.

Located in the basement of government offices, the Cabinet War Rooms were hurriedly converted on the eve of the war as emergency accommodation to protect the British Government against air attack. The 21 rooms were in operational use from August 27, 1939 to the Japanese surrender in 1945.

It is hard to imagine how the entire British war effort could have been coordinated from within the cramped conditions of the bunker's 21 rooms.

Churchill rarely slept in the bunker, preferring to defy the German bombers by watching the blitz of London from the roof of the building at night.

On a tour through the honeycomb of rooms, you can see the room where the war cabinet met, the huge world

Cabinet War Rooms

map used to plot army positions and the secret cubbyhole where Churchill held phone conversations with President Roosevelt. Many of the most important decisions of the war were made in the narrow and gloomy confines of the Cabinet Room, where Churchill and his War Cabinet met more than 100 times.

The tour passes through the map room, practically untouched since it was abandoned in August 1945. A stirring extract from one of Churchill's famous broadcasts can be heard in the background. The room which was

Exterior of the Cabinet War Rooms

kept for him as a bedroom, office and broadcasting suite remains just as it was during the war.

The free headset commentary, available in English, French, German, Italian and Spanish, helps enliven the tour, pointing out artefacts and describing their history.

ADDRESS

Clive Steps,
King Charles Street
☎ 0171-930-6961

GETTING THERE

Westminster or St. James's tube station

HOURS

Mon-Sun: 9.30am-6pm
last admission 5.15pm.
(Oct-Mar: opens 10am)

PRICES

Adult £4.40
Child £2.20
Senior £3.30
Student £3.30

DISCOUNT

Adult £1 off admission,
child, senior and student
70p off admission with
voucher on page 277.

Horse Guards Parade

10 Downing Street

The Cenotaph

Parliament Square

Other Attractions . . .

Half-way along Whitehall, you will pass **Horse Guards**, where two mounted sentries of the Queen's Household Cavalry and two foot soldiers are on duty between 10am and 4pm daily. The price of being in the British Army's most prestigious regiment is that you must stand motionless for a shift lasting two hours (or one

hour if you're on horseback). The Queen's Life Guards leave Hyde Park Barracks on horseback and arrive at Horse Guards via Constitution Hill and the Mall. *(Tiltyard, in front of Horse Guards or in Horse Guards Parade. ☎ 0839-123411. Mon-Sat:11am. Sun: 10am.)*

Through the arch is **Horse Guards Parade**, a large gravelled square which until recently was a civil servants' car park but has now been

Horse Guards Parade

cleared for pedestrians. Once a year it is filled with the royal military regalia of the Queen's Trooping of the Colour ceremony. There is a Changing of the Guard ceremony here every day of the week.

South from Horse Guards, on the west side of Whitehall, is the Prime Minister's official residence at **10 Downing Street.** Robert Walpole, who was the first Prime Minister to live at No.10, took up residence in 1735. Although it looks like a modest abode, the house includes a grand State Dining Room.

Unfortunately, you can only peer through the tall iron gates at the end of Downing Street, which were installed by a security-conscious Margaret Thatcher in 1990. Despite such precautions, an IRA mortar attack in 1992 narrowly missed the Cabinet Room, where Prime Minister John Major was meeting his most senior ministers. Next door, at No. 11, is the official

Winston Churchill in Parliament Square

residence of the Chancellor of the Exchequer, who is responsible for the nation's finances. The Foreign Secretary lives at No. 12.

Further along Whitehall, in the middle of the road, is

. . . Other Attractions . . .

the **Cenotaph** – the nation's chief memorial to its war dead. The royal family and all the senior politicians gather for a ceremony here on the Sunday closest to November 11, the anniversary of the end of the First World War.

Parliament Square contains statues of famous statesmen, including Benjamin Disraeli and Sir Winston Churchill. The latter statue, sculpted by Ivor Roberts-Jones in 1974, has an internal electric system to protect it from pigeons.

Jewel Tower

A collection of relics from the old Palace of Westminster, destroyed by fire in 1834, is displayed in the **Jewel Tower**, which is opposite the Houses of Parliament on Abingdon Street. Built by Edward III in 1366, it houses his valuables, including his jewels, robes, furs and gold vessels.

The three-storey tower, once surrounded by a moat, now includes an informative exhibit entitled 'Parliament, Past and Present'. The

exhibit traces the history of the British parliament, as well as the peculiar customs still observed by MPs and Lords. *(Abingdon Street,*

☎ 0171-222-2219. Apr-Sep: Mon-Sun: 10am-1pm, 2pm-4pm. Oct-Mar: 10am-1pm, 2pm-4pm. Adult £1.50, child 80p, senior £1.10, student £1.10. 2 admissions for the price of 1 with your London for less card.)

The Jewel Tower

Westminster Cathedral

The smaller church that stands beside Westminster Abbey is **St. Margaret's Church**, where Milton, Pepys and Churchill were all married. *(☎ 0171-222-6382. Open Mon-Sun: 9.30am-4.30pm.)*

St Margaret's Church

The Roman Catholic **Westminster Cathedral**, a ten-minute walk from Parliament Square, is overlooked by most visitors to London, but is well worth a detour. Work began in 1895 on this neo-Byzantine building, with its distinctive striped terracotta pattern and towering 274-foot (82-metre) campanile. Its interior, however, remains only half-decorated. Visit All Souls Chapel, with its 100 different types of marbles from around the world, and admire the stations of the cross, which were sculpted in 1913 by Eric Gill. *(Victoria Street ☎ 0171-798-9055. Open: Mon-Sun: 7am-7pm. Admission free.)*

Westminster Cathedral

. . . Other Attractions . . .

From the Cathedral, double back along Victoria Street and turn on to Broadway. Notice the series of sculptures by Jacob Epstein, Henry Moore and Eric Gill on the façade above St. James's Park tube station.

Guards Museum

The Guards Museum

A little to the north is Birdcage Walk, where the **Guards Museum** has a collection of ceremonial uniforms, weapons and memorabilia covering 300 years of history of the five regiments of foot guards. In addition to their other duties, these regiments have the task of protecting the Queen. The museum contains a large toy soldier centre that is popular with children. *(Birdcage Walk, St. James's Park, ☎ 0171-930-4466. Mon-Fri: 10am-3.30pm. January: closed. Adult £2, child £1, senior £1, student £1. 50% off admission with your London for less card.)*

Guards Chapel

The **Guards' Chapel**, inside Wellington Barracks on Birdcage Walk, was the scene of one of the worst bomb strikes of the Second World War, when 121 people were killed in 1944 by a Doodlebug rocket. The remains of the 19th-century apse were included in the rebuilt chapel, which opened in 1963. *Sun: service 11am.)*

Queen's Gallery

The Institute of Contemporary

Queen's Gallery, on the southern side of the palace grounds, displays a frequently-changing selection from the fabulous royal collection of paintings. *(Buckingham Palace Road, for exhibition details, call the visitor's office, ☎ 0171-839-1377. Mon-Sun: 9.30am-4.30pm. Adult £3.50, child £2, senior £2.50, family £10.)*

Royal Mews

The Queen's gold State Coach, used for coronations and jubilees, is the star attraction at the **Royal Mews**. Other carriages on display include the Glass Coach, which is used for royal weddings. *(Buckingham Palace Road, ☎ 0171-839-1377 for opening details. Adult £3.70, child £2.10, senior £2.60, student £2.60, family £10.)*

. . . Other Attractions

The Mall, a broad tree-lined avenue leading from Buckingham Palace to Trafalgar Square, forms the first part of the processional route from Buckingham Palace to Westminster.

Halfway down the Mall, opposite St. James's Park, John Nash designed the cream stucco Carlton House Terrace, where the **Institute of Contemporary Arts** is located. The Institute was established in 1947 to offer artists in Britain similar facilities to those enjoyed by American artists at New York's Museum of Modern Art. The Institute contains a cinema, art gallery and bar, which is one of the few in London that stays open until 1am. *(The Mall, ☎ 0171-930-0493. Mon: 12noon-11pm. Tue-Sat: 12noon-1am. Sun: 12noon-10.30pm. Mon-Fri: Adult £1.50, child free, senior £1, student £1. Sat-Sun: Adult £2.50, child free, senior £1.50, student £1.50. £1 off adult, senior and student admission with your London for less card. Cinema: £6.50. £1.50 off tickets with your London for less card.)*

The ICA

Open Spaces

St. James's Park (page 194), which was once marshy ground, has been a royal park ever since it was drained on Henry VIII's orders so that he could use it for hunting. In the 17th century, the first formal gardens with an aviary (hence Birdcage Walk) were created. Charles II had clandestine meetings with his mistress, Nell Gwyn, in the park. Over the next century, St. James's Park became notorious for prostitution.

Dean's Yard

These days, the park is well-maintained. It is perfect for a picnic and is a short walk from any of the sights of Westminster. There is a pretty lake, filled with geese and ducks, over which there is a bridge that offers superb views of both Buckingham Palace and Westminster.

Whitehall from St. James's Park

At lunchtime, the park is filled with civil servants escaping their offices in Whitehall. Even the Prime Minister occasionally takes a stroll in the park.

Dean's Yard, beside Westminster Abbey, is a secluded grassy square. It is private property belonging to the prestigious Westminster School, where playwright Ben Jonson was a pupil, but you are allowed to stroll around and view the exteriors of the surrounding medieval buildings.

Eating and Drinking

Compared with the neighbouring West End, there are relatively few restaurants and pubs in Westminster. Most are to be found at the northern end of Whitehall, on Victoria Street and around Victoria Station.

Tattershall Castle

There are a couple of floating bars and restaurants on the River Thames near the Embankment tube station. The **Tattershall Castle** pub and the **R.S. Hispaniola** restaurant are moored beside each other.

The Victoria area has several good wine bars that serve food, including **The Ebury Wine Bar** (see below) and **Carriages** (page 65).

Finnegan's Wake *(Strutton Ground, off Victoria Street)* is a newly refurbished Irish pub. It has Irish musicians performing five nights a week and Irish food, such as a Dublin Fry, is served all day. Beers include Guinness and the much-celebrated creamy ale Kilkenny.

Lord Moon of the Mall

Further west is **The Albert** *(52 Victoria Street)*, a large Victorian public house. It is richly decorated and has a magnificent staircase. Lots of MPs drink here and a Division Bell rings in the restaurant to signal important votes for which they must return to the House of Commons. Portraits of Prime Ministers, from the Marquis of Salisbury to John Major, hang on the staircase. The portrait of Mrs Thatcher was unveiled by the Iron Lady herself. Food is served in the bar from 11am to 10.30pm. The carvery restaurant is open from 12noon to 10pm.

Lord Moon of the Mall *(at the Trafalgar Square end of Whitehall)* is an attractive, spacious pub.

The Ebury Wine Bar

Modern British / Wine Bar

139 Ebury Street
☎ 0171-730-5447

Average meal: £10-15
for less discount: 25%
AM/VS/MC/DC

The Ebury Wine Bar serves good food at wine bar prices. It is well known for its bar snacks, pre-theatre suppers and à la carte menu. The restaurant has a great atmosphere and is popular with people of all ages.

Carriages

Modern British / Wine Bar

43 Buckingham Palace Road
☎ 0171-834-0119

Average meal: £10-15
for less discount: 25%
AM/VS/MC/DC

HOURS
Mon-Fri: 11am-11pm
Sat-Sun: closed

Carriages is located between Buckingham Palace and
Victoria Station. It is an ideal pit-stop for lunch or a
pre-theatre supper. A bar snack menu is available all
day and afternoon tea is served in summer.

Dino and Gianna

Italian / International

36 Vauxhall Bridge Road
☎ 0171-630-8400

Average meal: £5-10
for less discount: 25%
AM/VS/MC/DC

HOURS
Mon-Sat: 12noon-3pm,
6pm-11pm
Sun: 12noon-8pm

This friendly, family-run Italian restaurant offers good
value. It can be busy at lunchtime, but in the evening it
is relaxed. It is a great place to eat after a visit to the
Tate or a walk along the Thames.

Bella Pasta

Italian

152 Victoria Street
☎ 0171-828-7664

Average meal: £5-10
for less discount: 25%
AM/VS/MC/DC

HOURS
Mon-Thu: 11.30am-
11.30pm. Fri-Sat:
11.30am-12midnight
Sun: 12noon-11.30pm

Bella Pasta offers quality food with an emphasis on pizza
and pasta dishes. All of their restaurants have a pleasant,
continental atmosphere. It is ideal either for a relaxed
lunch or a romantic evening meal.

HOURS

Mon-Fri: 12.30pm-2.30pm,
6.30pm-10pm
Sat-Sun: 6.30pm-10pm

The Pavilion

French / Continental

Rochester Hotel,
69 Vincent Square
☎ 0171-828-6611

Average meal: £10-15
for less discount: 25%
AM/VS/MC/DC

The Pavilion offers fine continental cuisine in elegant surroundings. Its light and airy conservatory is an excellent venue for a relaxed dinner. Discounts are also available at the Rochester's Bar and Brasserie.

HOURS

Mon-Fri: 12noon-3pm,
5pm-11pm
Sat: 12noon-11pm
Sun: closed

Psistaria

Greek

82 Wilton Road
☎ 0171-821-7504

Average meal: £10-15
for less discount: 25%
AM/VS/MC/DC

Psistaria offers Greek Cypriot food at good prices. Its reputation is based on its grilled meats and seafood. Entertainment includes live music and belly dancing. No discount is available at the wine bar downstairs.

HOURS

Mon-Fri: 12.30pm-2pm,
7pm-11.15pm
Sat: 7pm-11.15pm
Sun: closed

Pomegranates

International

94 Grosvenor Road
☎ 0171-828-6560

Average meal: £15-20
for less discount: 25%
AM/VS/MC/DC

Pomegranates gives you a gastronomic tour of the world. Exotic dishes from afar are offered alongside traditional British fare. The food is complemented by an excellent, adventurous wine list.

West End

Introduction . . .

The **West End**, London's entertainment district, is packed with restaurants, bars, theatres, cinemas and nightclubs, not to mention thousands of shops.

The focal point is **Leicester Square** (pronounced 'Lester'), one of the few places in London where you will still find crowds of pleasure-seekers at 2am. Four

Piccadilly Circus

of London's biggest-screen cinemas are located around Leicester Square, where many Hollywood movies have their British première. The square is also home to some of the largest nightclubs, including the **Hippodrome**, on the corner of Charing Cross Road, and **Equinox**, on the north side.

The main thoroughfare from Leicester Square to **Piccadilly Circus** leads past the **Trocadero** (page 72), a popular entertainment centre with virtual reality games, a multi-screen cinema and gift shops.

Piccadilly Circus is one of London's busiest traffic junctions and, with its huge electronic billboards, is London's version of New York's Times Square. At its centre is the statue of **Eros**, the steps of which are a popular meeting spot.

Branching off from the Circus is **Shaftesbury Avenue**, which is lined with beautiful theatres and is London's more compact equivalent of Broadway. Sandwiched between Shaftesbury Avenue and Leicester Square is **Chinatown**, occupying only a handful of streets but containing dozens of Chinese restaurants (see page 81) and oriental shops.

North of Shaftesbury Avenue lies **Soho,** a strange mix of seediness and stylishness, with strip and peep shows sprinkled among classy restaurants and bars. The latter are frequented by

Theatres on Shaftesbury Avenue

fashion-obsessed folk from the many nearby advertising agencies and film companies.

The area is similar in some respects to New York's Soho, though the names have quiet different origins. While New York's Soho is an abbreviation of 'South of Houston Street', London's Soho dates back to the

. . . Introduction

16th century, when the area was Henry VIII's royal hunting ground. 'So-Ho' was the cry of the hunter who had spotted a hare or some other quarry.

Liberty department store

In the 17th century, the district was dotted with the mansions of dukes and earls, but the aristocrats eventually moved out, making way for immigrants and refugees. Even before the richer inhabitants left, Soho had acquired a reputation for tolerance and risqué entertainment which persists today.

INSIDER'S TIP

While restaurants around Leicester Square cater mainly for tourists, Londoners head for the choicer dining delights of Chinatown and Soho

Soho's main thoroughfare is **Old Compton Street**, running parallel to Shaftesbury Avenue. Continental-style pavement cafés have sprung up in recent years, though it is debatable whether London has the climate for evening *al fresco* meals. The street is the centre of the area's gay scene and has several gay bars, clubs and even a special taxi service.

One of London's distinctive characteristics is the way popular entertainment jostles for space beside historic and learned institutions. Nowhere is this more apparent than in the West End, where, only a short walk from the buzzing bars and clubs of Leicester Square, you find the magnificent halls of the **National Gallery** (pages 70-71) and **National Portrait Gallery** (pages 78-79).

The fountains in Trafalgar Square

The West End is also a mecca for shopaholics, with thousands of stores and boutiques lining **Regent Street**, **Oxford Street** and the many side streets leading off these main arteries. The bigger chain stores are to be found on Oxford Street, while the more exclusive department stores, such as **Liberty**, are either on or near Regent Street (see page 89).

East of Leicester Square lies **Covent Garden** (pages 74-75), a pedestrianized piazza where visitors and locals alike go to enjoy the street entertainment and visit the many interesting shops. Covent Garden is home to the **Royal Opera House**, Britain's premier venue for opera and ballet, which is undergoing a major refurbishment.

ADDRESS

Trafalgar Square
☎ 0171-747-2885

GETTING THERE

Charing Cross
tube station

HOURS

Mon-Sat: 10am-6pm
Wed: 10am-8pm
Sun: 12noon-6pm

PRICES

Admission is free
Free guided tours:
Mon-Fri: 11.30am
and 2.30pm
Sat: 2pm and 3.30pm.

National Gallery . . .

The National Gallery houses one of the world's foremost art collections.

With the majority of the gallery's 2,200 paintings on view at any one time, the best approach is to focus on what suits your taste.

'The Arnolfini Marriage' by Van Eyck

The gallery was founded in 1824 after the art-loving King George IV helped persuade the government of the day to buy the small but magnificent collection of the Russian-born merchant John Julius Angerstein, including works by **Raphael**, **Rembrandt** and **Van Dyck**. The first section of the present building was designed by William Wilkins and opened in 1838. The gallery's first director, Sir Charles Eastlake, spent a decade scouring Italy for Renaissance masterpieces. Sir Charles's 139 purchases turned the gallery into one of the most important public collections in Europe.

Nearly all the Old Masters are represented here. In addition to those already mentioned, there are works by **da Vinci**, **Botticelli**, **Michelangelo**, **El Greco**, **Goya**, **Rubens** and **Van Eyck**.

The most prestigious individual collections include a series of **Rembrandt** paintings, nine works by **Raphael**, several by **Holbein** and a section on **Cézanne** and other Impressionists.

National Gallery from Trafalgar Square

The **Sainsbury Wing**, opened in 1991 with a donation from a super-rich supermarket dynasty, contains the oldest paintings, including a magnificently restored altar piece, the *Wilton Diptych*. This wing contains the **Micro Gallery**, where you can create a mapped-out tour of your favourite paintings, with touch screens allowing you to view the entire collection on the computer. There are brief but illuminating notes on each work of art.

One of the most valuable collections of Italian art

. . . National Gallery

outside Florence is housed in rooms 57-61. The collection includes **Botticelli's** *Venus and Mars* and **Bellini's** *Doge Leonardo Loredan.*

Interior of the National Gallery

British art is gathered in room 34, including several works by **Thomas Gainsborough** and **Constable's** *The Hay-Wain –* perhaps the most famous British painting.

The excellent *Gallery Guide and Soundtrack*, which comprises a portable CD player and headphones, gives you a brief description of any of the 1,000 paintings on the main floor. This is available at the main

'Sunflowers' by Van Gogh

entrance and Sainsbury Wing foyer and is free, though donations are invited. A highlights tour of 30 great paintings is available in six languages: English, French, Italian, Spanish, German and Japanese.

There are three excellent shops in the gallery, selling art books, CD-ROMS and videos. The Brasserie restaurant in the Sainsbury Wing has all-day table service, with a good value daily chef's choice. The Prêt à Manger café in the main building is self-service and offers hot food, salads and snacks.

For the **National Portrait Gallery**, which is just behind the National Gallery, see page 78.

New: In late 1996, the National Gallery and the Tate Gallery (pages 56-57) agreed to swap dozens of masterpieces in an effort to redefine "modern" as post-1900. Several post-1900 paintings, including Monet's *Water Lilies,* have moved to the Tate. Pre-1900 works, like **Van Gogh's** *Farms near Auvers,* have moved to the National.

'The Hay-Wain' by John Constable

DON'T MISS

The anonymous *Wilton Diptych* (Room 53), **Van Eyck's** *The Arnolfini Marriage* (Room 56), **Bellini's** *The Doge Leonardo Loredan* (Room 61), **Botticelli's** *Venus and Mars* (Room 58), **El Greco's** *Christ Driving Traders from the Temple* (Room 7), **Gainsborough's** *Morning Walk* and **Constable's** *Hay Wain,* (Room 34), **Van Gogh's** *Sunflowers* (Room 44).

INSIDER'S TIP

Weekday mornings are the quietest time; enter by the Sainsbury Wing to avoid the crowds at the main entrance.

The Trocadero

The Trocadero is unashamedly aimed at the mass tourist market and is constantly packed with pleasure-seeking visitors.

Sonic the Hedgehog at Segaworld

Originally a gentlemen's tennis court, the 250-year-old Trocadero has been, at various times, a music hall, hotel and casino.

A £45 million refurbishment was completed in 1996, making it Britain's biggest hi-tech indoor entertainment complex. The governing concept is a 21st-century space 'mothership' and the aptly named Rocket Escalator carries visitors up 330 feet (100 metres) from the foyer to the top of the building. The central area is a mass of coloured neon lights and futuristic chrome plating.

ADDRESS

13 Coventry Street
☎ 0171-439-1791

GETTING THERE

Piccadilly Circus
tube station

INSIDER'S TIP

Summer 1997 sees the opening of the world's first indoor free-fall ride: 'The Giant Drop'.

Daytona Racetrack at Segaworld

Segaworld, the main attraction, features six themed 'futuractive' zones on eight floors. It is based on the Joypolis park in Yokohama, Japan, but is far larger and can hold 3,000 people at one time. The virtual reality rides vary in quality. *Aqua Planet* is an exciting undersea adventure, but *Beast in Darkness* is disappointing. *Space Mission* uses personal Mega Visor Displays with built-in stereo to take prospective starfighter pilots on a journey into space in search of enemy starships. The Daytona *Race Track*, with eight riders racing each other, has cameras showing the hilarious expressions on the riders' faces. Allow four hours for a visit. (☎ *0171-734-2777. Sun-Thu: 10am-12midnight. Fri-Sat: 10am-1am. £2 entry, plus cost of individual games/rides.*)

'Cosmic Pinball' at the Emaginator

Showscan's Emaginator offers a variety of simulated whiteknuckle rides, including a space-age roller coaster and desert buggy race. (☎ *0171-734-3271. Sun-Thu: 11am-10.15pm. Fri-Sat: 11am-11.30pm. £3.75 per ride, repeat ride on the same day £2.75. 50% off per person with the voucher on page 277.*)

Rock Circus

Rock and pop's biggest stars gather in wax for a musical version of Madame Tussaud's.

You wander around the galleries with a special head-set that plays the greatest hits of whichever singer you happen to be passing. A 20-foot 'video wall' plays archive film footage.

More than 50 rock and pop legends are represented, including **Madonna, Eric Clapton, Billy Idol** and **Tina Turner**. It concentrates on the 1960s-1980s but has a small, and growing, collection of stars from the 1990s. A model of **Lenny Kravitz**, complete with tattoos and a nipple ring

Michael Jackson

donated by the singer himself, is a recent addition. A team of 25 artists worked the model, which cost £35,000 to produce.

A small collection of rock memorabilia, including Eric Clapton's cowboy boots, is on display. While he sat for his wax model, Clapton played Layla for half an hour to maintain his concentration. He even shaved his beard off to allow the sculptor to achieve the correct jaw-line.

New addition: Pulp's Jarvis Cocker

The **Wall of Hands**, where the stars have left mouldings of their hands, is worth a look. You can measure your own hands against the imprints left by, among others, **Michael Jackson, Jon Bon Jovi** and **Gloria Estefan**. **Little Richard**'s are easily the biggest. More recent stars who have contributed to the wall include teen band **Boyzone** and **Dina Carol**.

A 20-minute 'concert' at the end of the 90-minute tour traces the history of rock music, claiming that its roots date back 100 years. Rare recordings and previously unseen

Bob Geldof and Tina Turner

archive footage are included, as well as a new acknowledgement of the black influence in modern music.

ADDRESS

London Pavilion,
Piccadilly Circus
☎ 0171-734-8025

GETTING THERE

Piccadilly Circus
tube station

HOURS

Sun-Mon and Wed-Thu:
11am-9pm.
Tue: 12noon-9pm
Fri-Sat: 11am-10pm

PRICES

Adult £7.50
Child £5.95
Senior £6.95
Student £6.95

DISCOUNT

£1.50 off admission per person with voucher on page 277.

Covent Garden . . .

The colourful, lively area around the old market buildings of Covent Garden is a favourite place for Londoners to socialise.

As much of the area is pedestrianised, it is ideal for strolling, browsing in quirky shops, enjoying the talents of the street entertainers or simply relaxing and watching the world go by in one of the many pavement cafés.

The name Covent Garden is derived from its former function as a convent garden. Until the 16th century, it was an area of market gardens growing produce for Westminster Abbey.

Designed by Inigo Jones in the 1630s, the square is one of the oldest in London. Initially a very up-market neighbourhood, the area became debauched in the 18th century, when there were so many brothels and gambling dens that it was dubbed the 'great Square of Venus'. Poets and dramatists such as Alexander Pope, John Dryden and Richard Sheridan used to congregate in the local coffee houses, gathering material for their savage caricatures.

In the 1830s, market buildings were constructed to replace the haphazard collection of stalls that had existed before. Designed by Charles Fowler, the new market hall was described in a contemporary London magazine as being "a structure at once perfectly fitted for its various uses; of great architectural beauty and elegance; and so expressive of the purposes for which it is erected, that it cannot by any possibility be mistaken for anything else than what it is."

The market became very popular among fashionable Londoners, who liked to mingle with the tradesmen and flower sellers. It is in Covent Garden that flower-girl Eliza Doolittle, the heroine of George Bernard Shaw's *Pygmalion*, first meets Professor Henry Higgins. The play was turned into the popular musical *My Fair Lady*.

The street market

The market hall in the centre of the piazza remained London's main fruit, vegetable and flower market until 1974, when it was transferred to Battersea. The attractive covered market buildings now house designer shops, cafés and dozens of stalls selling superior arts and crafts.

GETTING THERE

Covent Garden or Leicester Square tube stations

INSIDER'S TIP

The Covent Garden Festival, a celebration of opera and music theatre, takes place at venues around the area in late May and early June.

. . . Covent Garden

On the northern side of the square lies the **Royal Opera House** (page 203), London's most prestigious theatre, which is home to the Royal Opera and Royal Ballet. It is presently undergoing a major refurbishment.

Covent Garden central market

To the north, and through into Neal Street, there are gimmick shops and some of London's trendiest boutiques, plus plenty of lively bars and cafés. Many of Britain's most innovative designers have studios around **Seven Dials**, where seven streets meet.

On the western edge of the square is St. Paul's Church, known as the 'Actors' Church', because of the many theatres close by. Designed by Inigo Jones and completed in 1633, the interior is a simple double square, 100 feet by 50 feet. It is filled with memorials to famous actors and actresses, including the legendary Shakespearean actress Ellen Terry, who died in 1928 and whose ashes are preserved in the south wall.

The church also has a long association with puppetry, dating back to at least 1662 when the diarist Samuel Pepys watched 'a very pretty' Italian puppet play. The tradition is upheld with a puppeteers' festival in the church on the second Sunday in May.

The street entertainers – be they jugglers, sword-eaters, comedians or magicians – all have to audition to perform in the piazza. One of the best places from which to watch the street entertainers is the balcony of the Punch and Judy pub at the end of the market hall.

The Punch & Judy pub, overlooking the Piazza

The balcony stretches the whole width of the building, with a shelf along the wall which is lined with dozens of pints of beer in summer! Two floors down, the Punch and Judy cellar bar opens out into a pretty, stone-flagged sunken courtyard inside the market buildings.

The **Theatre Museum** (page 77) and **London Transport Museum** (page 77) are situated off the square.

REFLECTIONS

'Covent Garden market, when it was market morning, was wonderful company. The great wagons of cabbages, with growers' men and boys lying asleep under them, and with sharp dogs from market garden neighbour-hoods looking after the whole, were as good as a party' – *The Uncommercial Traveller*, Charles Dickens (1861)

Other Attractions . . .

London's **Chinatown**, between Leicester Square and Shaftesbury Avenue, is tiny in comparison with New York's but efforts have been made to give the area an Oriental feel. Three Chinese arches straddle the central pedestrianized avenue, Gerrard Street, and phone boxes have been turned into mini pagodas. There are plenty of Chinese arts and crafts shops and dozens of restaurants (see page 81).

Chinatown

Chinatown

The **Courtauld Institute** boasts one of the world's greatest collections of Impressionist works, as well as a small, but spectacular Post-Impressionist collection.

Somerset House

The galleries, covering a dozen rooms on two floors, are located in Somerset House, a fine Georgian building still partly occupied by tax collectors.

The core of the collection was put together by industrialist Samuel Courtauld between the two World Wars, though other donations have greatly enriched it since.

Works by **Pieter Brueghel**, **Rubens** and **Botticelli**, including the latter's *Holy Trinity with Saints John and Mary*, are the highlights of the early galleries.

The more modern paintings, which tend to be better known, include some **Degas** studies of dancers and almost an entire room devoted to **Cézanne**. One of **Manet's** most popular works, *Bar at the Folies-Bergère*, is on display along with a copy of his *Déjeuner sur l'herbe*, the first Impressionist painting.

Courtauld Institute

Van Gogh's famous *Self-Portrait with Bandaged Ear* is worth a visit in itself. The painter

'Dejeuner sur l'herbe' by Édouard Manet

mutilated himself in a guilt-ridden frenzy after threatening fellow artist and guest **Gauguin**, whose

. . . Other Attractions . . .

Tahitian works are also in the Courtauld. *(Somerset House, The Strand, ☎ 0171-872- 0220. Mon-Sat: 10am-6pm. Sun: 2pm-6pm. Adult £4, child £2, senior £2, student £2, free entry after 5pm. The galleries will be closed for a major restoration from August 31, 1997 until July 1, 1998.)*

The **Photographers' Gallery**, which showcases work from both leading and up-and-coming snappers, often has interesting exhibitions. The gallery has a café and specialist photographic bookshop. *(5 Great Newport Street, ☎ 0171-831-1772. Tue-Sat: 11am-7pm. Admission is free.)*

Photographers' Gallery

London Transport Museum

The **London Transport Museum**, on the east side of Covent Garden piazza, houses a collection of period buses and original tube trains, with plenty of hands-on exhibits aimed at children. You can sit in the driving seat of some of the old vehicles and climb on board a set of electric trams. The last tram was removed from London's streets in the early 1950s, but they are scheduled to make a comeback in the city's southern suburbs. A fine collection of commercial art, commissioned to adorn London's buses and tubes, is displayed in a special gallery and the museum shop sells some of the best examples in their original poster form. *(Covent Garden, ☎ 0171-379-6344. Sat-Thu: 10am-6pm. Fri: 11am-6pm. Adult £4.50, child £2.50, senior £2.50, student £2.50, family £11.)*

London Transport Museum

Close by, in a basement on Russell Street, the **Theatre Museum** charts the history of the English stage, with a collection of props, costumes and memorabilia. The best parts are the portraits of stage legends and an interactive display about the history of stage make-up, entitled *Slap*. The latter includes a section on the special effects from the smash-hit musical *The Phantom of the Opera*.

Visitors can take part in a range of daily activities, including costume workshops and make-up demonstrations, during which a specialist will give you a horrible scar or a werewolf face.

A costume workshop at the Theatre Museum

Theatre Museum

. . . Other Attractions . . .

There is also an exhibition illustrating the development of theatre from Shakespearean times to the present day. *(Russell Street, ☎ 0171-836-7891. Tue-Sun: 11am-7pm. Adult £3.50, child £2, senior £2, student £2, Family £8. £1 off adult admission, child, senior and student have free admission with voucher on page 277.)*

Theatre Royal

Around the corner, on Catherine Street, is the famous **Theatre Royal**, the world's oldest theatre still in use. It was here that the traditions of modern theatre, as we know it, were forged in the 18th century by the brilliant actor and manager David Garrick.

The Theatre Royal

The first theatre on this site was built in 1663. Kings George I and George III both survived assassination attempts while attending performances. Backstage tours include the under-stage machinery rooms, paint shops and the Royal Room. *(Theatre Royal Backstage Tours, Catherine Street, ☎ 0171-240-5357. Tours run Mon-Sun, call for times. Adult £4, child £3, senior £4, student £4. £1 off per person with your London for less card.)*

Heading south into the main thoroughfare of The Strand, which links the West End with the City, you will find several more old theatres.

St Mary-le-Strand

At the east end of the Strand, the road divides, with the crescent-shaped Aldwych curving round to create an island. At its centre stands the neo-classical **Bush House**, the headquarters of the BBC World Service.

South of Aldwych, you will find the tall narrow church **St. Mary-le-Strand** marooned in the middle of the road. Built in 1724, it has a distinctive wedding-cake layered tower and fussily decorated exterior inspired by Baroque churches in Rome.

Cleopatra's Needle

Cleopatra's Needle

Looping back towards the Thames via Lancaster Place, there is a pleasant walk along the river, passing **Cleopatra's Needle**. This 60-foot (18-metre) granite obelisk, carved in 1500 BC, was presented to Britain in 1819 by the then Turkish Viceroy of Egypt, Mohammed Ali.

Opposite St. Martin-in-the-Fields, on St. Martin's Place, is the **National Portrait Gallery**, containing

. . . Other Attractions . . .

the world's largest collection of portraits – 10,000 in all. Until fairly recently, only portraits of those who had died were displayed, so many of the paintings are of historical characters, such as Henry VIII and Shakespeare (the painting of whom – illustrated on page 154 – is the only one ever taken from life). More recently, a select few contemporary figures have been added, among them Paul McCartney of The Beatles and former Prime Minister Margaret Thatcher.

The National Portrait Gallery

The third floor, containing Victorian and early 20th-century works, has just been brilliantly redesigned by architect Piers Gough. The original windows of the 1896 building have been uncovered to shed daylight on what was formerly a dingy gallery. Partitions from the 1970s

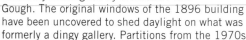

have been removed to reveal spacious Victorian interiors. *(St. Martin's Place, ☎ 0171-306-0055. Mon-Sat: 10am-6pm. Sun: 12noon-6pm. Admission is free. 10% discount on all goods at gallery shop (except books) with your London for less card.)*

National Portrait Gallery

Trafalgar Square, officially the centre of London, is easily accessible by tube and many of London's bus routes and all night buses call at stops

H.M. Queen Elizabeth II

around the square.

The thousands of pigeons that inhabit the square will willingly eat out of your hand and perch on different parts of your body. A tub of pigeon food costs 25p from a booth on the eastern side of the square. Unfortunately – and to the fury of many Londoners – the huge flock creates a nasty mess, which you may well skid on. The British government spends £100,000 a year removing up to a ton of pigeon droppings from Nelson's Column.

Trafalgar Square

The square is traditionally used for political demonstrations, most famously in 1990 when a protest against the 'poll tax' turned into a mass riot. Huge crowds gather on New Year's Eve, when barriers are erected to prevent revellers from climbing on Sir Edward Landseer's four bronze lions (1867) and from swimming in the fountains.

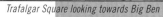

Trafalgar Square looking towards Big Ben

Admiralty Arch

London Brass Rubbing Centre

Victoria Embankment Gardens

. . . Other Attractions

Several fine buildings face the square, including the **National Gallery** to the north and **Admiralty Arch** – through which you can see the Mall and Buckingham Palace – to the south-west.

The church of **St. Martin-in-the-Fields,** with its distinctive tower and Corinthian columns, stands in the north-eastern corner of Trafalgar Square. There is a lively and modestly-priced café in the crypt, entered from the street to the south of the church.

Brass rubbing

In the crypt, you will also find the **London Brass Rubbing Centre**. You can create your own souvenir from Britain's age of chivalry by doing a 'rubbing' of one of the medieval brasses. *(The Crypt, St. Martin-in-the-Fields, ☎ 0171-930-9306. Mon-Sat: 10am-6pm. Sun: 12noon-6pm. £1.50-10. 20% off self-made rubbings with voucher on page 277.)*

Heading towards Whitehall, the horse-and-rider statue marooned on a traffic island just to the south of Trafalgar Square is of Charles I. Completed in 1633, it was removed during the English Civil War, but with the restoration of the monarchy in 1660, it was placed on the exact spot where the men who signed the king's death warrant were beheaded.

Open Spaces

There are very few green spaces in the densely packed West End and, as a result, any patch of grass tends to be packed with sun-seeking office workers in summer.

Soho Square

One of the most pleasant places to relax and have a picnic is **Victoria Embankment Gardens**, a narrow stretch of formal gardens alongside the Thames and close to Embankment tube station. Statues of famous British people line its walkways.

At the northern flank of the West End area lies the small, but attractive, **Soho Square**, which is surrounded by houses once inhabited by the nobility. These days, the buildings are mainly occupied by entertainment businesses such as 20th Century Fox. The mock-Tudor shed in the centre of the square conceals an air vent for the Tube.

Eating and Drinking . . .

Whatever you feel like eating, be it Afro-Caribbean, Indonesian or Tex/Mex, you will find it among the thousand-plus restaurants of the West End.

Chinatown, on and around Gerrard Street, has dozens of restaurants suitable for all budgets. You can buy a four-course meal for two for as little as £14. Turn up Wardour Street and follow the smell of roast duck.

Poons *(4 Leicester Street)* is modestly priced and serves delicious, authentic dishes. North of Chinatown is Soho, home of dozens of exotic restaurants and late-night cafés.

Gerrard Street

There are several themed restaurants in the Leicester Square/Piccadilly Circus area with menus based on burgers and steaks. These include **Planet Hollywood** *(13 Coventry Street)*, **Football, Football** *(57-60 Haymarket)*, which is stuffed with football memorabilia and the **Fashion Café** *(5-6 Coventry Street)* which has four supermodels as partners.

Al fresco dining in the West End

Planet Hollywood

On Aldwych you will find the Waldorf Hotel which is famous for its weekend tea dances (see page 256-257).

Several restaurants offer live entertainment. **Smollensky's** (page 88) has live music every night and magic shows for kids at lunchtime, while **Centre Stage** (page 86) has cabaret performers selected from the West End stage.

The many pubs and bars tend to be jam-packed at weekends. **All-Bar-One** *(48 Leicester Square)* is a bar/restaurant laid out like a wine cellar with huge windows allowing you to see and be seen. **De Hems** *(11 Macclesfield Street)* serves Dutch beer and has a party atmosphere most nights.

The Waldorf Hotel Tea Room

Around the corner on Greek Street is Soho's most celebrated pub, The **Coach and Horses**. It was immortalised in Keith Waterhouse's play, *Jeffrey Bernard is Unwell*, based on the life of the heavy drinking journalist who spent much of his time here.

. . . Eating and Drinking

The pub's décor is best described as basic, but the cartoons on the walls by Michael Heath are well worth seeing.

The Lamb and Flag

The listings magazine *Time Out* once nominated **The Polar Bear** *(30 Lisle Street)* as one of the worst pubs in the West End. The pub responded by putting up a large banner declaring itself 'One of the worst pubs in the West End' and takings immediately went up by 60%. It is mainly frequented by homesick New Zealanders.

The **Lamb and Flag** *(33 Rose Stree)* has a long and chequered history and its bar has retained its old-worldiness. An inn has stood on this site for 500 years.

New Jakarta

Indonesian

150 Shaftesbury Avenue
☎ **0171-836-2644**

Average meal: £5-10
for less discount: 25%
AM/VS/MC

HOURS

Mon-Fri: 12noon-2.30pm,
6pm-11.30pm
Sat: 12.30pm-2pm,
6pm-11.30pm
Sun: 5pm-10.30pm

New Jakarta offers good Indonesian food at reasonable prices. For two or more, the rijsttaffel is highly recommended. For lunch, the set menu is extremely good value.

My Old Dutch

Pancake House

131-132 High Holborn
☎ **0171-242-5200**

Average meal: £5-10
for less discount: 25%
AM/VS/MC/DC

HOURS

Mon-Sat: 12noon-11.30pm
Sun: 12noon-11pm

This speciality pancake house offers over 100 different toppings and fillings. Specially imported Dutch beers complement the pancakes. It is an excellent place for an economical lunch or dinner.

Celebrities Restaurant

Modern British

**The Hampshire,
Leicester Square**
☎ 0171-839-9399

Average meal: £15-20
for less discount: 25%
AM/VS/MC/DC

HOURS

Mon-Sat: 12.30pm-
2.30pm, 6pm-11pm
Sun: 12.30pm-2.30pm,
6pm-10pm

Celebrities Restaurant, located in the heart of Leicester Square, offers modern British cuisine in an intimate atmosphere. The wine list is excellent and the service is friendly and attentive.

 # Flicks Brasserie

International

**The Pastoria,
St. Martin's Street**
☎ 0171-930-8641

Average meal: £10-15
for less discount: 25%
AM/VS/MC/DC

HOURS

Mon-Fri: 11am-10pm
Sat: 5pm-10pm
Sun: closed

Just off Leicester Square, Flicks Brasserie is the ideal spot for a late-night drink, or something a little more substantial. It serves a selection of excellent international dishes.

Bella Pasta

Italian

22 Leicester Square
☎ 0171-321-1246

Average meal: £5-10
for less discount: 25%
AM/VS/MC/DC

HOURS

Mon-Sun:
11am-12midnight

This chain of Italian restaurants offers excellent value. They are great places to go for a quick lunch or a relaxed dinner. The discount also applies at 61 Shaftesbury Ave, 1 Cranbourne Street and 10 Irving Street.

HOURS

Mon-Fri: 12noon-3am
Sat: 6pm-3am
Sun: closed
Tue-Sat: disco

Boardwalk

American

18 Greek Street
☎ **0171-287-2051**

Average meal: £10-15
for less discount: 25%
AM/VS/MC/DC

The atmosphere is lively and informal at this stylish Soho restaurant. The American cuisine has a distinct Cajun flavour. There is a disco most nights, and live jazz on Mondays and Wednesdays.

HOURS

Mon-Sat: 12noon-
12midnight
Sun: closed

Si Señor

Mexican

2 St. Anne's Court
☎ **0171-494-4632**

Average meal: £10-15
for less discount: 25%
AM/VS/MC

This is the only Mexican restaurant in London owned by Mexicans. The spacious, bright décor enhances the fun and informal atmosphere. Try the taco tray or the excellent *fajitas*.

HOURS

Mon-Sat: 5.30pm-
11.30pm
Sun: closed

Los Locos

Tex / Mex

14 Soho Street
☎ **0171-287-0005**

Average meal: £10-15
for less discount: 25%
AM/VS/MC

Located just off Oxford Street, Los Locos is a lively Tex/Mex restaurant. After 11pm it becomes a nightclub, popular with Londoners and visitors alike. If you have dinner here you gain free entrance to the nightclub.

Wheeler's

Seafood

19 Old Compton Street
☎ 0171-437-2706

Average meal: £20-25
for less discount: 25%
AM/VS/DC

HOURS

Mon-Sat: 12.30pm-
2.30pm,
6pm-11.15pm
Sun: 12.30pm-2.30pm,
7pm-10.30pm

Wheeler's is London's most famous seafood restaurant. Its name has been synonymous with the finest fresh fish for over 100 years. It is a superb location for pre- or post- theatre dining.

Steph's

Modern British

39 Dean Street
☎ 0171-734-5976

Average meal: £10-15
for less discount: 25%
AM/VS/DC

HOURS

Mon-Thu: 12noon-3pm,
5.30pm-11.30pm
Fri-Sat: 5.30pm-
12midnight
Sun: closed

Steph's charming, intimate restaurant is a favourite with theatre-goers. It features an eclectic menu, with a strong, traditional British influence. Food is served in an informal, fun atmosphere by friendly attentive staff.

Pizza Piazza

Pizza

39 Charing Cross Road
☎ 0171-437-1686

Average meal: £5-10
for less discount: 25%
AM/VS/MC/DC

Pizza Piazza is an up-market pizza and pasta restaurant chain. This popular restaurant has an excellent location in the heart of the West End. Try the roasted artichoke topping on a wholemeal-based pizza.

HOURS

Thu-Sat: 10pm-1am
(show starts at 11pm)
Sun-Wed: closed

HOURS

Mon: 5.30pm-11.30pm
Tue-Sat: 12noon-3pm,
5.30pm-11.30pm
Sun: 12noon-4pm

HOURS

Mon-Sat: 12noon-2.45pm,
5.30pm-11.30pm
Sun: 12noon-2pm,
6pm-10.30pm

Centre Stage

Cabaret

**Mountbatten Hotel,
20 Monmouth Street
☎ 0171-379-6009**

Average meal: £30
for less discount: 25%
AM/VS/MC/DC

Centre Stage offers a two-course dinner with wine and intimate cabaret by artistes hand-picked from the West End stage. It is open only on Thursday, Friday and Saturday and you need to book in advance.

Eutens

Modern Afro-Caribbean

**4-5 Neal's Yard
☎ 0171-379-6877**

Average meal: £10-15
for less discount: 25%
AM/VS/MC/DC

This light and airy restaurant serves excellent Afro-Caribbean cuisine. The intriguing menu includes unusual dishes such as curried goat and *roti*. Green décor and numerous plants create a relaxed atmosphere.

Bhatti

Indian

**37 Great Queen Street
☎ 0171-831-0817**

Average meal: £10-15
for less discount: 25%
AM/VS/MC/DC

Bhatti is one of the finest Indian restaurants in London. Its menu is based on that used by India's Moghul royal family. The good value 'special dinner' is highly recommended.

Bella Napoli

Italian

101 Dean Street
☎ **0171-437-9440**

Average meal: £10-15
for less discount: 25%
AM/VS/MC/DC

HOURS

Mon-Sat: 12noon-11pm
Sun: closed

Bella Napoli is a friendly, family-run restaurant, which has been serving traditional Italian food for 25 years. The home-made pasta dishes are particularly recommended.

Nusa Dua

Indonesian

11-12 Dean Street
☎ **0171-437-3559**

Average meal: £10-15
for less discount: 25%
AM/VS

HOURS

Mon-Fri: 12noon-3pm,
6pm-11.30pm
Sat: 6pm-12midnight
Sun: 6pm-10pm

The extensive menu offers Indonesian, Singaporean and Malaysian dishes. Customers include businessmen at lunchtime and theatre-goers at night. Use the set menu to sample a wide range of dishes at an excellent price.

Ad Lib Restaurant

Modern British

Mountbatten Hotel,
20 Monmouth Street
☎ **0171-836-4300**

Average meal: £15-20
for less discount: 25%
AM/VS/MC/DC

HOURS

Mon-Fri: 12.30pm-
2.30pm, 5.30pm-11pm
Sat: 5.30pm-11pm
Sun: 6pm-10pm

The Ad Lib, decorated with West End and Broadway theatre memorabilia, is the perfect place to eat before or after you go out in the area. You can have a starter and main course before the theatre, and a dessert after.

Chi-Chi's

Tex / Mex

5-6 Henrietta Street
☎ **0171-240-2228**

Average meal: £10-15
for less discount: 25%
AM/VS/MC/DC

HOURS

Mon-Sun:
12noon-11.30pm

Chi-Chi's is a bright, open-plan bar and restaurant with a lively atmosphere. The menu is extensive and the *fajitas* are recommended. Try one of the excellent margaritas with your meal.

Old Orleans

American / Cajun

29-31 Wellington Street
☎ **0171-497-2433**

Average meal: £10-15
for less discount: 25%
AM/VS/MC/DC

HOURS

Mon-Sat: 12noon-11pm
Sun: 12noon-10.30pm

Old Orleans re-creates the ambience of the Deep South, in the heart of Covent Garden. The menu is an assortment of Cajun and Creole specialities, plus steaks, burgers, barbecue ribs and various Mexican dishes.

Smollensky's

American

105 The Strand
☎ **0171-497-2101**

Average meal: £10-15
for less discount: 25%
AM/VS/MC/DC

HOURS

Mon-Wed: 12noon-
12midnight
Thu-Sat: 12noon-12.30am
Sun: 12noon-10.30pm

Smollensky's serves modern and traditional American food. Its full and varied menu caters for every taste, including vegetarians. The atmosphere is young, relaxed and fun, with live music every night.

Shopping . . .

Oxford Street is London's main shopping artery. Stretching from Marble Arch to Tottenham Court Road, it contains almost two miles of chain stores, a number of 'megastores' such as the **Virgin** and **HMV** music shops, and numerous small boutiques.

Only buses and taxis are allowed along Oxford Street, but the traffic is still bumper to bumper. It is not much better on the wide pavements, which are flooded with shoppers when the shops are open.

Selfridges department store

Selfridges *(400 Oxford Street, ☎ 0171-629-1234)* is an enormous department store with a very long and grand façade of neo-classical columns. Above the main entrance sits a statue of the Queen of Time, riding the Ship of Commerce. London's up-market answer to Macy's, Selfridges was founded in 1909 by Chicago millionaire Gordon Selfridge. It sells almost everything, but specializes in popular designer fashion.

Two other, much better value department stores are **John Lewis** *(278 Oxford Street, ☎ 0171-629-7711)* and two large branches of **Marks & Spencer** *(173 Oxford Street, ☎ 0171-437-7722 and 458 Oxford Street, ☎ 0171-935-7954),* renowned for its reliable clothing, particularly underwear.

Selfridges

Liberty department store

Bond Street contains exclusive fashion stores, including special outlets of **Donna Karan** *(19 New Bond Street, ☎ 0171-495-3100)* and **Calvin Klein**.

A short distance along the elegantly curved **Regent Street** is **Liberty** *(210 Regent Street, ☎ 0171-734-1234),* probably London's most charming department store. Behind the striking black and white mock-Tudor façade is a labyrinth of rooms and alcoves selling tasteful gifts, clothes, scarves and exotic goods. It is most famous for its gorgeous fabrics.

Liberty

Close to Liberty is the toy emporium **Hamley's** *(188 Regent Street, ☎ 0171-734-3161),* which has several floors overflowing with everything from traditional toys to the latest computer games – many of which can be played with by children before they are bought. You could save a lot of money, however, by buying the same toy from a department store such as John Lewis which

REFLECTIONS

'London is *hot*...right across the board in London now there is daring and finesse' – Karl Lagerfeld (March 1997)

. . . Shopping

has a policy of being 'never knowingly undersold'.

Carnaby Street

Running parallel with Regent Street is the youth fashion showcase of **Carnaby Street**. Shops here sell leather jackets, jeans, nightclub wear and all manner of gimmicks. Carnaby

Regent Street

Street still encapsulates the Swinging Sixties for middle-aged British people, though it has re-invented itself for each generation of teenagers.

Further to the east is **Berwick Street Market**, a street market packed with stalls selling cheap fresh fruit and vegetables. Alongside the colourfully stacked stalls are several specialist popular music shops.

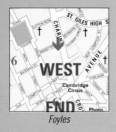

Foyles

Book lovers will be in seventh heaven on **Charing Cross Road**. There are dozens of specialist bookstores such as **Silver Moon** for feminist writing *(64 Charing Cross Road, ☎ 0171-836-7906)*, **Zwemmer's** for art *(24 Litchfield Street, ☎ 0171-379-7886)*, and **Forbidden Planet** for sci-fi *(71 New Oxford Street, ☎ 0171-836-4179)*. **Foyles** *(Charing Cross Road, ☎ 0171-437-5660)* is one of the largest general bookshops, although it is very old-fashioned.

Neal Street

A host of specialist and cult shops, ranging from a store selling hundreds of types of tea to one devoted to the cartoon character Tintin, are to be found on and around **Neal Street**, near Covent Garden. If you want to buy a kite, try **The Kite Store** *(69 Neal Street, ☎ 0171-836-1666)*. If it is beads you need, step into **The Bead Shop** *(43 Neal Street, ☎ 1071-240-0931)*. If your skateboard is seizing up, **Slam City Skates** *(16 Neal's Yard, ☎ 0171-240-0928)* will sort you out.

Neal's Yard

Neal's Yard, tucked away off Neal Street, is a mecca for vegetarians and healthfood fanatics. Mock-rustic shops specialize in cheeses, herbal remedies and other wholesome goods.

For fashion victims, **Floral Street** has major outlets of the top designers **Paul Smith** *(40-44 Floral Street, ☎ 0171-379-7133)* and **Nicole Farhi** *(11 Floral Street, ☎ 0171-497-8713)*. On the parallel street, **Long Acre**, is **Stanford's**, the world's oldest and largest map and guide shop *(12-14 Long Acre, ☎ 0171-836-1321)*.

Old Time Photographers

Photographic Portrait Shop

**Trocadero Centre,
Piccadilly Circus**
☎ 0171-734-8709

for less discount: 20%
AM/VS/MC/DC

HOURS

Sun-Fri: 11am-11pm
Sat: 11am-12midnight

Old Time Photographers offers you a unique souvenir photo service. First, choose the historical period in which you want to be photographed. Then, put on the relevant costume and have your portrait taken.

Piccadilly Souvenirs

Gifts

217 Piccadilly
☎ 0171-734-2175

for less discount: 20%
AM/VS/MC/DC

HOURS

Mon-Sat: 10.30am-9pm
Sun: 12noon-9pm

Packed with souvenirs and woollen goods, this store is designed for visitors. Located in Piccadilly Circus, it is a convenient place to purchase gifts. Items sold range from T-shirts to shortbread biscuits.

Bellini

Men's Suits

167 Regent Street
☎ 0171-494-1778

for less discount: 20%
AM/VS/MC/DC

HOURS

Mon-Sat: 9.30am-6.30pm
Sun: closed

Bellini sells designer label suits at reduced prices. Brands stocked include Hom, Fendi, Ferre, Versace, Zegna and Valentino. This discount is also available at Bellini's main branch at 77 New Bond Street.

HOURS

Mon-Sat: 10.30am-7pm
Sun: closed

Violet

Candles & Gifts

23a Beak Street
☎ **0171-734-3754**

for less discount: 20%
VS/MC

This fascinating shop sells candles of every shape, colour and scent. Some can be made to your personal specification while you wait. It is a great place to purchase a novelty gift or an unusual souvenir of London.

HOURS

Mon-Sat: 9am-6.30pm
Sun: 10am-4pm

Estridge

Woollen & Cashmere Clothing

60-62 Regent Street
☎ **0171-734-0195**

for less discount: 20%
AM/VS/MC/DC

Situated at the bottom of Regent Street close to Piccadilly Circus, Estridge specializes in cashmere, cotton and woollen knitwear for men and women. Many famous British clothing brands are sold here.

HOURS

Mon-Sat: 9.30am-6.30pm
Sun: 12noon-5pm

Grip

Jeans and Casualwear

27 Great Marlborough Street
☎ **0171-437-5068**

for less discount: 20%
AM/VS/MC/DC

Grip sells a wide range of European and American casual wear, such as leading brands of jeans for both men and women. It is a good place to buy fashionable clothes at reasonable prices.

Supreme

Woollen & Cashmere Clothing

31 Carnaby Street
☎ 0171-437-0768

for less discount: 20%
AM/VS/MC/DC

Mon-Sat: 9am-6.30pm
Sun: 10am-4pm

Carnaby Street was famous in the 1960s as the home of London fashion. Supreme specializes in top brand lambswool and cashmere products, as well as accessories from famous English clothing companies.

 # Carlyle and Forge

Menswear & Household

30-32 Foubert's Place
☎ 0171-437-5801

for less discount: 20%
AM/VS/MC

HOURS

Mon-Fri: 11am-7pm
Sat: 10.30am-6pm
Sun: closed

Carlyle and Forge is one of the most interesting stores in Soho. The ground floor presents, elegant, modern English men's clothing. The first floor sells unusual accessories and home furnishings.

 # Back Packer

Outdoor & Camping Goods

136 Charing Cross Road
☎ 0171-836-1160

for less discount: 20%
VS/MC

HOURS

Mon-Sat: 10.30am-6.30pm
Sun: closed

Back Packer has everything you need for outdoor activities, from a penknife to a tent, plus a wide range of sleeping bags and travelling accessories. It stocks major brands such as Karrimor, Vango and Dr. Marten's.

Marmalade

Men's Clothe

85 Oxford Stree
☎ **0171-439-167**

for less discount: 20%
AM/VS/M

HOURS

Mon-Sat: 9.30am-7pm
Sun: 11am-6pm

Marmalade specializes in high-fashion men's clothes both casual and formal. The designer clothes are notable for their unique styles. It is a great place to buy unusual up-to-the-minute men's designer wear.

Sherry's

Men's Fashio

24 Ganton Stree
☎ **0171-734-586**

for less discount: 20%
VS/M

HOURS

Mon-Fri: 10am-6.30pm
Sat: 9.30am-6.30pm
Sun: closed

If you like Mod clothes, you will love this shop. Sherry' specializes in 1960s-style clothing, and you will fin names such as John Smedley and Fred Perry on th shelves.

The Face

Men's Fashio

38 Beak Stree
☎ **0171-437-349**

for less discount: 20%
VS/M

HOURS

Mon-Sat: 10am-6.30pm
Sun: closed

The Face offers a full range of 1960s-style clothing Ben Sherman button-down shirts are among the mor popular items. For high quality woollen wear, try the Joh Smedley range.

Woollen Centre

Men's Tailored Suits

149 Regent Street
☎ 0171-437-7077

for less discount: 20%
VS/MC

HOURS

Mon-Sat: 9.30am-6.30pm
Sun: 11.30am-5.30pm

At the Woollen Centre, you can have a suit hand-tailored for you in one week. Choose a cloth and a style to suit your personal taste. The suit will then be made to your exact size and requirements.

Scottish Cashmere

Cashmere Goods

141 Regent Street
☎ 0171-437-4735

for less discount: 20%
VS/MC

HOURS

Mon-Sat: 9.30am-6.30pm
Sun: 11.30am-5.30pm

Scottish Cashmere stocks a full range of cashmere clothes. Choose from the wide selection of sweaters, scarves and other items. Famous brands sold include Johnstons and McArthur.

Awards

Men's & Women's Clothes

46 Carnaby Street
☎ 0171-734-1546

for less discount: 20%
VS/MC

HOURS

Mon-Sat: 9.30am-6.30pm
Sun: 12noon-5pm

Awards is situated in the heart of Carnaby Street. It stocks well-known brands and own-label items of quality. This discount also applies in the branch at 123a Kings Road, Chelsea.

HOURS

Mon-Sat: 9am-6.30pm
Sun: 10am-4pm

Court

Men's Clothes

187 Regent Street
☎ **0171-494-3590**

for less discount: 20%
AM/VS/MC/DC

Court has been making fine suits for forty years. Suits can be tailor-made within five days of the first fitting. Accessories such as raincoats, ties and cuff-links are also sold.

HOURS

Mon-Sat: 11am-11pm
Sun: 12noon-10.30pm

Cougar

Men's Clothes

151 Regent Street
☎ **0171-287-2426**

for less discount: 20%
AM/VS/MC/DC

This large Regent Street shop sells a complete range of menswear. It stocks top quality clothes and offers excellent, personal service. Brands include Savile Row shirts, Wellington waterproofs and Zegna.

HOURS

Mon-Sat: 10am-7pm
Sun: 12noon-6pm

Saks

Women's Fashion

1 Oxford Street
☎ **0171-437-4542**

for less discount: 20%
AM/VS/MC/DC

Saks is a popular women's fashion store located close to Tottenham Court Road. A wide selection of women's wear in different styles is sold. Souvenir London T-shirts can also be purchased.

Mayfair and St. James

Introduction . . .

Built to accommodate royal courtiers 300 years ago, Mayfair and St. James's remain the playground of the aristocracy and the seriously rich.

These areas boast the highest concentration of exclusive shops, luxury hotels and expensive art galleries. There are few attractions or sites open to the public in Mayfair and St. James's, the notable exception being the **Royal Academy of Arts** (page 100) with its world famous Summer Exhibition.

Hard Rock Café, Old Park Lane

Bordered by three royal parks – Hyde Park, Green Park and St. James's Park – Mayfair and St. James's are the most up-market of London's areas. It is no coincidence that the most expensive properties in the British version of the boardgame Monopoly are all here or close by, with Mayfair and Park Lane the most likely to bankrupt unlucky players.

Luxury service at a Mayfair hotel

Mayfair takes its name from the 15-day fair that was held in the area every May for almost 100 years until 1764, when wealthy residents protested about the noise and succeeded in closing it down.

Unlike Covent Garden and Soho, which were once fashionable with the aristocracy before going into decline, Mayfair has managed to retain its social cachet. Few aristocrats now live here, but hundreds of extremely wealthy foreign nationals have made their London homes in Mayfair in recent years.

Of the six great estates established in the 18th century, the Grosvenor estate was by far the largest, and remains intact in the hands of a direct descendant, the Duke of Westminster.

A traditional wine merchant

The original street pattern survives, punctuated by four very grand squares: Grosvenor, Hanover, Berkeley and St. James's. Many of the Georgian houses have had stucco facings and new porticos added, but most of the structure underneath is original.

. . . Introduction

The area first attracted aristocrats when **St. James's Palace** (page 101), originally one of Henry VIII's hunting lodges, became the official royal London palace after fire had destroyed Whitehall Palace in 1698.

The high concentration of the *haut monde* meant hundreds of fine craftsmen and purveyors of luxury

The Saudi Arabian embassy

goods set up shop locally. Many of these businesses are still open today, clustered on Jermyn Street and Bond Street, and you will find that far more shops in Mayfair and St. James's display the coveted Royal Warrant (denoting a supplier to the Royal family) than in any other area of London (see pages 106-110).

St. James's has long been known as 'Clubland', because of the large number of gentlemen's clubs in the area. Several can be found along **Pall Mall** (page 101), one of London's grandest streets, which was laid out in 1661 with extravagant mansions built for dukes and earls. The street began to acquire its present commercial character in the Victorian period, though two of Queen Victoria's grand-daughters, Princess Helena Victoria and Princess Marie Louise, lived here until 1947.

Large sections of Mayfair and St. James's have, in the last 50 years, been taken over by service industries seeking prestigious addresses for their headquarters. Banks, advertising agencies and luxury car showrooms now occupy the buildings around **Berkeley Square**.

Many of London's most famous hotels are to be found in Mayfair. Several, such as **Claridges** on Brook Street, have illustrious histories stretching back into the 19th century. The **Ritz Hotel** on Piccadilly is perhaps the most famous of Mayfair's exclusive hotels. A sister of the Paris Ritz, it opened in 1906 and still serves its legendary afternoon teas in the exotic Palm Court.

REFLECTIONS

'He had strayed simply enough into Bond Street, where his imagination... caused him now and then to stop before a window in which objects massive and lumpish, in silver and gold...were as tumbled together as if in the insolence of the Empire, they had been loot of far-off victories.'
– *The Golden Bowl,* Henry James (1904)

Claridges

Royal Academy of Arts

The Royal Academy **Summer Exhibition** is one of London's cultural highlights, showcasing the work of both established and up-and-coming artists and sculptors.

The painter Sir Joshua Reynolds was the first president of the Academy, which was founded as Britain's first formal art school in 1768, with George

The Royal Academy of Arts

III as patron. It has occupied its present home, Burlington House – one of the few aristocratic mansions left on Piccadilly – since 1837.

The Academy is approached through a courtyard, sadly used as a car park, around which are housed several other learned societies, including the Geological Society and the Royal Astronomical Society.

The Academy's permanent collection includes at least one work from every member in its history (one of the traditions of membership is that you must contribute a piece of your work). The artists Turner and Constable were members. Living members include artists David Hockney and Sir Hugh Casson, and architects Richard Rogers and Sir Norman Foster. Royal Academicians may put 'RA' after their name.

Interior of the Royal Academy

The prize exhibit is the *Taddei Tondo*, a sculpted disc of the Madonna and Child by Michelangelo. It is found at the top of the glass staircase, inside the astounding light-filled Arthur Sackler Galleries which were designed by Norman Foster and opened in 1991.

Several special exhibitions, for which there is an entry fee, are staged annually.

The Academy shop has an enormous selection of art books, prints, postcards and paraphernalia, which

'Taddei Tondo' by Michelangelo

are ideal as tasteful gifts to take back home.

There is a good restaurant serving excellent, reasonably priced food. It is open from 10am to 5.30pm.

ADDRESS

Burlington House, Piccadilly
☎ 0171-439-7438

GETTING THERE

Piccadilly tube station

HOURS

Mon-Sun: 10am-6pm. The Summer Exhibition is held Jun 1 - Aug 10.

PRICES

Prices vary between £4-6 depending on exhibition.

Other Attractions . . .

Wandering through the streets of Mayfair will afford a glimpse into the rarefied world of the folk who live in the area. Whether it be a gorgeous crystal chandelier spied through a window, or gentlemen in dinner suits accompanied by ladies in gowns making their way to evening functions, you will get a taste of the lavish lifestyle enjoyed here for more than 300 years.

Pall Mall

Pall Mall, lined with gentlemen's clubs and elite societies, was the first gas-lit street in London. It was illuminated to celebrate George III's birthday on June 4, 1807. Royal hangers-on have traditionally lived here, including Charles II's mistress, Nell Gwyn, at No. 79. Charles's dying words were 'Let not poor Nelly starve'.

Filled with privately educated, rich males, the Pall Mall clubs foster Britain's peculiar 'old boys network'. The clubs offer sports facilities for younger members and libraries where the older ones can snooze in plush leather armchairs behind a copy of *The Times*. **The Athenaeum** *(107 Pall Mall)*, flanking Waterloo Place,

Pall Mall

counts many aristocrats, top politicians and several bishops among its members. Traditionally, women have been banned from joining most of these clubs, but the **Oxford and Cambridge University Club** *(71 Pall Mall)* recently voted to admit women as full members.

St. James's Palace stands on the site of an 11th-century hospital for women lepers dedicated to St. James, hence the palace's name. A single sentry stands outside the Tudor brick building. Built by Henry VIII in 1532 as a hunting lodge, only the original octagonal towered Gatehouse and Chapel Royal remain. Foreign ambassadors are still described as being attached to the 'Court of St. James' and they are accredited here, before riding to Buckingham Palace in the Glass Coach *(Corner of Pall Mall and St. James's Street)*.

Guarding St. James's Palace

St James's Palace

Clarence House

Beside the palace is **Clarence House**, built by John Nash in 1825 for the Duke of Clarence, who became William IV. It is the home of the Queen Mother, who is undoubtedly Britain's best-loved royal. She greets well-wishers at the gates on her birthday, August 4.

. . . Other Attractions . . .

Spencer House

There are several other mansions in the immediate area that were built for dukes and duchesses, including **Marlborough House**, built in 1709 by Sir Christopher Wren and the 1820 **Lancaster House**, venue for the 1978 conference that ended white rule in Rhodesia (now Zimbabwe).

Spencer House is a magnificent mid-18th century Palladian mansion with eight finely decorated rooms open to the public. Its beautiful parquet floors, ornate plaster ceilings and classical murals were designed for the first Earl of Spencer, an ancestor of Diana, Princess of Wales. Look out for the ostentatious gilded palm tree columns in Lord Spencer's Room. *(27 St. James's Place, ☎ 0171-493-8111. Sun only: 10.45am-5.30pm. Aug & Jan closed. Adult £6, child £5, senior £5, student £5. Children under 5 not admitted.)*

St. James's Church

Christie's *(8 King Street, ☎ 0171-839-9060)*, the fine art auctioneers, and **Spink & Son** *(7 King Street)*, which sells antique coins and medals, are well worth a browse.

St. James's Square, at the end of King Street, has been one of London's most exclusive addresses since it was laid out in 1670. At one point in the 18th century, 14 dukes and earls lived here.

St. James's Church, completed in 1684, was the last of the many London churches built by Wren and was his personal favourite. It was destroyed in the Second World War bombing of London, but has since been restored. There is a craft market in the courtyard. *(197 Piccadilly, usually open Mon-Sun: 8am-7pm)*

St James's Church

On the north side of Piccadilly, behind the Royal Academy, is the **Museum of Mankind**. This is the ethnographic branch of the British Museum, celebrating the cultures of non-industrialised civilisations and fast-disappearing tribes. It has several reconstructed primitive buildings and dwellings, as well as some astounding religious icons, including one of the famous stone faces from Easter Island. There is a beautiful simplicity to the art, especially the West African carvings, which include two ivory leopards from Benin. The *Gilded Image* is a small, but fascinating, exhibition of gold artefacts from Central and South

Museum of Mankind

Museum of Mankind

. . . Other Attractions

America. All 300,000 artefacts in the collection will be moved to the main British Museum building at the end of 1997. The Café de Colombia on the ground floor serves wholesome food and is rarely busy. *(6 Burlington Gardens, ☎ 0171-437-2224. Mon-Sat: 10am-5pm. Sun: 2.30pm-6pm. Admission is free.)*

Shepherd Market

A few streets to the west stands the grand façade of

Michael Faraday

the **Royal Institution**, a scientific body founded in 1799. Several famous inventors were members, including Michael Faraday, the man who discovered the electromagnetic force. His old laboratory has been turned into the small **Faraday Museum**. *(21 Albemarle Street, ☎ 0171-409-2992. Mon-Fri: 10am-6pm. Sat-Sun: closed. Adults £1, child 50p, senior 50p, student 50p.)*

Faraday Museum

Hidden between Piccadilly and Curzon Street is an attractive enclave of shops and cafés known as **Shepherd Market** (page 104). It is a popular lunchtime and evening meeting place for Londoners, who come here to this residential haven to escape from the traffic.

Open Spaces

The largest open space in the area is **Green Park** (page 194), at the western end of Piccadilly. There are hundreds of well-maintained wrought iron benches lining the long, leafy avenues that criss-cross the park.

Berkeley Square

Grosvenor Square, at the northern end of Mayfair near Oxford Street, is the second largest square in London (only Lincoln's Inn Fields is bigger). It was the grandest address in London in the 18th and 19th centuries, when elegant terraces occupied all four sides and more than half the occupants had aristocratic titles. The west side was removed in the late 1950s to make way for the curiously ugly US embassy.

Berkeley Square

In the heart of Mayfair is **Berkeley Square**, where a group of tall plane trees provides leafy shade. This is a key address for upper class offspring, for whom the annual Berkeley Square Ball is *the* place to be seen. Annabel's, London's top night-club for the rich and famous, is also here.

Eating and Drinking

Most of the restaurants in Mayfair and St. James's serve the upper end of the market. They include the celebrity-packed **Le Caprice** *(Arlington Street, ☎ 0171-629-2239)* and Michel Roux Jnr's **Le Gavroche** *(Upper Brook Street, ☎ 0171-499-1826)*.

Many restaurants are tucked away in **Shepherd Market**, which is a warren of alleyways and passages leading off a square. In the 18th century, this area was a notorious den of gambling and prostitution. It still retains some of its old colour, but is, in addition, a charming, traffic-free location for a drink or meal. Several pubs and cafés have tables on the pavement.

Shepherd Market

Most of the better hotels have restaurants open to people who are not staying at the hotel. **Chez Nico** *(90 Park Lane, ☎ 0171-409-1290)*, at the Grosvenor House Hotel on Park Lane, serves classic French cuisine. The restaurant at **The Chesterfield** (see below) has won several awards.

For simple, but carefully cooked, American food, **Smollensky's** (see opposite) is popular.

If you arrange to meet someone in the Red Lion pub, make sure you know which one you are heading for, because there are two in this area and 22 more across London.

Chez Nico at 90 Park Lane

The **Red Lion** *(☎ 0171-930-4141)* of St. James's is a tiny 400-year-old pub hidden in a narrow alley known as Crown Passage, which runs between Pall Mall and King Street. The **Red Lion** *(☎ 0171-499-1307)* of Mayfair, on Waverton Street, has a blazing fire in winter and a forecourt for the summer.

The Chesterfield

Modern British

**The Chesterfield
35 Charles Street
☎ 0171-491-2622**

Average meal: £15-20
for less discount: 25%
AM/VS/MC/DC

HOURS

Mon-Fri: 12noon-2pm,
6pm-10pm. Sat: 5.30pm-
9.30pm. Sun: 12noon-
2pm, 7pm-10pm

This elegant hotel restaurant, located in the heart of fashionable Mayfair, has won numerous awards for the quality of its dining experience. The superb menu offers an exciting choice of speciality dishes.

Bullochs

International

116 Piccadilly
☎ 0171-499-3464

Average meal: £20-25
for less discount: 25%
AM/VS/MC/DC

HOURS

Mon-Fri: 12.30pm-
2.30pm, 6pm-11pm
Sat: 6pm-11pm
Sun: 7pm-10pm

Bullochs serves high quality food in an exclusive
atmosphere. It offers a modern and romantic setting in
which to have a pleasant meal. The extensive menu
changes with the seasons.

Smollensky's

American

1 Dover Street
☎ 0171-491-1199

Average meal: £10-15
for less discount: 25%
AM/VS/MC/DC

HOURS

Mon-Sat: 12noon-
12midnight
Sun: 12noon-10.30pm

Smollensky's serves modern and traditional American
food. The full and varied menu caters for every taste,
including vegetarian. On weekends, Smollensky's
specializes in children's entertainment.

Bella Pasta

Italian

64 Duke Street
☎ 0171-495-1110

Average meal: £5-10
for less discount: 25%
AM/VS/MC/DC

HOURS

Mon-Sun: 11am-11pm

Bella Pasta serves good-value Italian food from
restaurants all over London. Best known for its pasta
dishes, it also serves pizzas. It is a great place for a
reasonably priced dinner.

Shopping . . .

Many of the exclusive stores in Mayfair and St. James's proudly announce that they supply to members of the royal family, with the title 'By appointment to...' and the appropriate royal coat of arms. There are currently around 800 Royal Warrant holders.

A traditional hat shop

Brace yourself for the very expensive price tags on the luxury goods sold in this neighbourhood. Many people just come to window shop at the exquisitely displayed stores.

Bond Street

Bond Street is the main north-south shopping artery. Silver, paintings and antiques are found in the southern section, while to the north are designer-label clothing and shoe shops.

Gucci *(33 Old Bond Street, ☎ 0171-629-2716)*, **DKNY** *(27 Old Bond Street, ☎ 0171-499-8089)* and, most recently, **Calvin Klein** *(41 New Bond Street, ☎ 0171-491-3900)*, all have major outlets on Bond Street.

Asprey & Co. *(165-169 New Bond Street, ☎ 0171-493-6767)*, the prestigious jewellers serving the royal family, marks the junction of **Old Bond Street** (laid out in 1686) and **New Bond Street** (1721). This is where Prince Charles bought Diana's engagement ring.

Fenwicks, on the corner of Brook Street, is a department store selling Bond Street quality goods at more affordable prices.

Burlington Arcade

Running parallel with Bond Street is **Savile Row**, a byword for fine gentlemen's tailoring.

Burlington Arcade, beside the Royal Academy, is one of London's oldest shopping arcades, dating from 1819. The mahogany-fronted shops sell English fancy goods and finery. Rules of propriety, including an ancient ban on whistling, are enforced by Beadles, top-hatted ex-soldiers who are happy to give advice and directions.

Burlington Arcade

Piccadilly has several traditional English shops, including **Simpson** *(203 Piccadilly, ☎ 0171-734-2002)*, a fashion department store. The most prestigious store is **Fortnum & Mason** *(181 Piccadilly, ☎ 0171-734-8040)*, London's top grocer which supplies delicacies like turtle soup and exotic teas to

. . . Shopping

the Royal Household.

Jermyn Street is famous for selling all the accessories required by a young lord. Several of the shops are patronised by the royal family.

Bates the Hatter *(21 A Jermyn Street,* ☎ *0171-74-2722)* sells deerstalkers, top hats and other high society head gear; **Floris** *(89 Jermyn Street,* ☎ *0171-930-2885)* supplies perfumes to the Queen; **Paxton & Whitfield** *(93 Jermyn Street,* ☎ *0171-930-0259)*, founded in 1740, sells the world's finest cheeses; and **Prestat** (page 110), in nearby Princes Arcade, sells chocolates to the Queen. **St. James's Street** has several very fine shops, notably **Berry Brothers & Rudd** Wine Merchants *(3 St. James's)* and **Lock & Co.** *(6 St. James's)*.

Jermyn Street

 # Taylor

Men's Barber & Gift Shop

74 Jermyn Street
☎ **0171-930-5544**

for less discount: 20%
AM/VS/MC/DC

HOURS

Mon-Fri: 8.30am-6pm
Sat: 8.30am-6pm
Sun: closed

Established in 1854, Taylor is run by the great-grandson of the founder. This exclusive gentlemen's hairdresser is renowned for its service and sells a superb range of high quality gentlemen's accessories.

 # London House

Classic English Clothes

445 Oxford Street
☎ **0171-491-0010**

for less discount: 20%
AM/VS/MC/DC

HOURS

Mon-Sat: 9.30am-6.30pm
Sun: 11am-5pm

London House specializes in classic English clothing for men and women. The range includes cashmere and woollen sweaters and cardigans, rainwear, blazers, shirts, ties, hats and scarves.

HOURS

Mon-Sun: 9.30am-6pm

Mackenzie's

English & Scottish Wear

169 Piccadilly
☎ 0171-495-5514

for less discount: 20%
AM/VS/MC/DC

Mackenzie's, located between The Ritz Hotel and Fortnum & Mason's, is a perfect place to buy traditional English clothing, such as wax jackets. A 20% discount is also available at Forbes menswear at 166 Piccadilly.

HOURS

Mon-Wed: 10am-6pm
Thu-Fri: 10am-8pm
Sat: 9.15am-5.30pm
Sun: closed

Cobella

Hair & Beauty

52 Shepherd Market
☎ 0171-409-0606

for less discount: 20%
VS/MC

Cobella is one of London's outstanding hair and beauty salons. It has won many awards including 'London Stylists of the Year'. A full range of hair and beauty treatments is available.

HOURS

Mon-Fri: 9.30am-5.30pm
Sat: 9.30am-4pm
Sun: closed

Bucci

Leather Goods

16 Prince's Arcade
☎ 0171-734-1846

for less discount: 20%
AM/VS/MC/DC

Situated in Prince's Arcade, Bucci sells the finest quality leather accessories. Exclusive handbags, belts, wallets and executive cases, many hand-crafted and hand-finished, are stocked.

Astleys

Pipes

16 Piccadilly Arcade
☎ 0171-499-9950

for less discount: 20%
AM/VS/MC/DC

HOURS

Mon-Sat: 10am-6pm
Sun: closed

Established in 1862, Astleys stocks a vast range of pipes and pipe accessories. Enthusiasts will marvel at the beautiful oak-fitted period shop. Astleys specializes in fine Briar and Meerschaum smoking pipes.

House of Cashmere

Menswear & Cashmere

471 Oxford Street
☎ 0171-493-3493

for less discount: 20%
AM/VS/MC

HOURS

Mon-Sat: 9.30am-6.30pm
Sun: 11am-5pm

House of Cashmere, situated close to Selfridges, stocks menswear, cashmere knitwear and textiles. A wide range of items, including well-known brands such as Daks, can be purchased.

Benson and Clegg

Gentlemen's Accessories

9 Piccadilly Arcade
☎ 0171-409-2053

for less discount: 20%
AM/VS/MC/DC

HOURS

Mon-Fri: 8.30am-5pm
Sat: 8.30am-12noon
Sun: closed

Benson & Clegg stocks a fine selection of gentlemen's accessories. Of particular note are the cuff-links and ties, but it also specializes in blazer buttons and engraving. Special orders can be taken.

John Bray

Men's Suits

78-79 Jermyn Street
☎ 0171-839-6375

for less discount: 20%
AM/VS/MC/DC

Well-dressed gentlemen of all ages shop for clothes on Jermyn Street. John Bray specializes in modern-style designer suits from famous designers like Versace and Corneliani.

Adele Davis

Women's Clothes

10 New Bond Street
☎ 0171-493-2795

for less discount: 20%
AM/VS/MC/DC

Adele Davis is located in the heart of the Mayfair shopping district. It stocks women's accessories, designer wear and handbags. Major brands include Versace, Fendi, Valentino and Dior.

Prestat

Chocolates

14 Prince's Arcade
☎ 0171-629-4838

for less discount: 20%
AM/VS/MC/DC

Prestat opened in 1903 and is chocolate maker to the Queen. All of the chocolates are hand-made and sold only through this outlet. Specialities include truffles, chocolate figures and brandy cherries.

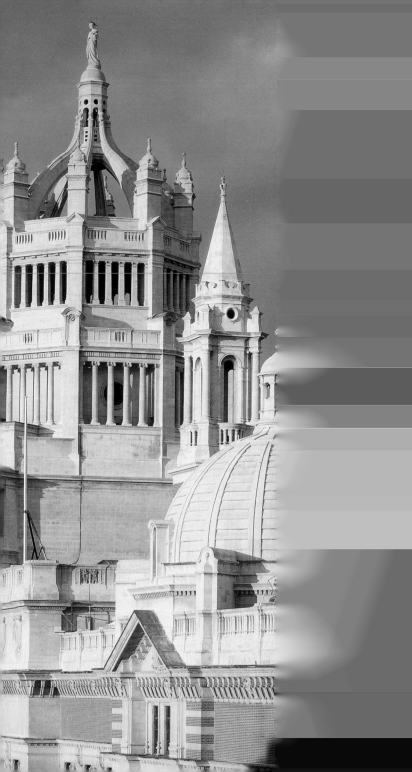

Introduction . . .

London's upper crust inhabits the elegant streets of South Kensington and Chelsea, which have hundreds of fine shops, great restaurants and several historic institutions. All of these combine to make this perhaps the capital's most complete area.

Kensington Palace

For the visitor, South Ken (as it is known to locals) is Museumland. Several of the world's finest museums – the **Victoria & Albert** (page 114), the **Science** (page 115) and the **Natural History** (page 116) – are located in this area.

South Ken is flanked to the north by the vast green expanse of **Kensington Gardens** and **Hyde Park** (page 121). Chelsea, to the south, includes one of the most attractive stretches of the **River Thames**.

South Ken acquired its fine museums during the Victorian period, when Prince Albert decided to channel the profits from the **Great Exhibition** (page 26) into lasting cultural institutions.

REFLECTIONS

'It seems as if only magic could have gathered this mass of wealth from all the ends of the earth - as if none but supernatural hands could have arranged it thus, with such a blaze and contrast of colours' – Charlotte Brontë on visiting the Great Exhibition in Hyde Park (1851)

North of the museums lie a number of colleges and the **Royal Albert Hall** (page 118), where the Promenade Concerts (better known as the 'Proms') take place from July to September. Across the road from the Hall, on the edge of Kensington Gardens, is the enormous **Albert Memorial** (page 118), which is undergoing lengthy restoration. A ten-minute walk into the park brings you to **Kensington Palace** (page 114).

The Cast Room at the V & A

With its fine museums and seats of learning like Imperial College, the area became highly fashionable in the last century, resulting in a network of streets lined with impressive Italianate terraced houses. Today, these are inhabited by wealthy Londoners and foreign nationals from every country.

London is one of the world's most cosmopolitan cities and nowhere is this more manifest than in South Ken. Several embassies are located here and many foreign diplomats live in the area. It has French, German and

. . . Introduction

Islamic institutes, a French Lycée, dozens of language schools and hundreds of foreign restaurants, cafés and delicatessens.

Knightsbridge, the exclusive shopping street, boasts Britain's grandest department store, **Harrods** (page 117).

Chelsea has an even older pedigree than South Ken. It became fashionable in the early 16th century when statesmen like Sir Thomas More lived here. During the latter half of the last century, Chelsea was a haven for

Punks on the King's Road

artists, writers and intellectuals, including Thomas

Carlyle and Oscar Wilde. The area's artistic character has mutated over time, with 1960s flower-power people and, later, the mods and punks of the 1970s claiming a special affinity with the **King's Road**.

This famous road is so-named because, until the 18th century, it was a private royal highway running down to the palaces at Hampton Court and Kew. Today, the King's Road

Royal College of Organists

stretches for more than a mile through the heart of Chelsea. Since the 1960s, it has been one of London's trendiest shopping streets. Wacky fashion designer Vivienne Westwood has a shop at No. 430. There are also hundreds of cafés, bars, fine antiques shops and clothes stores. On Saturday, the 'beautiful people' arrive to parade up and down the street in their latest outfits.

INSIDER'S TIP

Ignore signs at South Kensington tube station for the underpass to the museums – the route above ground is more interesting and almost as quick.

The oldest part of Chelsea is by the river, close to Battersea Bridge. To the left of the bridge is **Chelsea Old Church**, the south chapel of which was built in 1528 for Sir Thomas More's own use. The church contains a monument to More and, outside, there is a colourful statue of him in his Lord Chancellor's robes.

Royal Albert Hall

The road running alongside the river is the famous **Cheyne Walk**, which has been one of the city's most fashionable addresses since the 18th century. George Eliot, Henry James and Dante Gabriel Rossetti are among the famous writers and artists who have lived here.

Victoria & Albert Museum

This vast museum is a treasure trove of art drawn from the world's great cultures. Thousands of exquisite, decorative objects are displayed in an imposing Victorian building.

Founded in 1852, the V&A (as it is usually known) houses priceless collections of sculpture, jewellery, glass, silver, furniture, ironwork, ceramics, photographs and costumes.

ADDRESS

Cromwell Road
☎ 0171-938-8500

If you only have a couple of hours, the best way to see the V&A is simply to browse through a few galleries, dwelling on objects that appeal. In late 1996, the V&A introduced a compulsory entrance charge, thereby provoking a fierce debate about access to Britain's cultural heritage. The likely result is that visitor numbers will fall and the galleries will become less crowded.

Don't miss the two cast rooms, which include an astonishing actual-size replica of **Trajan's Column**, which was so tall it had to be cut in two. Ironically, this copy contains more detail than the original in Rome, which has been eroded by 20th-century pollution. Michelangelo's *David* is also reproduced here.

Victoria & Albert Museum

GETTING THERE

South Kensington
tube station

HOURS

Mon: 12noon-6pm
Tue-Sun: 10am-6pm

PRICES

Adult £5
Child (under 18) free
Senior £3
Student £3

INSIDER'S TIP

For major exhibitions book in advance on 0171-938-8638

Look out for **Tippo's Tiger**, an Indian sultan's 18th-century life-size wooden model of a tiger mauling a British soldier – complete with wind-up sound effects of roars and screams. Other highlights include the **Gloucester Candlestick**, **Ardabil Carpet**, **Eltenburg Reliquary** and **Chinese Jade Geese Box**.

The V&A's spectacular glass collection, comprising 7,000 objects dating from 2,000 BC to the present day, has recently been re-displayed in the high-tech **Glass Gallery** after an absence of fifty years. Other redesigned galleries include the T.T. Tsui **Gallery of Chinese Art**, with its exotic jade and rhino horn carvings, and the Toshiba **Gallery of Japanese Art**, with its elaborate Samurai armour.

The Silver Galleries and the **Raphael Gallery**, were re-opened at the end of 1996 after major refurbishment,

Galleries at the V & A

New: The British Galleries, which represent some 10% of the entire gallery space of the V&A, will close for redevelopment from July 31, 1997 for four years.

Science Museum

Mankind's greatest inventions, including dozens of planes, trains and automobiles, as well as imaginative

demonstrations of scientific discoveries and principles, are on display at the Science Museum.

Making science fun is the emphasis throughout and, of all London's museums, the

Science Museum

Science Museum has made the greatest effort to meet the hands-on demands of today's visitors.

The museum's seven floors contain more than 10,000 exhibits, so – unless you're planning to spend all day here – it is best to head for a few highlights.

The massive machines in the **Land Transport** hall (on the ground floor) include a collection of steam trains and the oldest Rolls Royce.

More than 20 aircraft are on display in the third floor **Flight Gallery**. These include a copy of the Wright brothers' 1903 *Flyer*, Amy Johnson's *Gipsy Moth* and a group of fighter planes from the two world wars.

Next door is the **Flight Lab**, with hands-on demonstrations of flight principles, including a hot-air balloon and a pedal plane. There is an admission

charge for the popular flight simulator.

The **Launch Pad**, a superb attraction for young children, has dozens of giant toys which demonstrate scientific principles. The gallery includes sound dishes that project your voice to the other side of the room, a "shadow box" that catches

The Flight Gallery

your shadow and other games which are demonstrated by friendly green-shirted "Explainers".

The museum has four cafés, two gift shops, a bookshop, a post office and a bureau de change.

New: the **Secret Life of the Home**, revealing how everyday appliances work, opened in the basement in 1996. **A Science of Sport** exhibition is running until October 1998.

ADDRESS

Exhibition Road
☎ 0171-938-8000

GETTING THERE

South Kensington
tube station

HOURS

Mon-Sun: 10am-6pm

PRICES

Adult £6
Child £3.20
(under 5 free)
Senior £3.20
Student £3.20

Admission is free Mon-Fri:
after 4.30pm.

DON'T MISS

Wright Brothers' plane,
Apollo Space Craft and
George III's scientific
instruments.

INSIDER'S TIP

Go before 11am as the
most popular galleries fill
up with kids on busy days

Natural History Museum

ADDRESS

Cromwell Road
☎ 0171-938-9123

GETTING THERE

South Kensington
tube station

HOURS

Mon-Sat: 10am-5.50pm
Sun: 11am-5.50pm

PRICES

Adult £6
Child (under 17) £3
Senior £3.20
Student £3.20
Family £16
Free Mon-Fri: after
4.30pm, Sat-Sun:
after 5pm

DON'T MISS

Earth Galleries, Dinosaur
Gallery, Blue Whale, slice
of Giant Sequoia.

What was once a lifeless collection of specimens in glass cases has recently been transformed with the help of exciting virtual reality displays. The museum occupies a fine neo-Gothic building, with a glorious 675-foot (200-metre) pink and gold terracotta

Natural History Museum

façade. It is not just a major attraction, but also an important research institution, with a staff of 800 maintaining and studying the 68 million objects in its collection.

The museum is divided into two main sections: the **Life Galleries** and the spectacular new £12 million **Earth Galleries.** The Life section starts with a hall dominated by an 85 foot plaster cast of a **Diplodocus** skeleton. Around it are displayed some of the wonders of the natural world, including a model of a sabre-tooth tiger.

The new **Dinosaur Gallery** features three robotic life-size Deinonychi ripping apart a Tenontosaurus. There are also 14 complete dinosaur skeletons. The **Ecology Gallery** has a reconstructed patch of rain forest in a rather politically correct exhibition on green issues.

An unparalleled collection of stuffed birds and animals, some dating back to the 18th century, can be found in the **Bird Gallery**. The museum's most famous exhibit is the full-size model of a blue whale, stretching the length of the **Whale Hall**.

The Earth Galleries, the first of which opened in 1996, are still being completed. They start with an audiovisual **Story of the Earth**, which includes simulated erupting volcanoes. The **gemstones** collection contains a dazzling display of Siberian

The Earth Galleries

diamonds, indigo-blue lapis lazuli from Afghanistan and many more precious stones.

One of the most visually-stunning galleries is **The Power Within**, which includes a reconstruction of Japan's Kobe earthquake, complete with moving floors and shaking walls. In another gallery, one of the world's highest escalators carries you through a massive revolving metal globe 35 feet (10 metres) in diameter.

Harrods

The green and gold doormat at the entrance to the world's most famous department store bears the slogan "Enter a Different World".

Harrods at night

Harrods is neither the world's biggest nor the oldest department store, but it is without doubt the classiest, and thousands enter its doors every day just to browse. There are 300 departments on seven floors, selling everything from pets to polo mallets.

The store's history dates back to 1849, when a wholesale tea merchant, Henry Charles Harrod, took over a small grocer's shop in what was then the village of Knightsbridge. His son, Charles Digby Harrod, took control in 1861 and within 20 years had branched out into perfumes, stationery and patented medicines, employing 100 assistants. In December 1883, the store was destroyed by fire, but Harrod still managed to dispatch all his Christmas orders. Customers were so impressed that, when rebuilding work finished a year later, turnover doubled.

The huge **Food Halls** on the ground floor are a must for any visitor. The lavish displays of exotic foods include 350 cheeses and 151 varieties of tea. Other memorable sections include the **Egyptian Hall**, the elegant **Georgian Restaurant** and the **Fine Jewellery Room**.

Liveried doormen

Harrods' Food Halls

Unfortunately, Harrods' prestige made it an attractive target for IRA bombers, who struck twice at the store, in 1983 and 1993. Though five people were killed in the first bomb, Harrods continued undaunted and in 1985 was bought by the Al Fayed brothers for £615 million.

Throughout the year, the store's façade is beautifully illuminated at night by 12,500 light bulbs. Sales are held in January and July, the first days of which attract upwards of 300,000 people.

ADDRESS

Knightsbridge
☎ 0171-730-1234

GETTING THERE

Knightsbridge
tube station

HOURS

Mon-Tue and Sat:
10am-6pm
Wed-Fri: 10am-7pm

INSIDER'S TIP

A dress code has been introduced banning shorts, vest T-shirts and backpacks.

Other Attractions . . .

Royal Albert Hall

The **Royal Albert Hall**, overlooking Kensington Gardens, is the grandest concert hall in London. Modelled on Roman amphitheatres, the round building was originally to be called the Hall of Arts and Science, but Queen Victoria changed the name to the Royal Albert Hall in memory of her husband. The high frieze around the top of the red-brick building is the work of various artists and depicts 'The Triumph of the Arts and Sciences'.

The hall's former notorious echo was discovered during prayers at the opening ceremony in 1871, when the 'Amen' reverberated around the building. The

Royal Albert Hall

acoustics improved after saucer-like shapes were suspended from the ceiling in 1968. The popular 'Proms' series of classical concerts (page 198) take place at the hall from July to September. *(Kensington Gore, ☎ 0171-589-3203.)*

Opposite the Royal Albert Hall, sheathed in corrugated plastic, is the 180-foot (54-metre) **Albert Memorial**. Queen Victoria took a close interest in Sir George Gilbert Scott's design for this national memorial to Prince Albert. The Gothic canopy is inlaid with polished stone, enamels and mosaics. The base has 169 life-size figures carved in white marble. Seven tiers of statuary rise above the base. The memorial's iron frame had rusted badly by the time it was placed under wraps in 1990. The design and the restoration work are explained in the **Albert Memorial Visitor Centre** on site.

Royal College of Organists

Queen's Tower

The most bizarrely decorated building in the area is the **Royal College of Organists**. The ornate cream and maroon plasterwork is capped by a frieze depicting youths and maidens playing musical instruments. *(Behind the Royal Albert Hall.)*

Royal College of Music

The neo-Gothic **Royal College of Music** building contains a collection of 600 musical instruments, some dating from the 15th century. Instruments played by George Handel, Franz Haydn and other great composers are on display. *(Prince Consort Road, ☎ 0171-589-3643. Wed only: 2pm-4.30pm. Adult £1.20, child £1, senior £1, student £1.)*

. . . Other Attractions . . .

The 280-foot (84-metre) **Queen's Tower**, on Imperial College Road, is all that remains of the huge Imperial Institute built in the 1880s. The rest of it has been demolished to make way for the office blocks of Imperial College.

Brompton Oratory

Queen's Tower

South Kensington has hundreds of Italianate terraces and mansions with colonnaded entrances and uniformly whitewashed façades. The finest are to be found in Onslow Square and along Queen's Gate.

Queen Victoria is one of the historical figures you can hear talking at the **National Sound Archive**. Order what you want to hear in advance. *(29 Exhibition Road, ☎ 0171-412-7440. Mon-Fri: 10am-5pm. Thu: 10am- 9pm. Admission is free.)*

Brompton Oratory

The Italian baroque **Brompton Oratory**, next to the V&A on Brompton Road, is London's grandest Catholic church. It was built in 1880-1884 and is based on the church of Chiesa Nuova in Rome. The main features of interest are the striking, white stone façade, the magnificent Italian altar-piece and the stunning 200-foot (60-metre) high dome. The Oratory, famous for its acoustics, is a renowned concert venue. *(Thurloe Place, Brompton Road, ☎ 0171-589-4811. Mon-Sun: 7am-8pm)*

The National Army Museum

Chelsea Physic Garden, overlooking the Thames on Chelsea Embankment, contains a collection of rare trees, herbs and plants. This small but fascinating garden was founded by the Apothecaries' Company in 1676. It boasts the world's first rock garden and a statue of Sir Hans Sloane, the 18th-century physician who bequeathed his antiquities to found the British Museum. *(66 Royal Hospital Road, Swan Walk, ☎ 0171-352-5646. Apr-Oct: Wed: 2pm-5pm. Sun: 2pm-6pm. Admission £3.50, child £1.80, senior £1.80, student £1.80.)*

Chelsea Physic Garden

A short walk from the garden, along Royal Hospital Road, is the **National Army Museum**. It is mainly of interest to the military-minded. The skeleton of Marengo, Napoleon's charger, and a 420 square foot model of the Battle of Waterloo with 70,000 model

. . . Other Attractions

soldiers, are two of the most popular exhibits. A new permanent exhibition, *The Rise of the Redcoat*, tells the story of the British Army from Agincourt to the American Revolution. *(Royal Hospital Road, ☎ 0171-730-0717. Mon-Sun: 10am-5.30pm. Admission is free.)*

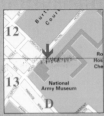

National Army Museum

The **Commonwealth Experience,** is the latest of London's galleries to 'go interactive'. The old Commonwealth Institute, founded in the 1960s as a

Commonwealth Experience

celebration of the various cultures that make up the British Commonwealth, re-opens in May 1997 with two special features. 'Heliride' takes visitors on a simulated helicopter ride over Malaysia. 'Interactive World' offers hands-on explanations of natural phenomena, like why the sky is blue. *(Kensington High Street, ☎ 0171-371-3530. Mon-Sun: 10am-5pm. Last admission 4.30pm. Adult £4.45, child £2.95, senior £3.45, student £3.45.)*

Commonwealth Experience

A short distance from the Galleries, tucked away on Holland Park Road, is **Leighton House**, home of one of Queen Victoria's favourite artists, Frederic Leighton. There are paintings by Leighton and his contemporaries, including works by all the leading Pre-Raphaelites. Evening concerts are held in Leighton's vast studio. *(Holland Park Road, ☎ 0171-602-3316. Mon-Sat: 11am-5.30pm. Sun: closed. Admission is free).*

Leighton House

Leighton House was once part of a Victorian artists' colony around Holland Park. Holman Hunt, who painted the *Light of the World* which hangs in St. Paul's Cathedral (page 136-137), lived at No.18 Melbury Road, while sculptor George Frederick Watts, whose equestrian figure *Physical Energy* stands in Kensington Gardens, lived at No.6.

More Victorian art and decoration is on display at **Linley Sambourne House**. The house ostensibly celebrates the work of Sambourne, the famous 19th-century *Punch* magazine cartoonist, but is in fact a superbly preserved example of late Victorian taste, complete with William Morris wallpaper. *(18 Stafford Terrace, ☎ 0181-742-3438. Mar-Oct: Wed: 10am-4pm. Sun: 2pm-5pm. Adult £3, child £1.50, senior £2.50, student £3.)*

Open Spaces

There is a hidden green space behind Brompton Oratory surrounded by pretty pastel-painted cottages. It is small, but ideal for picnics as the trees offer some shade.

For longer walks, **Hyde Park** (page 188) and **Kensington Gardens** (page 190) can easily be reached from most parts of South Kensington and Chelsea. These two linked parks combine to make central London's largest green expanse, stretching from the West End to Kensington Palace. Dozens of paths criss-cross the parks through open and wooded areas, making them ideal for either walking or playing ball games. On fine days, you will find thousands of Londoners relaxing in the sunshine.

Holland Park

Holland Park, which contains central London's largest area of woodland, lies at the western end of Kensington High Street. The remains of Holland House, a 17th-century stately home, stand in the centre of the park. There are three formal gardens: the Rose Garden, the Iris Garden and the Dutch Garden. The latter contains a statue by the English sculptor Eric Gill. In summer, open-air plays and concerts are held in the Court Theatre. There is an inexpensive café at the top of the main field, with tables and chairs set under the trees.

The largest open space in Chelsea is **Ranelagh Gardens**, where the famous Chelsea Flower Show is held in the third week of May. The gardens alongside the River Thames afford excellent views of Sir

Holland Park

Christopher Wren's **Royal Hospital**, completed in 1686 and now known as the Chelsea Hospital. It was founded by Charles II as a home for veteran soldiers and it is still used for this purpose. The 'Chelsea Pensioners', as the residents are known, are easy to identify by their distinctive winter blue and summer scarlet uniforms.

Ranelagh Gardens

Just across the river, reached by either Chelsea Bridge or Albert Bridge, is **Battersea Park**. The **London Peace Pagoda**, built in 1985 beside the river, is the park's distinctive landmark. A children's zoo, a deer park and a boating lake are among the other amenities.

Eating and Drinking

South Kensington and Chelsea both have a diverse range of international restaurants. Old Brompton Road, Fulham Road, King's Road and Kensington High Street all have dozens of good places to eat and drink.

In Knightsbridge, **Walton Street** has a number of classy eateries, including **Turner's** *(87-89 Walton Street)* and **San Martino** *(103 Walton Street)*. Brompton Cross, where the Fulham and Brompton Roads meet, has several trendy cafés. **Joe's Café** *(126 Draycott Avenue, ☎ 0171-225-2217)* attracts the 'fashion crowd'.

Within a stone's throw of South Kensington tube station is an eclectic mix of venues. Try **Francofill** (page 125) for freshly-baked French treats or the authentically Polish **Wodka** (page 124).

Walton Street

HOURS

Mon-Sun: 12noon-3pm,
6pm-12midnight

HOURS

Mon-Sat: 12.30pm-
1.30am
Sun: 5.30pm-1am

Thai Terrace

Thai

14 Wright's Lane
☎ 0171-938-2227

Average meal: £10-15
for less discount: 25%
AM/VS/MC/DC

In recent years, Thai cuisine has become very popular in London. This large restaurant is renowned for the quality of its food. The ground floor is comfortable and relaxed, while the upper floor is more traditional.

Borshtch 'n' Tears

Russian

46 Beauchamp Place
☎ 0171-589-5003

Average meal: £10-15
for less discount: 25%
AM

Borshtch 'n' Tears has been offering fine Russian food since 1965. The portions are generous and the atmosphere is always lively. Every evening the informal ambience is enhanced by live Russian music.

Khan's of Kensington

Indian

3 Harrington Road
☎ 0171-581-2900

Average meal: £10-15
for less discount: 25%
AM/VS/MC/DC

HOURS

Mon-Sat: 12noon-2.30pm,
5.30pm-11.30pm
Sun: 1pm-11pm

Khan's is the perfect place to enjoy a relaxed lunch. House specialities include *murgh makhni* and *Karachi gosth*. The wine bar is a good place to meet friends for a drink.

Footlights

International

1 Kensington High Street
☎ 0171-795-6533

Average meal: £10-15
for less discount: 25%
VS/MC

HOURS

Mon-Thu: 12noon-11pm
Fri-Sat: 12noon-11.30pm
Sun: 12noon-10.30pm

Footlights is located almost on the doorstep of Kensington Palace. It is situated in a large, impressive building that was once a bank. A wide range of Mexican and traditional English dishes are served.

 # Made in Italy

Italian

249 King's Road
☎ 0171-352-1880

Average meal: £10-15
for less discount: 25%
AM/VS/MC

HOURS

Mon-Fri: 12noon-3pm,
6pm-11.30pm
Sat: 12noon-12midnight
Sun: 12noon-11pm

Good-value Italian food is offered at this popular restaurant, where the dining areas, on three levels, have a rustic Italian charm. It is best known for its large reasonably priced pizzas.

Wodka

Polish

12 St. Alban's Grove
☎ 0171-937-6513

Average meal: £10-15
for less discount: 25%
AM/VS/MC/DC

HOURS

Mon-Fri: 12.30pm-
2.30pm, 7pm-11pm
Sat: 7pm-11pm
Sun: 7pm-10.30pm

Wodka is the best-known Polish restaurant in London. The décor is modern and the food, which offers great variety, is classic Polish cuisine. To finish, try one of the frozen vodkas.

Phoenicia

Lebanese

11-13 Abingdon Road
☎ 0171-937-0120

Average meal: £10-15
for less discount: 25%
AM/VS/MC/DC

HOURS

Mon-Sun:
12noon-12midnight

Phoenicia is one of the best Lebanese restaurants in London. It is also one of the most reasonably priced, even before the discount. The set meals offer an easy-to-follow introduction to Lebanese food.

Bugis Street Brasserie

Asian

Gloucester Hotel,
Ashburn Place
☎ 0171-411-4234

Average meal: £5-10
for less discount: 25%
AM/VS/MC

HOURS

Mon-Sun: 12noon-11pm

Bugis Street Brasserie serves inexpensive multicultural dishes from Asia. The décor is contemporary and the atmosphere lively. Try the chef's special seafood *ho fun* or the *laksa*.

South West 7

Modern British

**Gloucester Hotel,
Courtfield Road**
☎ 0171-411-4212

Average meal: £10-15
for less discount: 25%
AM/VS/MC/DC

HOURS

Mon-Fri: 12noon-3pm,
5.30pm-10.45pm
Sat-Sun: 5.30pm-
10.45pm

This sophisticated restaurant serves contemporary British food in a spacious and relaxed atmosphere. Try the grilled sea bream with leek compote and saffron risotto.

My Old Dutch

Pancake House

221 King's Road
☎ 0171-376-5650

Average meal: £5-10
for less discount: 25%
AM/VS/MC/DC

HOURS

Sun-Mon: 12noon-11pm
Tue-Thu: 12noon-11.30pm
Fri-Sat: 12noon-
12midnight

This inexpensive restaurant serves enormous, tasty pancakes. The menu has over 100 flavours of pancakes and waffles. There is a full bar with seasonally imported Dutch beers.

Francofill

French

1 Old Brompton Road
☎ 0171-584-0087

Average meal: £5-10
for less discount: 25%
AM/VS/MC

HOURS

Mon-Sat: 11am-11pm
Sun: 12noon-10.30pm

Francofill serves freshly baked rolls filled with selected meats and sauces. It also has a wide selection of traditional French favourites. It is a pleasant, informal place to have a quality, high-speed meal.

HOURS

Mon-Sun:
12noon-12midnight

Pizza Chelsea

Pizza

93 Pelham Street
☎ 0171-584-4788

Average meal: £5-10
for less discount: 25%
AM/VS/MC/DC

Pizza Chelsea is located in the heart of the museum district. It is best known for its good-value pizzas. For something unusual, try the Thai duck or Chinese prawn pizzas.

Spago 2

Italian

45 Kensington High Street
☎ 0171-937-6471

Average meal: £10-15
for less discount: 25%
AM/VS/MC

HOURS

Mon-Sun:
12noon-12midnight

Spago 2 is a great place to take a break from shopping. You could pop in for a cup of coffee or settle down for a proper meal. It specializes in pizza and pasta dishes. Try the spaghetti *vongole veraci*.

Bella Pasta

Italian

60 Old Brompton Road
☎ 0171-584-4028

Average meal: £5-10
for less discount: 25%
AM/VS/MC

HOURS

Sun-Thu:
10.30am-11.30pm
Fri-Sat:
10.30am-12midnight

Bella Pasta serves unpretentious Italian food. It is best known for its home-made pizza and pasta dishes. The discount also applies at Bella Pasta restaurants located at 155 Earls Court Road and 313 Fulham Road.

Rotisserie Jules

French

338 King's Road
☎ 0171-351-0041

Average meal: £5-10
for less discount: 25%
AM/VS/MC

HOURS

Mon-Sun:
11.30am-11.30pm

Open long hours, Rotisserie Jules is popular with visitors and residents alike. The menu offers a good range of exciting chicken dishes. It is ideal either for an afternoon snack or a reasonably priced meal.

Marlborough Room

Modern British

**The Vanderbilt Hotel,
76 Cromwell Road**
☎ 0171-589-2424

Average meal: £10-15
for less discount: 25%
AM/VS/MC/DC

HOURS

Mon-Sat: 12.30pm-
2.30pm, 5.30pm-10pm
Sun: 12.30pm-2.30pm,
6.30pm-10pm

The Marlborough Room features British cuisine in an elegant setting. Being only a short walk from Harrods and the major shopping area, it is a superb place to relax after a hectic day of sightseeing or shopping.

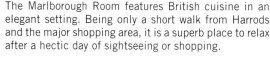 Café Lazeez

Indian

93-95 Old Brompton Road
☎ 0171-581-9993

Average meal: £10-15
for less discount: 25%
AM/VS/MC/DC

HOURS

Mon-Sat: 11am-1am
Sun: 11am-10.30pm

Winner of several awards, including "Best Indian Restaurant 1996", it is regarded as one of the top Indian restaurants in Europe. There are three dining environments: *al fresco*, café/bar and formal.

Shopping

The presence of Harrods (page 117) has made **Knightsbridge** one of London's most exclusive shopping areas, especially for high fashion.

Harvey Nichols

The other major department store, **Harvey Nichols** (*Knightsbridge,* ☎ *0171-235-5000*), is now largely devoted to expensive women's clothes and has the finest window displays in London. **The Fifth Floor Café** is popular with elegant 'ladies who lunch'.

There are several expensive designer fashion shops on Sloane Street, Walton Street and Beauchamp (pronounced 'bee-cham') Place, which are all nearby.

Brompton Cross, at the eastern end of the Fulham Road, has several 'design' shops, the most famous of which is the **Conran Shop** (*81 Fulham Road,* ☎ *0171-589-7401*) occupying Michelin House. It specializes in classic designer furniture, such as Kandinsky chrome and hide chairs and Travieso steel bedframes.

Kensington High Street

Kensington High Street (known locally as 'High Street Ken') is a smaller, and more up-market, version of Oxford Street, with larger stores at the eastern end and specialist shops further west. **Barkers of Kensington** (*63 High South Kensington Street,* ☎ *0171-937-5432*), close to High Street Kensington tube station, is an art deco-style department store, recommended for its men's fashion. You can buy a pair of Church's brogues, Calvin Klein jeans or a Pour Homme shirt.

Branching off the High Street, leading up to Notting Hill Gate, is **Kensington Church Street**, where you will find many up-market antique shops.

Cashmere Gallery

Woollen & Cashmere Clothing

25 Brompton Road
☎ **0171-838-0048**

for less discount: 20%
AM/VS/MC/DC

HOURS

Mon-Sat: 9am-6.30pm
Sun: 10am-4pm

Cashmere Gallery specializes in wool, cotton and cashmere products. All of the top brands are stocked in a range of colours and sizes. It also sells men's and women's clothing accessories.

Paul and Shark

Men's Clothing

24 Brompton Arcade
☎ **0171-581-0846**

for less discount: 20%
AM/VS/MC/DC

Paul and Shark sells classic Italian designed clothes. A complete range of men's clothes is available. All items are made from natural materials such as cotton, wool, cashmere or silk.

HOURS

Mon-Sat: 10am-6.30pm
Sun: closed

Cashmere Stop

Cashmere & Silk Clothing

4a Sloane Street
☎ **0171-259-6055**

for less discount: 20%
AM/VS/MC/DC

In this classic shop, all goods are either cashmere (pure or mix) or silk. An extensive collection of top brand sweaters is stocked. Cardigans, jackets, overcoats, capes and accessories are also available.

HOURS

Mon-Sat: 10am-6.30pm
Sun: 11am-5.30pm

Createx

Children's Clothing

25-27 Harrington Road
☎ **0171-589-8306**

for less discount: 20%
AM/VS/MC/DC

Createx sells high quality, stylish French and Italian designer children's clothes. It provides a "top-to-toe" service that includes accessories such as hats, with each item complementing the outfit.

HOURS

Mon-Fri: 9.30am-6pm
Sat: 10am-6pm
Sun: closed

Gallops

Men's Clothing

16 Old Brompton Road
☎ 0171-589-1734

for less discount: 20%
AM/VS/MC

HOURS

Mon-Sat: 8.30am-6.30pm
Sun: closed

Gallops has been selling luggage to Londoners since the turn of the century. It carries a wide selection of travel and leather goods, and also operates a 24-hour repair service if your luggage has been damaged.

Hari's

Hair & Beauty

305 Brompton Road
☎ 0171-581-5212

for less discount: 20%
AM/VS/MC/DC

HOURS

Mon-Sat: 10am-6.30pm
Sun: closed

On the lower floors is Hari's hairdressing salon, while the top two floors offer a comprehensive beauty facility. The service is friendly and attentive, with all customers being offered tea or coffee.

Natural Fact

Clothing & Accessories

192 King's Road
☎ 0171-352-4283

for less discount: 20%
VS/MC

HOURS

Mon-Fri: 8.30am-8pm
Sat: 8.30am-7pm
Sun: 12noon-6pm

Natural Fact sells leisure clothes, denims, sweaters and nightwear. Natural body products, foam and bath oil, shampoos and conditioners are also sold. There is also a wide range of gifts, all of which can be boxed.

Hitite

Women's Fashion

157 King's Road
☎ 0171-351-1915

for less discount: 20%
AM/VS/MC/DC

HOURS

Mon-Sat: 10am-7pm
Sun: 11am-7pm

Hitite, which stocks the latest street wear, is especially popular with young, fashion-conscious Londoners. It sells everything from top club wear to sunglasses and hats.

 # Linea

Ladies & Men's Clothing

4 Harriet Street
☎ 0171-235-8881

for less discount: 20%
AM/VS/MC/DC

HOURS

Mon-Sat: 10am-6pm
Sun: closed

Linea is located just around the corner from Harvey Nichols. It specializes in designer clothes for both men and women. Major brands include Fendi, Vestimenta and Alea.

 # Obsessions

Gifts

23 Old Brompton Road
☎ 0171-589-0071

for less discount: 20%
AM/VS/MC/DC

HOURS

Mon-Sat: 10.30am-
6.30pm
Sun: closed

Obsessions is full of novel items and unusual gifts. Here you will find everything from alarm clocks to underwear. Whoever you are buying for, Obsessions will have something appropriate.

Make-up Centre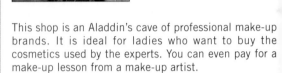

Make-up

26 Bute Street
☎ **0171-584-2188**

for less discount: 20%
AM/VS/MC/DC

HOURS

Mon-Fri: 10am-6.30pm
Sat: 10am-5.50pm
Sun: closed

This shop is an Aladdin's cave of professional make-up brands. It is ideal for ladies who want to buy the cosmetics used by the experts. You can even pay for a make-up lesson from a make-up artist.

Leather Classics

Leather Garments

113 King's Road
☎ **0171-352-2480**

for less discount: 20%
AM/VS/MC/DC

HOURS

Mon-Sat: 10am-7pm
Sun: 12noon-6pm

This fashionable King's Road store sells a wide range of stylish leather jackets. Motorcycle racing jackets and a wide range of leather clothing are stocked. Among the brands available are Avirex and Red Skins.

Museum Store

Gifts

50 Beauchamp Place
☎ **0171-581-9255**

for less discount: 20%
AM/VS/MC/DC

HOURS

Mon-Sat: 9am-5pm
Sun: closed

The Museum Store stocks gifts from museums around the world, including traditional and contemporary pieces. It sells many unusual, exclusive items from around the world.

City of London

Introduction . . .

The compact area known as **'the City'**, spelled with a capital 'C', is not to be confused with the wider city of London.

The City is Europe's financial centre, where the world's leading banks and financial services companies are located. Also known as the 'Square Mile' (for that is the area it covers) the City is a rabbit warren of narrow streets and tall office blocks.

The Barbican Centre

Paradoxically, this is at once the most ancient and most modern part of London. Its boundaries are still roughly equivalent to those of the old Roman walled city, but its skyline is now dominated by high-rise buildings, many built during the 1980s commercial property boom. The great exception, of course, is the magnificent domed **St. Paul's Cathedral** (pages 136-137).

The narrow, winding, medieval street pattern remains, and there are clues to the City's long history in many of the street names, such as Bread Lane, Milk Street and Poultry. Cheapside, now full of banks and company headquarters, was once London's main shopping street.

Tower Bridge

INSIDER'S TIP

The tube journey to the City can be crowded during morning and evening rush hours. For a scenic ride to St. Paul's catch a bus on the Strand.

Visit on a weekday if you want to find restaurants, pubs and shops open, or at the weekend to avoid the crowds.

Other than a few medieval churches and the **Tower of London** (pages 138-139), the City's oldest surviving buildings mainly date from the reconstruction that followed the **Great Fire** of 1666, which ravaged two-thirds of the area. This destroyed old St. Paul's Cathedral along with the City's medieval slums (where over 75,000 people had died the previous year in the **Great Plague**). More recently, many beautiful buildings were razed to the ground during the Second World War bombing 'Blitz' of 1940-41.

Lloyd's of London building

As a result of all the necessary building and rebuilding through the ages, the City is a confusing maze of streets and a hotchpotch of architectural styles.

Some of the City's modern office architecture is impressive, notably the space-age **Lloyd's of London**

. . . Introduction

building (page 146) and the huge **Broadgate** development (page 148) around Liverpool Street Station, with its open-air ice rink and plentiful modern sculptures.

Only 8,000 people actually live in the City. It is a ghost town in the evenings and at weekends, when offices are closed. However, more than 300,000 commuters flood into the City's offices each weekday morning. Do not, however, expect warm greetings from City workers going about their business; as the poet T.S. Eliot put it: "A crowd flowed over London Bridge...each man fixed his eyes before his feet".

City skyline from St. Paul's

The City still enjoys the semi-autonomous status conferred upon it by William the Conqueror. It is controlled by 'The Corporation of London', a select, somewhat mysterious and very powerful group. A range of feudal titles – Beadle, Alderman, Sheriff and the Lord Mayor – are conferred each year on

Commuters on London Bridge

members of the Corporation. Genuine democracy has yet to invade this anachronistic old boys' club, which draws its electors from the City's 90 **Livery Companies** (page 147). In the City, the Lord Mayor ranks above all, except the Sovereign. He (there has only ever been one woman) is invested on the second Saturday in November with a grand pageant, known as the **Lord Mayor's Show** (page 247).

REFLECTIONS

' There are not more useful members in a common-wealth than merchants. They knit mankind together in a mutual intercourse of good offices, distribute the gifts of nature, find work for the poor, add wealth to the rich, and magnificence to the great.' – Joseph Addison, writing about The Royal Exchange (1711)

While most visitors to the City come just to see St. Paul's or the Tower of London, there is a wealth of smaller churches and museums tucked away, which are well worth seeking out. **Dr. Johnson's House** (page 143) celebrates the life of one of England's greatest men of letters and has many 18th-century

Lord Mayor's Show

artefacts, including first editions of Johnson's great dictionary. Sir Christopher Wren's **St. Bride's Church** (page 143) has one of the most beautiful steeples ever built and interesting Roman mosaics in the crypt.

St. Paul's Cathedral . . .

Sir Christopher Wren's masterpiece is London's greatest architectural treasure.

St. Paul's is a majestic building with the second largest cathedral dome in the world (after St. Peter's in Rome). It is venerated by the British as a place of public triumph and is where, instead of the more traditional Westminster Abbey, Prince Charles chose to marry Lady Diana Spencer in 1981.

The modern St. Paul's is the fourth cathedral dedicated to London's patron saint to be built on the site – the first was a wooden building founded by King Ethelbert in the 7th century.

Wren began planning the present cathedral only days after the Great Fire of London destroyed old St. Paul's in 1666. The only monument to survive the fire was that of **John Donne**, the poet and Dean of St. Paul's. It can still be seen in the south choir aisle.

St. Paul's Cathedral

Wren had a furious row with the Church authorities over his original plan, which they considered too "modern". The architect himself oversaw the 33 years of construction. In 1697, Parliament became frustrated with the slow progress of the project and halved Wren's £200 salary. But Wren, though approaching 70, remained in close control of the building work and was regularly hoisted 300 feet (90 metres) up into the great stone lantern that sits above the dome. It was his son, however, who laid the final stone.

Wren is buried in the crypt, where his simple tomb is easy to miss. However, immediately under the dome is the inscription: "Reader, if you seek his monument, look around you."

St. Paul's in fact has two domes: the smaller dome seen from the inside and a larger, outer shell rising 60 feet (18 metres) above it. In between the two domes is a brick cone, a clever architectural device to support the great weight of the lantern. Sir James Thornhill's frescoes on the inner dome depict scenes from the life of St. Paul.

ADDRESS

Top of Ludgate Hill
☎ 0171-236-4128

GETTING THERE

St. Paul's tube station

HOURS

Mon-Sat: 8.30am-4pm
Sun: closed to sightseers

Sunday organ recitals are at 5.15pm.
Orchestral Sunday services in July are at 11am.

PRICES

Cathedral only:
Adult £3.50
Child £2
Senior £3
Student £3

Combined ticket to cathedral and galleries:
Adult £6
Child £3
Senior £5
Student £5

DISCOUNT

£1 off combined ticket to cathedral and galleries per person with voucher on page 279.

. . . St. Paul's Cathedral

Relatively few monuments or paintings adorn St. Paul's, though Holman Hunt's copy of his own. **The**

'The Light of the World' by Holman Hunt

Light of the World, one of the finest Pre-Raphaelite paintings, is in the south aisle (the original is in Keble College, Oxford).

The 530 steps to the **Golden Gallery** are gruelling, but are divided into three stages, with a viewing point at each. There is a separate entrance charge for the galleries.

The first leg, much the easiest, takes you up to the **Whispering Gallery** where the extraordinary acoustics allow you to hear words whispered into the wall at the other side of the dome, 107 feet away. This was a favourite place for lovers in the Victorian period, who would whisper secret messages to each other.

The next flight of steeper, spiralled stairs leads to the **Stone Gallery**, with grand views and benches on which to rest.

Even more magnificent is the view across London from the **Golden Gallery**, though for this pleasure you will have to climb another 160 fire-escape type steps. On the way up, don't miss the small spy window through which you can view the monochrome marble floor a dizzying drop below.

Interior of St. Paul's

You can see many famous landmarks from the viewing galleries, including the Houses of Parliament to the west and Tower Bridge to the east. On a clear day, the galleries offer views stretching across to the distant hills that surround London.

For a less energetic experience, the **Crypt** contains the tombs of some of Britain's greatest war heroes, including those of Nelson and Wellington. More recent memorials commemorate the hundreds of men who died in the Falklands and Gulf Wars. The **Treasury** at the west end of the crypt displays ancient chalices and gorgeously embroidered robes used for state occasions.

DON'T MISS

Whispering Gallery,
John Donne's memorial,
The Light of the World.

INSIDER'S TIP

St. Paul's is very popular, so try to go before 11am if you want to appreciate the peaceful holiness of the Cathedral.

Tower Hill
☎ 0171-709-0765

Tower Hill tube station

Mar-Oct:
Mon-Sat: 9am-6pm
Sun: 10am-6pm

Nov-Feb:
Sun-Mon: 10am-5pm
Tue-Sat: 9am-5pm

 # Tower of London . . .

The **Crown Jewels** might be the most famous exhibit, but every inch of this ancient palace-fortress is steeped in history.

Tower of London

The Tower has served many functions in its nine centuries: it was the fortress of William the Conqueror, the palace of medieval kings, the prison of Sir Thomas More, Anne Boleyn, Sir Walter Raleigh and, most recently, Rudolph Hess. It has also housed the Royal Mint, making the nation's money, and is now the stronghold for the priceless Crown Jewels.

The Tower is guarded by 40 Yeoman Warders, popularly known as **Beefeaters**. They are all ex-servicemen and wear elaborate red and dark blue Tudor tunics with large, round hats.

The Beefeaters' guided tours, free with the entrance price, are superb, with just the right mix of history and humour. They tell you about the kings and queens who were murdered or executed in the Tower, but also point out where Errol Flynn was filmed holding up a three-ton portcullis in *Robin Hood*.

The Ravenmaster

The **Bloody Tower** is so named because of the many dastardly crimes committed inside, including the murders of the boy king Edward V and his ten-year-old brother in 1483. Shakespeare famously blamed the murders on Richard of Gloucester, young Edward's protector. This theory is attractive from a theatrical perspective as the hunchbacked villain of Shakespeare's history plays benefits from his crime by becoming Richard III. However, many historians have since sought to redeem Richard's reputation.

The oldest part of the fortress is the **White Tower**, built by William the Conqueror in the 11th century. The Tower's Chapel of St. John is ringed by graceful columns which have been restored to their original appearance.

The **Instruments of Torture** gallery in the White Tower contains the execution block used for the last public

. . . Tower of London

beheading on Tower Hill, which took place in 1747. The grooves cut by the falling axe can still be seen.

Most of the **Royal Armouries'** enormous collection of weapons and suits of armour has been moved to a special museum in Leeds. However, there is still a small collection of royal armour in the Tower.

St. Thomas's Tower, built in the 13th century, has been restored to show how it would have looked during the reign of Edward I.

Imperial State Crown

Queuing at the **Jewel House**, which was refurbished in 1994, is made relatively painless as the line is filtered through three rooms. Each of the rooms has a large video screen telling the history of the Crown Jewels.

The Jewels themselves are viewed from a conveyor belt, which glides you past glass cases, inches from the crowns and sceptres.

The Queen Mother's crown contains the legendary **Koh-i-noor** diamond. Charles II's sceptre is fitted with the 530-carat **Star of Africa** – the world's largest cut diamond.

Security is so tight at the Jewel House that the gift shop feels confident enough to sell a board game in which the aim is to steal the Crown Jewels.

A Yeoman of the Watch

Traitors' Gate, which connects with the River Thames, is where prisoners would arrive by boat. Elizabeth I entered the Tower through this gate in 1554 when her sister, Queen Mary, briefly imprisoned her on suspicion of treason.

Tower Green, which is lined with benches, is an ideal place to have a picnic lunch. Look out for the huge ravens that live within the Tower and have been protected by Royal Decree since the reign of Charles II. Legend has it that, should they desert the Tower, the kingdom will fall. Just to be safe, they have their wings clipped.

New: The Crowns and Diamonds Exhibition, tracing the history of the royal crowns in Britain, opened in the Martin Tower in December 1996.

Medieval actor guides

PRICES

Adult £8.50
Child £5.60
Senior £6.40
Student £6.40

DISCOUNT

10% off admission per person with voucher on page 279.

INSIDER'S TIP

Get there for opening time to avoid the hordes (especially in summer) and bring a snack, as there's no café in the Tower (although there is a new Prèt á Manger just outside)

DON'T MISS

Crown Jewels, Chapel of St. John, Royal Armouries, Henry VIII's codpiece.

ADDRESS

1 Tower Hill Terrace
☎ 0171-709-0081

GETTING THERE

Tower Hill tube station

HOURS

Apr-Oct: Mon-Sun:
9.30am-5.30pm
Nov-Mar: Mon-Sun:
9.30am-4.30pm

PRICES

Adult £6.95
Child £4.95
Senior £4.95
Student £4.95

DISCOUNT

£1 off admission per
person with voucher on
page 279.

Time ride

🖼 Tower Hill Pageant

This 'time ride' aboard computerized cars takes you on a 15-minute journey through 26 moving-model

Rebuilding the City

scenes, which depict the history of London from earliest Roman settlement to modern metropolis.

A digital clock in the roof of the car tells you the date as you pass through each era in London's history, including the Viking invasions, the plague years and the Great Fire of 1666.

A rat scuttles across one scene and figures whirr into action as you pass. The best scenes are those brought to life with sounds and smells, the most pleasant being the aroma of spices in a tableau of London's docks. Less convincing, perhaps thankfully, is the supposed foul smell that emanates from the plague scene.

There is a series of striking holograms, one of which depicts two severed heads skewered on stakes (the fate of traitors executed at Tower Hill).

Early settlement

In-car commentary during the rides is available in English, French, Spanish, Italian, German, Dutch and Japanese.

At the end of the ride is the small, but excellent, **Waterfront Finds Museum**, which contains 1,000 artefacts from Roman and medieval London dredged up from the riverbed and banks of the Thames. The Roman banks of the Thames were 100 metres inland from the current riverside wall. Over the centuries, the banks steadily advanced as city dwellers sought to extend their properties. A rich hoard of medieval finds has come from excavating behind the wooden walls, or revetments, built by successive generations. Rubbish once dumped as in-fill behind these walls has given fascinating insights into the Roman, Saxon and medieval ways of life.

Tower Bridge Experience

London's most famous landmark is a triumph of Victorian engineering.

Ten men died during the eight-year construction of the bridge, the main frame of which contains 12,000 tons of steel to support the great weight of the two arms (known as bascules). Several daredevil pilots

have flown through the 200-foot (60-metre) wide and 100-foot (30-metre) high gap between the towers – the first was Frank McLean in 1912. At least one later attempt proved fatal.

Tower Bridge

In 1952, a red double-decker bus (No. 78), passing through traffic lights stuck on green, jumped a three-foot gap as the bridge was opening.

An historical tour retraces the origins of the bridge, from its conception through to the present day, using an animatronic worker called 'Harry' as a guide.

The high-level walkways connecting the twin towers have incredible views both up and down the Thames. The unique panorama of London is the highlight of the tour, even though the view is partially obstructed by steel girders.

The mechanically-minded will be fascinated by the displays on the design and operation of the bridge, which culminate in the **Engine Room** containing the massive steam-driven pumps used to raise the two arms.

If you are lucky, you will witness the bridge being raised to allow a ship to pass through. When the bridge first began operating, this used to happen 6,000 times a year, hence the high-level walkways allowing pedestrians to continue crossing the bridge. Declining traffic on the Thames means the bridge is now only lifted around 500 times annually. In summer, however, it can be raised up to ten times a day. If you call ☎ 0171-378-7700, a recorded message will give the times when the bridge will be lifted the following week.

ADDRESS

River Thames
☎ 0171-378-1928

GETTING THERE

Tower Hill
tube station

HOURS

Apr-Oct: Mon-Sun:
10am-6.30pm
Nov-Mar: Mon-Sun:
9.30am-6pm

PRICES

Adult £5.70
Child £3.90
Senior £3.90
Student £3.90

DISCOUNT

£1 off admission per
person with voucher
on page 279.

The engine room

Other Attractions . . .

The area on the western edge of the City is the centre of legal London, which includes the labyrinthine **Royal Courts of Justice** on the Strand and the beautiful **Inns of Court**, where Britain's top barristers practise. **Lincoln's Inn** is the best-preserved of the four Inns of Court (the others are Gray's Inn, Middle Temple and

Lincoln's Inn

Inner Temple). Famous alumni include Sir Thomas More and Oliver Cromwell. Some of the buildings (including the Chancery Lane Gatehouse) date from the 15th century and are best appreciated by taking a stroll around the gardens. The chapel was remodelled by Inigo Jones in 1620. *(Chancery Lane, ☎ 0171-405-1393. Mon-Fri: 12noon-2pm. Sat-Sun: closed. Admission is free.)*

Barristers at the Inns of Court

On the north side of Lincoln's Inn stands the exquisite **Sir John Soane's Museum**. Because it is off the beaten track, most visitors to London miss this treasure-trove of lovely, and often peculiar, works of art collected in the early 19th century by Bank of England architect Sir John Soane. The collection is housed on several floors of three linked Georgian houses, artfully redesigned by Sir John with domes, skylights and mirrors that play tricks with space and light. Hogarth's famous morality tale, *The Rake's Progress*, hangs in a picture gallery with false walls that open to reveal yet more pictures. The vast sarcophagus of Seti I stands in a colonnaded atrium, surrounded by classical statues. There is an excellent free lecture tour on Saturdays at 2.30pm and a special tour takes place on the first Tuesday of every month from 6pm-9pm. *(13 Lincoln's Inn Fields, ☎ 0171-405-2107. Tue-Sat: 10am-5pm. Sun-Mon: closed. Admission is free.)*

Sir John Soane's Museum

Just outside the City boundary is the ancient district of **Clerkenwell**, which in medieval times was a hamlet with abundant springs that supplied water to local monasteries. Remnants of two of the monasteries survive. The **Order of St. John's Museum** is housed in a 16th century gatehouse on the south side of Clerkenwell Road. *(St. John's Gate, Clerkenwell Road, ☎ 0171-253-6644. Mon-Fri: 10am-5pm. Sat: 10am-4pm. Sun: closed. Guided tours Tue and Fri-Sat: 11am and 2.30pm. Admission is free.)*

Order of St John's Museum

Charterhouse, founded by the Carthusians in 1371,

. . . Other Attractions . . .

but rebuilt in the Tudor period, is tucked away off St. John Street. (☎ 0171-253-3260. Apr-Jul: guided tour Wed: 2.15pm. Adult £3, child £2, senior £2, student £2.) Clerkenwell became a fashionable spa in the 18th century, but a huge influx of people meant the area was a slum by the Victorian period. Despite redevelopment, some of the old street pattern and atmosphere remain, with traditional artisans like lockmakers and printers still plying their trade.

The **House of Detention**, on Clerkenwell Close, is a museum built on the site of a gaol dating back to 1616. The guided tour through dark labyrinths and cells gives a graphic account of the appalling conditions suffered by the prisoners, who were forced to wear masks and forbidden to talk. (Clerkenwell Close, ☎ 0171-253-9494. Mon-Sun: 10am-6pm (last admission 5pm). Adult £4, child £2.50, senior £3, student £3. £1 off admission with your London for less card.)

House of Detention

Fleet Street sign

The main thoroughfare linking the City with the West End has a series of different names: the **Strand** becomes **Fleet Street** at a point just past the Royal Courts. Fleet Street was once the headquarters of nearly all the national newspapers and its name is still used as a sobriquet for the British press. The last paper moved out several years ago, but some of the stylish buildings remain, including the *Daily Telegraph's* Art Deco edifice.

St Bride's Church

At the eastern end of Fleet Street stands **St. Bride's**, adopted by journalists and printers as their mother church. Of special interest is the graceful multi-tiered steeple, the tallest ever designed by Sir Christopher Wren, which inspired a local baker to create the first multi-layered wedding cake. The crypt contains Roman mosaics, which only came to light when the church was hit during the Blitz, and a small museum that catalogues Fleet Street's newspaper history. (Fleet Street, ☎ 0171-353-1301. Mon-Sun: 9am-5pm. Free admission.)

Hidden in a cul-de-sac north of Fleet Street is **Dr. Johnson's House**. This is one of the best of the capital's string of writers' museums created inside the former homes of famous literary Londoners. A host of memorabilia includes first editions of Dr. Johnson's great dictionary, which was put together in the attic and first published in 1755. The house was

Dr. Johnson's House

. . . Other Attractions . . .

Dr Johnson's House

Story of Telecommunications

Old Bailey

Smithfield Market

rescued from demolition by Lord Harmsworth in 1911 and opened to the nation. Today, it is one of the City's few surviving residential houses of its age. *(Gough Square, ☎ 0171-353-3745. May-Sep: Mon-Sat: 11am-5.30pm. Sun: closed. Oct-Apr: Mon-Sat: 11am-5pm. Sun: closed. Adult £3, child £1, senior £2, student £2. 50% discount with London for less card)*

'Justice' on top of the Old Bailey

British Telecom's **Story of Telecommunications Museum**, on Quick Street, includes a collection of early telegraph machines and telephones. There are gadgets such as the latest videophones, but it is mainly of interest to the technically-minded. *(145 Victoria Street, ☎ 0171-248-7444 or ☎ 0800-289689. Mon-Fri: 10am-5pm. Admission is free.)*

North of Fleet Street, off Farringdon Lane, is the **National Museum of Cartoon Art**, where exhibitions are sometimes held. Phone ahead for details. *(15-17 St. Cross Street, ☎ 0171-405-4717.)*

The **Central Criminal Court,** nicknamed **The Old Bailey** after the street on which it stands, is Britain's most famous criminal court and is where many of the highest profile cases are heard. Visitors can watch trials from the public galleries. The dome of the huge courthouse is topped by the gold statue of Justice, holding sword and scales in outstretched arms. The notorious **Newgate Prison**, whose inmates included Daniel Defoe, Ben Jonson and Casanova, stood on this site until 1902. *(Old Bailey, ☎ 0171-248-3277. Mon-Fri: 10.30am-1pm and 2pm-4pm. Free admission.)*

North of Newgate Street lie the sprawling ancient and modern buildings of **St. Bartholomew's Hospital**, London's oldest hospital. It was founded in 1123 by Henry I's court jester, who said he was acting on the orders of St. Bartholomew, which had been delivered in a visionary experience in Italy. The painter William Hogarth was made a governor in 1734 and two of his most famous paintings, *The Good Samaritan* and *The Pool of Bethesda*, now hang on the main staircase. *(West*

. . . Other Attractions . . .

Smithfield, ☎ 0171-601-8888.)

The long, low Victorian buildings of **Smithfield Market**, modernized in the early 1990s, accommodate London's main meat market. *(West Smithfield, best views are from Grand Avenue).* The legendary

Smithfield Market

Bartholomew Fair was held here from 1123 until its suppression for debauchery in 1855. Several pubs in the area, including the Fox and Anchor (page 149), open at 7am to serve huge cooked breakfasts to market traders and other early risers.

A Penny Black

The **National Postal Museum** contains a collection of rare stamps, including several Penny Blacks, the World's first postage stamp. *(King Edward Building, King Edward Street, ☎ 0171-600-8914. Mon-Fri: 9.30am-4.30pm. Sat-Sun: closed. Admission is free.)*

National Postal Museum

The Museum of London

The **Museum of London** traces more than 2,000 years of London's social history – from the tiny Roman town to the sprawling modern metropolis. There is a wealth of information on London, but you would need to have a strong interest in the city's history to want to spend the recommended minimum of two hours.

Museum of London

Each of the museum's galleries, arranged in chronological order, covers a different era. The Roman gallery has recently been revamped to reflect new discoveries, but by far the best gallery chronicles the life of the 'Imperial Capital', from the Victorian to the Edwardian periods. The Suffragettes' collection includes the chains women used to lock themselves to the railings outside the Prime Minister's house in Downing Street.

The 'London Now' gallery, which opened in 1997, brings the museum up-to-date with artefacts relating to London's recent history – from a Ford Cortina to punk fashion. The tour of the museum ends with the magnificent gold Lord Mayor's State Coach. *(London Wall, ☎ 0171-600-3699. Tue-Fri: 10am-5.50pm.*

Roman lamp in the shape of a human foot

. . . Other Attractions . . .

Royal Exchange

Sun: 12noon-5.50pm. Mon: closed. Adult £3.50, child £1.75, senior £1.75, student £1.75, family £8.50. Free admission Tue-Sat after 4.30pm.)

St. Stephen Walbrook is the Lord Mayor's parish church. Built by Sir Christopher Wren in 1672-1679, it has an ornate dome and intricately carved pulpit canopy. The central polished stone altar is by Henry Moore. *(39 Walbrook, ☎ 0171-626-8242.)*

The Royal Exchange

Some of the City's most splendid buildings, such as the **Mansion House** (built in 1753 as the Lord Mayor's residence) and the **Royal Exchange** (originally founded in 1565 as a centre for commerce, but rebuilt in 1844) are, sadly, not open to the public. The colonnaded facades of these buildings, however, are well-known City landmarks.

Mansion House

Beside the Royal Exchange is the **Bank of England**, known as Old Lady of Threadneedle Street. Established by William III in 1694 to raise money for his war against France, the Bank now regulates the banking industry and issues bank notes. The Bank's museum, entered from Bartholomew Lane, displays gold bars and historical bank notes. *(Bartholomew Lane ☎ 0171-601-5545.)*

Leadenhall Market is a beautiful Victorian arcade nestling amid the office blocks of the financial district. Meat, poultry and fish have been sold here since the 14th century. In addition to an old-style fishmonger and other traditional shops, the arcade

Leadenhall Market

now houses pubs and restaurants popular with City workers. *(Gracechurch Street. Mon-Fri: 10am-6pm. Sat-Sun: closed.)*

Leadenhall Market

At the back of Leadenhall Market is the astonishing **Lloyd's of London** building *(Lime Street, ☎ 0171-327-6210.)* – an enormous, complicated steel structure designed by modernist architect Richard Rogers (famous for creating the Pompidou Centre in Paris, another 'innards on the outside' building). It houses the world's biggest insurance market and is best seen by night, when blue

. . . Other Attractions

fluorescent lights make it look like a spaceship.

The 202-foot (62-metre) column north of London Bridge is known simply as **'Monument'**. Designed by Wren, it commemorates the Great Fire of London in 1666 and is said to be 202 feet west of where the fire started in Pudding Lane. You can climb the 311-step spiral staircase to the viewing platform. *(Monument Street, ☎ 0171-626-2717. Apr-Sep: Mon-Fri: 9am-5.30pm. Sat-Sun: 2pm-5.30pm. Oct-Mar: Mon-Sat: 9am-3.30pm. Sun: closed. Adult £1, child 25p, senior 25p, student 25p)*

Lloyd's of London

The City's **Livery Companies** hark back to the medieval craftsmen's guilds, though modern members may have little or no connection with the trade from which they take their name. The livery companies occupy halls dotted around the City, including Fishmongers' Hall, Merchant Taylor's Hall and Apothecaries' Hall. These and others can be viewed either free of charge or for a small fee, though advance booking is usually

Monument

necessary. *(Tickets are sold by the London Information Centre, ☎ 0171-332-1456.)*

On the north-eastern fringe of the City is an area known as **Spitalfields**. The area's most striking piece of architecture is **Christ Church** *(Commercial Street, ☎ 0171-247-7202)*, with its 205-foot (62-metre) spire. The finest view of Nicholas Hawksmoor's church, completed in 1729, is from the western end of Brushfield Street. The church lay derelict for much of this century, but reopened after restoration in 1987. It now hosts classical concerts and the Spitalfields Festival in June.

Petticoat Lane is one of London's most famous street markets, trading every Sunday for more than 200 years. The Huguenots sold petticoats here and the market still specializes in clothing, though mostly of the cheap variety. *(Centred on Middlesex Street. Sun: 9am-2pm. Mon-Sat: closed.)*

Lloyd's of London

Monument

Spitalfields

Petticoat Lane Market

Open Spaces

There are no parks and few gardens in the City, where all available open spaces and benches tend to be filled by office workers taking a break.

Lincoln's Inn Fields

Lincoln's Inn Fields, a 17th-century square between Kingsway and Chancery Lane, is shaded by tall plane trees. It also has tennis courts and a café frequented by lunching lawyers. At the other end of the social spectrum, homeless people tend to sleep in the bushes.

Broadgate Arena

The **Broadgate** complex, around and above Liverpool Street Station, is an impressive 1980s office development with plenty of piazzas and a liberal scattering of outdoor sculpture. Among the most striking of the office blocks is Exchange House, suspended over the railway line by means of huge supporting steel arches. **Broadgate Arena** doubles as an ice-rink and a performance space.

Broadgate Arena

St. Paul's Churchyard, the tiny garden at the rear of St. Paul's Cathedral, was the centre of London's book trade from 1500 until it was obliterated in the Second World War by the Blitz.

North of Moorgate, off City Road, lies **Bunhill Fields**, a peaceful old cemetery shaded by great plane trees and with lots of benches. The cemetery, last used for a burial in 1854, dates from the mid-17th century. The Corporation of London created a burial ground here for use in the Great Plague. In fact, few plague victims were buried at Bunhill, and it was mainly used for burying dissenters. The grim-looking spiked gate at the north-east corner was erected to deter body-snatchers. Most of the cemetery is fenced off, but you can see the monuments to John Bunyan (1628-1688), Daniel Defoe (1660-1731) and William Blake (1757-1827). In the adjoining Quaker graveyard lies George Fox (1624-1691), who founded the Society of Friends.

St Paul's Churchyard

Bowls in Lincoln's Inn Fields

Eating and Drinking

There are plenty of restaurants and pubs serving City office-workers, but most close early in the evening once the commuters have gone home.

There are several good restaurants near Bank tube station and in the Broadgate complex. Many visitors, however, join busy City folk in opting for traditional pub grub.

The Old Bell

Smithfield, to the north of the City, was once renowned for the pubs that served hearty breakfasts to the blood-splattered meat porters from the meat market. **The Fox and Anchor** *(115 Charterhouse Street)* still serves English breakfast with pints of ale from 7am to 3pm, but the porters are now outnumbered by men in suits on the way to their offices. North of Smithfield Market is **Vic Naylor's** (page 150), a lively bar and restaurant which stays open late.

Ye Olde Cheshire Cheese *(15 Fleet Street)* is probably the City's most famous pub. Once patronized by Dr. Samuel Johnson and Charles Dickens, this restored old tavern has six cosy bars and three restaurants. The ground-floor bar has a faded sign above the door that reads 'Gentlemen Only', but this is not to be taken seriously.

The Fox and Anchor

The Fox and Anchor

The Old Bell *(95 Fleet Street)* was built by Christopher Wren and was initially used by the workers who were building St. Bride's church nearby. It serves a good selection of traditional food.

St. Paul's Wine Vaults *(Knightrider Street)* is handy for a £10 set lunch after visiting St. Paul's Cathedral. Built in 1665, this was the Horn Tavern mentioned by Dickens in *Pickwick Papers*. Mr Pickwick, incarcerated in Fleet Prison, asked the pub to send him two bottles of good wine.

Ye Olde Cheshire Cheese

The Lamb Tavern *(Leadenhall Market)* is a favourite place for pin-striped City gents to come at lunchtime and in the early evening, though the pub gets much quieter after 9pm. The best of the four floors are the cavernous smoking bar in the basement and the top bar, with its tall windows and fine views of the market's intricate cast-ironwork. Food is available on all the levels.

The Lamb Tavern

HOURS

Mon-Fri: 11.30am-3.30pm
Sat-Sun: closed

HOURS

Mon-Fri: 12noon-3pm,
6pm-11pm
Sat-Sun: closed

HOURS

Mon-Fri: 12noon-
12midnight
Sat: 7pm-1am
Sun: closed

Corvino and Balcone

Italian / Brasserie

71 Middlesex Street
☎ **0171-247-6461**

Average meal: £10-15
for less discount: 25%
AM/VS/MC/DC

Corvino has formal dining on the ground floor and a balcony brasserie. In both areas, the food is classical Italian with fresh pasta and other dishes. Both restaurants are popular at lunchtime.

Terraza Est

Italian

109 Fleet Street
☎ **0171-353-2680**

Average meal: £10-15
for less discount: 25%
AM/VS/MC/DC

Terrazza Est is unique: every weekday evening, from 7.30pm-11pm, opera is performed in the restaurant. Located close to St. Paul's, it serves excellent Italian food.

Vic Naylor's

Traditional English

38-40 St. John Street
☎ **0171-608-2181**

Average meal: £10-15
for less discount: 25%
AM/VS/MC

This large, fashionable restaurant has the feel of a New York bar. The daily specials are fresh from London markets. Busiest at lunchtime, it stays open until late in the evening.

South of the River

Introduction . . .

Long neglected, the south bank of the Thames has enjoyed a remarkable renaissance in recent years. New

theatres and galleries have been opened, old pubs restored and decaying dock buildings transformed into elegant shopping arcades.

The river is now lined by an attractive walkway, from which there are stunning views across to London's more salubrious north bank. The walk from Lambeth Bridge to Tower Bridge, a little over two miles, takes you past many of London's most famous landmarks. There are more

View of Westminster from the river's south bank

than ten museums *en route* and a couple of good riverside pubs serving lunch.

The area between Blackfriars Bridge and Tower Bridge, known as **Southwark**, has a long and chequered history. With most forms of entertainment banned in the City in the 16th and 17th centuries, Southwark

was home to dozens of theatres, bear gardens, brothels and taverns. Shakespeare's **Globe Theatre** (page 154), now reconstructed, and the **Rose** were two of the best known theatres which attracted City dwellers across London Bridge.

The character of the area changed in the 18th and 19th centuries, with docks and warehouses built along the Thames. Some

County Hall from across the Thames

of these buildings have since been demolished to make way for offices. Others, like **Hay's Galleria** (page 162), have been imaginatively restored and put to new use.

The construction of the railways in the 19th century cut great swathes through Southwark and, to the west, Lambeth. Two of London's biggest train stations, Waterloo (from where the Channel Tunnel trains depart) and London

Hay's Galleria

. . . Introduction

Bridge, are located in the vicinity. Avoid the ugly road junctions around Waterloo Station, which are awkward to negotiate on foot.

Londoners living north of the Thames sometimes sneer at Southwark and Lambeth. While the dreary residential area beyond the riverside has little to attract the visitor, the south bank of the Thames is packed with curiosities and cultural attractions. Stylish new riverside restaurants, like the one at the **Oxo Tower** (page 162) with its fantastic views , now attract London's 'beautiful people' across the river.

The exterior of the Globe

South Bank Centre

There are museums to suit all tastes dotted along the south bank, including the **Design Museum** (page 156) for the style-conscious, the **London Dungeon** (page 155) for the bloodthirsty and **Bankside Gallery** (page 158) for watercolour enthusiasts.

The **South Bank Centre** (page 161) beside Waterloo Bridge, is London's premier arts complex. Inspired by the 1951 Festival of Britain, the centre is housed in a mass of concrete, which people either love or hate. The **Royal Festival Hall**, now almost 50 years old and still one of London's top classical concert venues, was the first part of the centre to be built. Several other leading arts institutions were later established here, including the **Royal National Theatre** (page 197), with its three stages, and the **Hayward Gallery**. The **National Film Theatre** and the **Museum of the Moving Image** (page 159) have added film to the list of art forms celebrated at the centre.

The Hayward Gallery

Several major developments are planned for the south bank of the Thames to help bring more visitors across the river. A new footbridge has been proposed, connecting St. Paul's Cathedral with **Bankside Power Station**, which is being converted into the Tate Gallery's museum of modern art. There is also a plan to mark the new millennium by erecting a transparent canopy over the windswept promenades of the South Bank Centre.

7

ADDRESS

New Globe Walk
☎ 0171-928-6406

GETTING THERE

London Bridge
tube station

HOURS

Mon-Sun: 10am-5pm

PRICES

Adult £5
Child £3
Senior £4
Student £4

DISCOUNT

Adult £1 off admission,
child, senior and student
50p off admission with
voucher on page 279.

William Shakespeare

Shakespeare's Globe

This meticulous reproduction of Shakespeare's original Globe Theatre – constructed using Elizabethan building techniques – offers authentic performances and guided tours.

The late Sam Wanamaker did not live to see the fulfilment of his 40-year dream of re-creating the 'Wooden O-shaped' thatched theatre, where many of the greatest plays in the English language were first performed. However, shortly before the legendary American director died in 1993, he saw the shell of the new Globe erected.

Theatregoers at the Globe

The original Globe was built in 1599, and rebuilt 14 years later following a fire. Shakespeare died in 1616, but the theatre continued to perform his work until the Puritans closed it in 1642.

Standing a short distance from the site of the original, the new theatre specializes in plays by Shakespeare and his contemporaries. The enormous cost of the new Globe – £30m at the last count – was the result of painstaking efforts to re-create the original, right down to the lime and goats hair used for plaster. The story of the construction is told in a special exhibition.

The design of the theatre, three sheltered tiers in a circle around the open-air stage, means no-one is more than half the length of a tennis court from the stage. Seats in the three galleries, which accommodate 1,000 people, cost £5-20. An extra 500 'groundlings' (who stand in the yard around the stage) pay a flat rate of £5.

The picturesque riverside location is relatively quiet – only the occasional passing helicopter drowns out the actors' lines. The wooden benches can get uncomfortable during a three-hour Shakespeare play, but cushions are available. The first public performance at the new Globe in 1996 had to be halted after an actor, swinging down to the stage by a rope, broke his leg.

Attached to the Globe theatre is a smaller, indoor theatre, built according to a design by Inigo Jones.

🏛 London Dungeon

Every grisly form of torture and death is featured in this nightmarish tour which uses moving models to reconstruct the goriest episodes of history.

The idea for the museum came from housewife Annabel Geddes, whose children were bored by the lack of 'blood and thunder' at the nearby Tower of London. The Dungeon's location under Victorian railway arches makes for a suitably cavernous and gloomy atmosphere.

Jack the Ripper

Bloodcurdling screams echo around the halls as you pass barbaric scenes of execution, with lifelike effigies being hanged, boiled, garrotted and guillotined. Even the guides enter the chilling spirit of the show, dressed as vampires with white faces and necks smeared with blood.

There are likely to be queues for the two special shows – **Jack the Ripper** and the **Guillotine**. The Ripper, in particular, is well worth the wait. A guide takes you on a walk through the re-created slums of

Terror in the dungeon

smog-filled Victorian London where the notorious serial killer terrorized the population by chopping out the vital organs of prostitutes.

New: With **Judgement Day**, the London Dungeon has taken its gruesome theme one stage further by actually turning the visitor into the victim. This new attraction reconstructs the grim final journey prisoners took to the Bloody Tower before execution. You face a sombre judge as he dons the dreaded black cap to pronounce a sentence of death on you and your fellow prisoners. You are then herded on board a barge to travel along a specially constructed waterway through a mock-up of Traitors' Gate at the Tower of London. From there you are taken to meet your fate!

Warning: young children may well find all this too frightening.

ADDRESS

Tooley Street
☎ 0171-403-0606

GETTING THERE

London Bridge tube station

HOURS

Mon-Sun: 10am-6.30pm
Last admission 5.30pm

PRICES

Adult £7.95
Child £4.50
Senior £4.50
Student £6.95

DISCOUNT

£2 off admission per person with voucher on page 279.

The executioner's axe

Other Attractions . . .

Classic designs of mass-produced items – including collections of bizarre hairdryers and modish TV sets – are on display at the **Design Museum**. Housed in an uninspiring tier of white blocks, it faces the Thames east of Tower Bridge. *(Butler's Wharf, Shad Thames ☎ 0171-403-6933. Mon-Fri: 11.30am-6pm. Sat-Sun: 12noon-6pm. Adult £4.75, child £3.50, senior £3.50, student £3.50.)*

Bramah Tea and Coffee Museum

Close by, at Butler's Wharf, is the **Bramah Tea and Coffee Museum**. The 350-year history of the tea and coffee trade is told in a lively exhibition that includes a collection of 1,000 coffee–makers and teapots. The museum was founded in 1992 by Edward Bramah, a former

Bramah Tea and Coffee Museum

tea planter and taster who is an acknowledged world expert on the traditional British tea-drinking habit. Butler's Wharf is an appropriate place for the museum, for it was used for three centuries to unload millions of chests of tea and coffee. The museum includes a café and shop selling 'slow-infusing' Bramah teas. *(The Clove Building, Maguire Street, ☎ 0171-378-0222. Mon-Sun: 10am-6pm. Adult £3.50, child £2, senior £2, student £2. 50% off admission with your London for less card.)*

Britain at War Experience

The **Britain at War Experience**, on Tooley Street next to the London Dungeon, celebrates the famous British 'stiff upper lip' when the country stood alone against Hitler in the Second World War. It begins with an air raid simulation: you wait in a bombed out department store and then walk through the charred

Britain at War

remains of a cinema, pub and houses. Original newsreels and radio broadcasts give an authentic 1940s flavour. Artefacts include a child's 'Mickey Mouse' gas mask. *(64-66 Tooley Street, ☎ 0171-403-3171. Apr-Sep: Mon-Sun: 10am-5.30pm. Oct-Mar: Mon-Sun: 10am-4.30pm. Adult £5.50, child £2.95, senior £3.95, student £3.95. £1 off admission per person with voucher on page 281.)*

HMS Belfast

HMS *Belfast*, a floating naval museum since 1971, was the Royal Navy's largest Second World War battle cruiser. Its six torpedoes and 14-mile range guns helped it sink the German cruiser *Scharnhorst* in 1943. The network of cabins, which is open to the public,

. . . Other Attractions . . .

accommodated a crew of 800. The tour includes the heavily armoured Shell Rooms and Magazines, the

HMS Belfast

Mess Decks, Officers' Cabins and Sick Bay. You can see inside the gun turrets and operate the light anti-aircraft guns. *(Morgan's Lane, Tooley Street, ☎ 0171-407-6434. Mar-Oct: Mon-Sun: 10am-6pm. Nov-Feb: Mon-Sun: 10am-5pm. Adult £4.40, child £2.20, senior £3.30, student £3.30.)*

Golden Hinde

The **Golden Hinde**, moored at St. Mary Overie Dock near London Bridge, is a full-scale reconstruction of Sir Francis Drake's famous galleon in which he circumnavigated the globe in the 16th century. *(St. Mary Overie Dock, Cathedral Street, ☎ 0171-403-0123. Mon-Sun: 10am-5pm. Adult £2.30, child £1.50, senior £1.90, student £1.90.)*

The Golden Hinde

Just west of London Bridge lies **Southwark Cathedral**, a fine medieval church, parts of which date from the 12th century. The early 15th-century tomb of poet John Gower, a contemporary of

Southwark Cathedral

Geoffrey Chaucer, is in the north aisle. A memorial to Shakespeare stands in the south aisle. John Harvard, who founded Harvard University, was baptized here in 1607 and a chapel has been named after him. *(Montague Close, ☎ 0171-407-3708. Mon-Sun: 9am-6pm. Suggested donation £2.)*

Bankside Gallery

The Clink Exhibition stands on the site of the old Clink Prison, a dungeon attached to the Bishop of Winchester's

Southwark Cathedral

House, where dissenting clerics were sent for punishment. In medieval times, this was London's red-light district and the museum re-creates the brothels

Clink Exhibition

. . . Other Attractions . . .

in lurid detail. *(1 Clink Street, ☎ 0171-403-6515. Mon-Sun: 10am-6pm. Adult £3.50, child £2.50, senior £2.50, student £2.50, family £8.)*

Bankside Gallery holds regular art exhibitions at its attractive Thames-facing location, midway between Blackfriars Bridge and Southwark Bridge. It is the headquarters of the Royal Watercolour Society and Royal Society of Painter-Printmakers. Many of the works on view are for sale. *(48 Hopton Street, ☎ 0171-928-7521. Tue-Fri: 10am-5pm. Sun: 1pm-5pm. Sat and Mon: closed. Adult £3.50, child free, senior £2, student £2. £1 off admission per person with your London for less card.)*

Bankside Gallery

The new **London Aquarium**, has one of Europe's largest collections of fish and marine life. Two huge twin tanks focus on species from the Atlantic and Pacific Oceans. The Pacific tank is mainly populated by sharks. *(County Hall, beside Westminster Bridge, ☎ 0171-967-8000. Mon-Sun: 10am-6pm. Adult £6.50, child £4.50, senior £5.50, student £5.50, family £20.)*

London Aquarium

The **Florence Nightingale Museum** tells the remarkable story of the 'Lady of the Lamp', who nursed the wounded soldiers of the Crimean War (1853-1856) and four years later founded the first school of nursing at St. Thomas's Hospital. Drawing on original documents, personal artefacts and photographs, the museum commemorates Florence Nightingale's unique contribution to medical care and

Florence Nightingale Museum

hospital standards. The exhibition includes the lamp which she carried and which was to become her symbol. There is also a dramatic representation of the Lady with war wounded at Scutari. *(2 Lambeth Palace Road, ☎ 0171-620-0374. Tue-Sun: 10am-4pm. Mon: closed. Adult £2.50, child £1.50, senior £1.50, student £1.50. Adult £1 off admission, child, senior and student 50p off admission with your London for less card.)*

Florence Nightingale Museum

The **Museum of Garden History** lies in and around the 14th-century tower of St. Mary's Church on Lambeth Palace Road. Charles I's royal gardeners are buried here and the museum includes a 17th-century style garden. *(Lambeth Palace Road, ☎ 0171-261-1891. Mon-*

. . . Other Attractions . . .

Fri: 10.30am-4pm. Sun: 10.30am-5pm. Sat: closed. Admission is free.)

Lambeth Palace

Lambeth Palace *(Lambeth Palace Road)*, overlooking the Museum of Garden History, has been the London residence of the Archbishop of Canterbury, the head of the English Church, since 1207. It is closed to the public, but there is an impressive twin-towered redbrick Tudor gatehouse.

The **Old Vic** is one of London's finest theatres. Opened in 1816, it became a celebrated venue for Victorian 'music hall' entertainment before turning to more serious Shakespearean drama early this century. It was beautifully restored in 1983 and offers guided tours by arrangement. *(Waterloo Road, ☎ 0171 928 7618.)*

The fun-filled **Museum of the Moving Image** (MOMI) takes you for a hands-on tour from the earliest magic lanterns to the latest movie special effects.

Film buffs will enjoy the classic film clips shown in a series of mini cinemas, but MOMI is also an ideal place for kids, with dozens of gadgets on which to play.

Actors demonstrate movie techniques and give you potted histories as you explore. Artists help you draw your own cartoon strip, which you can then watch in motion. Aspiring actors and actresses can take part in a screen test styled on the heyday of Hollywood.

Museum of the Moving Image

The final section is the most fun. You can record yourself reading the news, pretend to be Superman or Supergirl flying over London and be interviewed by Britain's top film critic, Barry Norman.

The film clips are shown in appropriate surroundings, such as the early Russian propaganda screened on board a Lenin Agitprop train.

Lambeth Palace

Old Vic

The Old Vic

MOMI

. . . Other Attractions

The classic film footage shown on various screens includes pioneering movies from around the world.

The TV section, however, is biased towards the BBC and caters mainly for British tastes.

Precious Images, an Oscar-winning 'short' which presents 500 film extracts in six minutes, is particularly worth seeing. *(Southbank, Waterloo, ☎ 0171-401-2636. Mon-Sun: 10am-6pm. Last admission 5pm. Adult £5.95, child £4, senior £4.85, student £4.85, family £16.)*

Imperial War Museum

Some of the world's most lethal inventions are on display in the **Imperial War Museum,** housed in what was once the infamous Bedlam mental hospital.

The imposing 47-foot (14-metre) V2 rocket stands in the main exhibition hall, among an array of tanks, fighter planes, heavy artillery and an atomic bomb (minus warhead). Hitler's deadliest weapon, the V2, delivered a ton of explosive unseen and unheard by its victims.

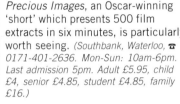

The two 'experiences' – **Trench** and **Blitz** – are the real highlight of the museum. In portraying the horror of war, they have helped undo the museum's former reputation for glorifying conflict.

Sopwith Camel

As you wander through a First World War trench, passing soldiers huddled in dugouts and manning the walls, the sound of machine gun fire rattles overhead.

The Blitz experience begins in an air raid shelter, where the seats vibrate with the impact of bombs. Then you emerge into a devastated street, where the only motion is the rotating wheel of an upturned pram.

You can experience a Second World War bombing mission on the **Operation Jericho** flight simulator, for which there is an extra charge.

The museum keeps abreast of recent conflicts and has acquired US General Norman Schwarzkopf's Gulf War uniform. *(Lambeth Road, ☎ 0171-416-5000. Mon-Sun: 10am-6pm. Adult £4.50, child £2.25, senior £3.50, student £3.50, family £12. Free admission after 4.30pm.)*

Imperial War Museum

Open Spaces

The three-mile riverside footpath, on the south bank of the Thames from Lambeth Bridge to Tower Bridge, is one of the finest walks in London.

Riverside Walk

Well removed from traffic, the footpath is partly tree-lined and has lots of benches that make excellent picnic spots.

There are astounding views across the river incorporating many of London's finest buildings and landmarks, such as the Houses of Parliament, St. Paul's Cathedral, the Tower of London and Tower Bridge. You will also see some of London's more interesting modern structures, including Charing Cross Station and the controversial South Bank Centre.

Tower Bridge from the South Bank

On the way, there are several fascinating sites, including the reconstructed Shakespeare's Globe Theatre (page 154), Southwark Cathedral (page 157) and HMS *Belfast* (pages 156-157).

Gabriel's Wharf

A few hundred yards east of the South Bank Centre is **Gabriel's Wharf**, a charming collection of craft shops, cafés and bars surrounding a pretty piazza.

There are few decent-sized open spaces in the area immediately south of the Thames. **Jubilee Gardens,** running alongside the Thames, is sandwiched between the South Bank Centre and County Hall (formerly the home of the defunct Greater London Council and now being turned into a hotel, conference centre and aquarium).

Jubilee Gardens

The only sizeable public park in the area is the **Geraldine Mary Harmsworth Park,** beside Lambeth Road. Dominated by the Imperial War Museum, it occupies the central block of what was the Bethlehem Royal Hospital, or 'Bedlam' for short. This notorious mental asylum had been a tourist attraction in the 17th and 18th centuries, with visitors coming to gape at the patients who were chained in their cells and regularly whipped. Hence the English word 'bedlam', meaning madhouse. Recreational visitors were banned in 1770, when it was decided that they 'tended to disturb the tranquillity of the patients' by 'making sport and diversion of the miserable inhabitants'. The hospital closed in 1930.

Geraldine Mary Harmsworth Park

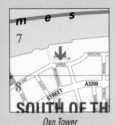
Oxo Tower

Eating and Drinking

Most of the more interesting pubs and restaurants overlook the River Thames on Bankside and near the **South Bank Centre**.

The roof top Harvey Nichols's Restaurant, Bar and Brasserie, at **Oxo Tower** *(Barge House Street)* has wonderful views up and down the Thames. The newly refurbished tower is one of London's riverside landmarks.

Sir Terence Conran has a row of Thameside restaurants with spectacular views of Tower Bridge. **Le Pont de la Tour** *(36D Shad Thames)* is the grandest, serving expensive modern French cuisine. Less pricey is Conran's Italian restaurant, **Cantina del Ponte** *(36E Shad Thames)*. Booking is essential for these restaurants, especially for the tables outside on the river terrace.

Dining South of the River

Hay's Galleria *(Tooley Street)*, a soaring atrium full of cafés and shops, is the most visually striking of the wharf developments south of the river. The weird fountain sculpture in the centre of the arcade is very ugly, but children love it. At the end of the Galleria is **Horniman's**, a spacious pub which serves lunch and dinner on weekdays.

For a grand view across the river of St. Paul's Cathedral, the big riverside terrace of **The Founders Arms** *(52 Hopton Street)* near to Blackfriars Bridge would be hard to beat. Indeed it has a sign by the door boasting of 'The finest view in London'. The restaurant serves lunch and dinner.

Hay's Galleria

The Anchor *(34 Park Street)* is a charming 18th-century restored riverside pub. Sam Wanamaker used to eat here while overseeing the development of the new Globe Theatre (page 154).

The George Inn, Southwark

George Inn

The **George Inn** *(77 Borough High Street)* is London's only surviving traditional galleried coaching inn. Owned by the National Trust, it is both a bar and a restaurant with live entertainment in summer in the cobbled yard.

Bloomsbury and Marylebone

Introduction . . .

Over the last 100 years, **Bloomsbury** has become a byword for intellectual and literary endeavour. The Bloomsbury Group, a subversive and brilliant circle of writers that included Virginia Woolf and Lytton Strachey, lived and worked in the area in the early decades of this century.

The presence of the **British Museum** (page 166-167) and University College, plus a number of other learned institutions and several hospitals, confirm the intellectual pedigree of the area. It is home to thousands of students and a long-established publishing industry. The spirit of the Bloomsbury Group, who believed in the 'pleasures of human intercourse and the enjoyment of beautiful objects', is still apparent.

Hotel Russell

There are several fine Georgian squares, the largest of which is **Russell Square** behind the British Museum. Much of the distinctive architecture was built under successive Dukes of Bedford in the 18th and early 19th centuries.

North of Bloomsbury are three major train stations serving the north of England and Scotland: Euston, St. Pancras and King's Cross. St. Pancras, with its newly restored curved red brick façade and clock tower, is one of London's greatest Victorian Gothic buildings.

Fitzrovia is the area immediately to the west of Tottenham Court Road. Writers such as Dylan Thomas named the neighbourhood after the pub they drank in: the Fitzroy Tavern. Most of the area's cafés and restaurants, are to be found along Charlotte Street. The 580-foot (174-metre) **BT Tower** dominates Fitzrovia. Built in 1965, this cylindrical jumble of transmitters and radio masts once had a revolving restaurant at the top, but it is now closed to the public. For a while, it was London's tallest building, but it was superseded by the NatWest Tower (which, in turn, has been gazumped by Canary Wharf in Docklands).

A Lewis Chessman (British Museum)

Wigmore Street is a pleasant, up-market shopping street, much quieter and more civilized than Oxford Street, which

REFLECTIONS

I came home from the Elgin Marbles melancholy. I almost wish the French had them; we do not deserve such productions. There they lie, covered with dust and dripping with damp, adored by the artists, admired by the people, neglected by the Government...and reverenced and envied by foreigners because they do not possess them.' – Benjamin Haydon (1815)

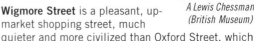

. . . Introduction

runs parallel and to the south. Renowned chocolate manufacturer Bendick's, at No.53, was founded soon after the First World War by Captain Benson and Mr

Dickson. Christopher's Place, an alleyway running south off Wigmore Street near the James Street junction, is where London's upper crust comes to shop.

Grand Georgian architecture covers much of **Marylebone**. Edward Harley, the 2nd Earl of Oxford, bought the land in 1713 and developed it to accommodate the rapid westward expansion of London. The area became

A typical Bloomsbury house

highly fashionable from the 1760s, when George II's daughter, Amelia, lived at No.16 Cavendish Square.

There is a maze of smart streets, some with chic little shops, running off Marylebone High Street. Among the many exclusive addresses in the area is **Harley Street**, synonymous with the prestigious private medical practices that have been here since the 1840s.

There are dozens of imposing mansions in Marylebone. The finest, built by the architect Robert Adam in the 1770s, include Chandos House on Chandos Street and Home House on Portman Square. Adams's 125-foot (37-metre) wide **Portland Place** is London's grandest 18th-century street. Appropriately, it is the home of the Royal Institute of British Architects (No.66).

The smart, cream-coloured stucco terraces and villas around **Regent's Park** were built by John Nash for high society families in the early 19th century. The buildings were intended to circle the park in two continuous rings, but the developers ran out of money. The grandest section is the 800-foot (240-metre) façade of Cumberland Terrace, where Mrs Wallis Simpson lived at No.16 in the early days of her relationship with King Edward VIII.

Many visitors come to Marylebone simply to visit **Madame Tussaud's** (pages 168-169), but close by is an enchanting and often overlooked museum: the **Wallace Collection** (page 171) has fabulous paintings, armour and porcelain on display.

INSIDER'S TIP

The prettiest part of Bloomsbury lies north of the British Museum between Coram's Fields and Tavistock Square. Woburn Walk, with its bow-fronted buildings dating from 1822, is particularly beautiful.

Madame Tussaud's

ADDRESS

Great Russell Street
☎ 0171-636-1555

GETTING THERE

Russell Square or
Tottenham Court Road
tube stations

HOURS

Open:
Mon-Sat: 10am-5pm
Sun: 2.30pm-6pm

Guided Tours of museum:
Mon-Sat: 11.15am and
2.15pm
Sun: 3pm and 3.30pm

Guided Tours of library:
Mon-Fri: 2.15pm and
4.15pm

PRICES

Admission is free.

Guided tours of the
museum: £6

Guided tours of the library
are free

DISCOUNT

£1 off price of guided
tours of the museum with
voucher on page 281.

 # British Museum . . .

The two and a half miles of galleries in the British Museum contain fragments of the seven wonders of

British Museum

the ancient world, amid countless other treasures from the very early histories of Greece, Rome, Egypt, China and other great cultures.

Six million people a year visit the British Museum, making it the most popular attraction in London.

Probably the best-known exhibit is the **Elgin Marbles**, the Parthenon sculptures taken from Athens by Lord Elgin in 1801. The 2,500-year-old marble friezes are the subject of a long and bitter campaign by Greece to persuade Britain to return them home.

The **Rosetta Stone** – initially discovered by Napoleon's soldiers in the Nile delta – was acquired during the same period. Its importance derives from the inscriptions in three languages, which enabled scholars to unlock the mystery of Egyptian hieroglyphs. In 1997 the Egyptian government dropped its demand for the return of the Rosetta Stone.

Rosetta Stone

The wizened remains of **Lindow Man**, slaughtered by druids and dumped in a peat bog 2,000 years ago, offer the peculiar experience of staring into the only face to survive from prehistoric Britain.

Many of the galleries and rooms are worth visiting simply for their stunning visual impact. The vast copper-domed **Reading Room** is astounding, though the effect may be diminished when the books lining the walls move to the new British Library at St. Pancras. Karl Marx wrote *Das Kapital* here and, in 1902, Lenin also came here to study.

. . . British Museum

The 19th-century American writer Washington Irving described the Reading Room as being filled with 'great cases of venerable books and odd personages at long tables poring intently over dusty volumes, rummaging among mouldy manuscripts and taking copious notes'. More poetically, Thackaray wrote: 'What peace, what love, what truth, what beauty … are here spread out'.

INSIDER'S TIP

Visit early in the morning
or after 3pm on
weekdays to avoid large
school parties

Pause at the entrance to the 100-metre-long **King's Library** and notice how the oval ceiling decorations appear circular with the perspective. The Library is due to house a new exhibition on the Age of Enlightenment.

The **Mexican Collection** – laid out inside a re-created temple – is the museum's commendable first attempt to display objects in their native context.

Egyptian Sculpture Gallery

The two-acre space at the centre of the museum is being transformed in the years up to the millennium. The **Great Court** scheme, designed by architect Sir Norman Foster, includes new mezzanine floors, a restaurant and a translucent canopy covering the whole area.

In the late 1990s, the museum has come under severe financial pressure to abandon its policy of free admission. At the time of writing, the trustees had made no change but stated that a charging policy was 'under active review'.

New: The **HSBC Money Gallery** opened in January 1997. Devoted to the history of money over the last 4,000 years, it traces changing forms of payment, starting with the grain, metal and shells used in ancient Mesopotamia, Egypt and China. The new **Celtic Europe Gallery**, scheduled to open in the summer of 1997, will display Celtic coins and Roman jewellery recently unearthed in Alton, Hampshire.

DON'T MISS

Elgin Marbles (Room 8),
the Mausoleum at
Halikarnassos (Room 12),
Rosetta Stone (Room 25),
Lindow Man (Room 37),
Lewis Chessmen (Room
42), Portland Vase
(Room 70)

Portland Vase

Surprisingly, you are allowed to take photos in the museum.

ADDRESS

Marylebone Road
☎ 0171-935-6861

GETTING THERE

Baker Street tube station

HOURS

Mon-Fri: 10am-5.30pm
Sat-Sun: 9.30am-5.30pm
Closed Christmas Day

The Garden Party

 # Madame Tussaud's . . .

The chance to be photographed shoulder-to-shoulder with your favourite movie star, world leader or member of the British royal family makes Madame Tussaud's collection of more than 400 wax figures London's most popular visitor attraction with an admission fee.

Diana, Princess of Wales

It is also one of the oldest, for Madame Tussaud opened her first exhibition around the corner on Baker Street in 1835. Her skill as a wax artist helped save her from the guillotine in revolutionary France – she was only freed on the condition that she sculpt the severed heads of aristocrats. Tussaud's own models of Benjamin Franklin and Voltaire are still on display.

The first room, known as the **Garden Party** and laid out as an English country garden, contains contemporary figures such as Oprah Winfrey, Mel Gibson, Liz Taylor, Arnold Schwarzenegger and Boris Becker. This is one of the best places to take pictures.

Supermodels past and present are represented by Jerry Hall and the recently-added Naomi Campbell. Hall's 1990 sitting is re-created in a special exhibition, which demonstrates the technology behind the model-making.

The **Hollywood** section is split into two – **Legends**, which features the likes of Marilyn Monroe, and **Superstars**, which includes Sylvester Stallone and Pierce Brosnan. Some of the most entertaining exhibits re-create famous movie scenes, such as the 'rolling boulder' episode in Indiana Jones and the Temple of Doom.

Jürgen Klinsmann

Royalty and world leaders are displayed downstairs in the **Grand Hall**. Here you can see Henry VIII and his six wives – brought together in wax as they never were in life. Several American presidents line up together, with Bill Clinton on the podium for a second term. The wax artists have had to add a few pounds to Helmut Kohl,

. . . Madame Tussaud's

who has grown steadily fatter since he first joined the cast at Madame Tussaud's. One of the most uncannily

The American Presidents

lifelike portraits is of French President Jacques Chirac.

The British royal family is grouped at the end of the room. The previous, somewhat unflattering, model of Princess Diana was improved recently, after she agreed to a new sitting, the first since before she was married. While Diana is now positioned on the edge of the royal group, Fergie (the Duchess of York) has been removed completely.

The most popular section, the **Chamber of Horrors**, was refurbished in 1996. It contains displays of infamous serial killers, like Charles Manson, and working execution models. A few genuine historical artefacts are on display, including the actual guillotine blade that beheaded Marie Antoinette. Among the infamous British murderers featured is John Christie, hanged in 1953 for murdering his wife and strangling five other women. His execution is re-created in gruesome detail, with a clock counting down, a lever being pushed and a trapdoor opening. The lights black out as Christie takes 'the drop'. The accompanying sound effects send shivers down the spine.

The Chamber of Horrors

This is not, however, the most disturbing part of the Chamber. Visitors who are even remotely squeamish should avoid the end of Jack the Ripper alley, where lies a chillingly-real disembowelled victim. At the entrance to the Chamber, there is an 'escape route' for those wanting to bypass the Horrors.

The exhibition ends with the **Spirit of London** – a ride though the history of the capital in a vehicle resembling a London black cab. Unlike in the rest of the museum, the figures in this section move and speak thanks to sophisticated computer and robotic technology.

PRICES

Adult £8.95
Child £5.90
Senior £6.75
Student £8.95

DISCOUNT

£1.50 off admission per person with voucher on page 281.

A breathtaking 3-D trip through the solar system in the huge domed auditorium is the centrepiece of the London Planetarium, which adjoins Madame Tussaud's.

Built on the site of a cinema destroyed in the Second World War Blitz, the Planetarium opened in 1958. Its great green copper dome has become a

Space Zone

familiar London landmark. When the model of Saturn was fixed to the top of the dome, it acquired the nickname 'Sputnik' after the first spacecraft launched the year before the building opened.

The main show uses the world's most advanced star projector, the £1 million Digistar Mark 2, which is capable of displaying more than 9,000 stars. Entitled **Planetary Quest**, the 30-minute narrated show invites you to imagine you are a space traveller and uses 3-D images to challenge how you look at the universe. Highlights include a trip across the canyons of Mars, an exploding supernova, Neptune's hurricane storms and a close-up view of the rings and moons of Saturn. Perhaps the most exciting sequence is the Big Bang, when the projector simulates the beginning of the universe. You will also be sent zooming through central London.

You can kill time before the show begins at the three exhibition areas outside the auditorium – **Launch Zone**, **Planet Zone** and **Space Zone** – which have hands-on demonstrations, including a gravity well.

Wax portraits of famous astronomers and astronauts

Inside the dome of the Planetarium

help give a human dimension when explaining often difficult concepts about space and time. Interactive video screens are available for those who want to find out more. An effigy of theoretical physicist and motor neurone sufferer Stephen Hawking can be heard discussing the mystery of black holes. He explains his theories on time travel, but adds a word of caution: "The best evidence we have that time travel is not possible, and never will be, is that we have not been invaded by hordes of tourists from the future."

ADDRESS

Marylebone Road
☎ 0171-935-6861

GETTING THERE

Baker Street tube station

HOURS

Mon-Sun: 10am-5pm
Shows every 40 minutes

PRICES

Combined ticket with
Madame Tussaud's
Adult £11.20
Child £7.10
Senior £8.70
Student £11.20

DISCOUNT

£2 off the combined ticket to Madame Tussaud's with voucher on page 281.

Wallace Collection

After fighting through the masses at the British Museum and the National Gallery, the tranquil corridors and rooms of this elegant town house offer a gentle respite for art lovers.

Bequeathed to the nation in 1897 by the widow of art collector Sir Richard Wallace, the sumptuous collection of paintings, armour, porcelain and furniture is displayed in the

The Wallace Collection

perfectly proportioned Hertford House. Overlooking one of London's most charming residential squares, the house dates back to the 18th century, when it was built by the Duke of Manchester as a lodge for the good duck shooting nearby.

The Wallace Collection was mostly put together by Sir Richard, his father and his grandfather. Their eclectic interests included Oriental armour, 18th-century French paintings and Limoges enamels. Sir Richard, a philanthropist, was knighted for helping British people trapped by the Franco-Prussian war.

The conditions of Lady Wallace's bequest were that nothing be added or taken away, and this is reflected in the museum's graceful old-world atmosphere.

The most famous painting in the collection is **Frans Hals'** *The Laughing Cavalier*, famous for the swaggering self-confidence expressed in the subject's face and the gorgeous detail of his coat. However, there are hundreds of delightful, lesser-known exhibits, such as a collection of gold snuff boxes and carved furniture inlaid with tortoiseshell.

'The Laughing Cavalier'
by Franz Hals

The 25 galleries fill two floors. Fine paintings by **Jean Fragonard** hang on the opulent white marble staircase. The iron and bronze balustrade flanking the staircase was originally in Louis XV's Palais Mazarin, but was torn down and later bought by Sir Richard and shipped to London. One upper room is filled with the world's foremost private collection of French 18th-century paintings and furniture.

There are dozens of places to sit and quietly absorb the beauty, including a pretty courtyard.

ADDRESS

Hertford House,
Manchester Square
☎ 0171-935-0687

GETTING THERE

Bond Street or Baker
Street tube stations

HOURS

Mon-Sat: 10am-5pm
Sun: 2pm-5pm

PRICES

Admission is
free

DON'T MISS

Velazquez's *Lady with a Fan* (Room 22), Titian's *Perseus and Andromeda* (Room 22), Hals' *Laughing Cavalier* (Room 22), views of Venice by Canaletto (Room 17), Arms and Armour (Rooms 8-11).

Dickens House

The great Victorian novelist Charles Dickens (1812-70) lived in this house from March 1837 to December 1839. It is the only one of his many London homes to survive.

His years here were among his most creative. It was in this house that he wrote *Oliver Twist* and *Nicholas Nickleby*, and also finished *The Pickwick Papers*. The

latter was so popular in America that readers gathered at the dock to meet the ship carrying each new instalment.

The exterior of Dickens House

The museum contains a wealth of Dickens memorabilia, including letters, manuscripts, furniture, pictures, first editions of his novels and personal possessions. The earliest known portrait of Dickens, painted by his aunt when he was 18, hangs in one of the rooms (which have been reconstructed to their 1830s appearance).

The author's brother-in-law, Henry Burnett, recalled an evening spent in the house when Dickens excused himself and went to a corner of the living room to work on *Oliver Twist*. He encouraged everyone to go on talking and sometimes himself chipped in with a remark, 'the feather of his pen still moving rapidly from side to side'.

Dickens's first two daughters were born in this house

and his wife's 17-year-old sister died here. He was still happily married at this stage and it wasn't until 20 years later, at the height of his fame, that he deserted his wife for the 18-year-old actress Ellen Ternan.

The house was bought by the Dickens Fellowship in 1924 and opened the following year as a museum. It is run by an independent charitable trust.

By the end of 1839, Dickens had moved into No.1 Devonshire Terrace, beside Regent's Park. Unfortunately, this building was demolished in 1960 to make way for an office block.

The Drawing Room

ADDRESS

48 Doughty Street
☎ 0171-405-2127

GETTING THERE

Russell Square
tube station

HOURS

Mon-Sat: 10am-5pm
Sun: closed

PRICES

Adult £3.50
Child £1.50
Senior £2.50
Student £2

DISCOUNT

Adult admission for the price of student admission with your *London for less* card.

Other Attractions . . .

The **Percival David Foundation of Chinese Art** has an important collection of Chinese porcelain dating from

the 10th to the 18th centuries. The 1,500 items were given to London University by the scholar and collector Sir Percival David, in 1951. *(53 Gordon Square, ☎ 0171-387-3909. Mon-Fri: 10.30am-5pm. Sat-Sun: closed. Admission is free.)*

St. Pancras Station

St. Pancras Station, on Euston Road, is one of London's grandest Victorian Gothic buildings. It was only recently revealed in its original glory, after several years of restoration. Next door, to the west, is the new **British Library** *(96 Euston Road, ☎ 0171-412-7000)*, a remarkable piece of modern architecture described by Prince Charles as 'a dim collection of brick sheds groping for some symbolic significance'!

Pollock's Toy Museum contains a captivating collection of historical toys from around the world. Toy maker Benjamin Pollock's famous Victorian paper theatres, complete with puppets, are displayed in one room. Pollock, who had a quaint little shop in London's East End in the early decades of this century, was the last of the 'toy theatre sheet' publishers. He kept the art going until

his death in 1937, whereafter the tradition was sustained by some of his loyal customers.

Pollock's Toy Museum

The six child-sized rooms, connected by narrow winding staircases, are filled with toy treasures. These include a collection of 19th-century dolls houses, hand-painted model soldiers and vintage teddy bears. There are also folk toys from the Alps, Russia, Poland and the Balkans. Toy theatre performances take place during the school

St Pancras Station

The British Library

British Library

Pollock's Toy Museum

. . . Other Attractions

All Souls, Langham Place

holidays. *(1 Scala Street, entrance to museum at 41 Whitfield Street ☎ 0171-636-3452. Mon-Sat: 10am-4.30pm. Sun: closed. Adult £2.50, child £1, senior £2.50, student £2.50. Adult, senior and student £1 off admission and child 50p off admission with London for less card.)*

All Souls, Langham Place, built in 1824, is architect John Nash's only London church. Best seen from Regent Street, the church has a distinctive round frontage and slender spire. BBC lunchtime and evening classical concerts are frequently recorded here. *(Langham Place, ☎ 0171-580-3522. Mon-Fri: 9.30am-6pm. Sun: 9am-9pm with services at 9am, 11am and 6.30pm. Sat: closed.)*

The **Sherlock Holmes Museum** claims to be at 221b Baker Street, the famous fictional address of Sir Arthur Conan Doyle's sleuth. But the museum is actually located at Nos.237-239. The rooms are in the Victorian style, but there is little of interest to the Holmes fan and the expensive entrance price is hardly justified by what you see. *(237-239 Baker Street, ☎ 0171-935-8866. Mon-Sun: 9.30am-6pm. Adult £5, child £3, senior £5, student £5.)*

Russell Square

Open Spaces

Regent's Park (page 192), London's second largest open space, lies to the north of Marylebone.

Some of the splendid Georgian Squares of Bloomsbury are open to the public, with **Russell Square** an ideal place to picnic after visiting the British Museum. The enormous plane trees provide shade and a small café sells refreshments.

Bedford Square

The poet T.S. Eliot worked at No. 24 Russell Square in the late 1920s. On the east side of the square stands London's finest surviving Victorian hotel, the Hotel Russell, opened in 1890. The façade is a glorious mass of red terracotta, colonnaded balconies and pinnacles with two central, copper-capped towers.

Bedford Square, located on the west side of the museum beside Tottenham Court Road, is perhaps the most attractive London square. It is surrounded by symmetrical 18th-century terraces.

Eating and Drinking

Groups of cafés and restaurants can be found on the narrow streets south of the British Museum, on Charlotte Street and further west on Marylebone High Street and around Baker Street tube station.

The **Fitzroy Tavern** *(16 Charlotte Street)* was a meeting place for literary folk in the 1920s and 1930s. The basement 'Writers and Artists Bar' is lined with pictures of famous customers, including author George Orwell and poet Dylan Thomas.

For traditional British food, try the **Edwardian Carvery** (page 176) at the Kenilworth Hotel. **Mandeer** (page 177), an inexpensive vegetarian Indian restaurant, is just off Tottenham Court Road.

Fitzroy Tavern

Ascots Restaurant

Modern British

**The Berkshire,
350 Oxford Street
☎ 0171-629-7474**

Average meal: £15-20
for less discount: 25%
AM/VS/MC/DC

The award-winning Ascots is located just off Oxford Street. It is a high-class restaurant with country-house-style décor. Fine cuisine is served in sumptuous surroundings.

HOURS

Mon-Fri: 12.30pm-2.30pm,
5.30pm-10.30pm
Sat-Sun: 5.30pm-10.30pm

Brasserie St. Martin

French

**Marlborough Hotel,
9 Bloomsbury Street
☎ 0171-636-5601**

Average meal: £10-15
for less discount: 25%
AM/VS/MC/DC

After a visit to the British Museum, this restaurant is a perfect place to relax. It serves delightful French cuisine in an informal, light-hearted setting. Sit back and enjoy the top-quality French food and wine.

HOURS

Mon-Sat: 12noon-2.30pm,
5pm-10.30pm
Sun: 6pm-10pm

HOURS

Mon-Sun:
12.30pm-2.30pm

HOURS

Mon-Fri and Sun:
12.30pm-2.30pm,
5.30pm-10pm
Sat: 5.30pm-10pm

HOURS

Mon-Fri: 11.30am-2.30pm,
6pm-11pm
Sat: 6pm-11pm
Sun: closed

The Cliveden Room

Modern British

**The Grafton,
130 Tottenham Court Road
☎ 0171-388-4131**

Average meal: £10-15
for less discount: 25%
AM/VS/MC/DC

The Cliveden Room, situated in the heart of the busy shopping district, has the atmosphere of an English country house. Both the cuisine and the wine list are superb.

Edwardian Carvery

Modern British

**Kenilworth Hotel,
97 Great Russell Street
☎ 0171-637-3477**

Average meal: £10-15
for less discount: 25%
AM/VS/MC/DC

No trip to London is complete without trying roast beef and Yorkshire pudding, and this is the perfect place to sample great British cuisine. The atmosphere is informal and the service of a high standard.

Caldesi

Italian

**15-17 Marylebone Lane
☎ 0171-935-9226**

Average meal: £10-15
for less discount: 25%
AM/VS/MC/DC

Caldesi's classic Italian menu specializes in reasonably priced fresh pasta dishes. The Victorian décor and corner tables make it perfect for a quiet dinner. In the summer, outside tables enable customers to enjoy *al fresco* dining.

Langham's Brasserie

French

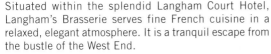

**Langham Court Hotel
31-35 Langham Street**
☎ 0171-436-6622

Average meal: £10-15
for less discount: 25%
AM/VS/MC/DC

HOURS

Mon-Fri: 12.30pm-2.30pm,
6.30pm-10pm
Sat-Sun: 6.30pm-10pm

Situated within the splendid Langham Court Hotel, Langham's Brasserie serves fine French cuisine in a relaxed, elegant atmosphere. It is a tranquil escape from the bustle of the West End.

 # Mandeer

Indian vegetarian

**The Basement,
21 Hanway Place**
☎ 0171-323-0660

Average meal: £10-15
for less discount: 25%
AM/VS/MC/DC

HOURS

Mon-Sat: 12noon-3pm,
5.30pm-10pm
Sun: closed

Opened in 1967 by Ravi Shankar, Mandeer retains its 1960s feel. Its slogan is: 'Peace, love and food at groovy prices'. The self-service luncheon menu is certainly excellent value.

 # Bertie's Brasserie

Modern British

**The Savoy Court,
19 Granville Place**
☎ 0171-408-0130

Average meal: £10-15
for less discount: 25%
AM/VS/MC/DC

HOURS

Mon-Sun: 12noon-2.15pm,
6pm-9.15pm

Bertie's Brasserie, with a discreet location off Oxford Street, features a host of great-value dishes throughout the day. The atmosphere is welcoming and the food excellent.

Tottenham Court Road

Shopping

Tottenham Court Road, which starts at the eastern end of New Oxford Street, is where people go to buy cheap computers and other electrical goods. Prices here can be well below normal high street rates, though take care not to be duped into buying second-rate equipment. Compare prices in several shops and always check the details of the guarantee. Half way up Tottenham Court Road is a major branch of the yuppie furniture store, **Habitat**.

Wigmore Street, which runs parallel with Oxford Street, has dozens of up-market shops. **St. Christopher's Place**, an alleyway near the Wigmore Street/James Street junction, has a cluster of exclusive establishments.

Chess and Bridge

Chess and Bridge Sets

369 Euston Road
☎ 0171-388-2404

for less discount: 20%
AM/VS/MC

This shop is an Aladdin's cave of chess and bridge boards, sets and software. It also stocks the largest collection of chess books in Europe. It is a great place to purchase a gift for the keen chess or bridge player.

Yves Rocher

Beauty Centre

7 Gees Court
☎ 0171-409-2975

for less discount: 20%
VS/MC

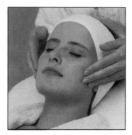

This modern beauty centre offers women every kind of beauty treatment. Among the services offered are manicures, facials and massages. Leg waxing and make-up sessions are also available.

Bayswater and Notting Hill

Introduction. . .

Most of Bayswater was built in the 1830s and 1840s, when wealthy merchants were attracted by the easy

Bayswater Road - Sunday art market

access to the City and property prices cheaper than the more fashionable Belgravia. However, the extravagant terraces and mansions, which were heavily influenced by John Nash's Regent's Park development, fell into disrepair in the early part of the 20th century.

Since the 1970s, Bayswater has undergone a remarkable period of gentrification and the majority of terraces have been fully restored to their Victorian grandeur. The best examples of the architecture are Hyde Park Gardens and the graceful curving façade at the corner of Kendal Street and Connaught Street.

Queensway is Bayswater's ever-busy hub, lined with restaurants, cafés and shops, many of which stay open very late. There are dozens of tacky souvenir shops and over-priced stores specialising in leather goods and other wares aimed at the tourist market. However, the image of Queensway has been boosted by the luxurious marble aisles of **Whiteley's**, an old department store that lay derelict for almost a decade before re-opening in 1989 as an attractive shopping mall.

Unfortunately, the seedy side of Bayswater has not been entirely expunged and the streets around Paddington train station are still infested with inferior restaurants exploiting the tourist trade. For better choice and quality of food, head for **Westbourne Grove** or further west into the Notting Hill area.

Whiteley's shopping centre

Bayswater and Notting Hill are two of London's most cosmopolitan neighbourhoods. A vibrant Arab community lives around Queensway, while Notting Hill is home to a large West Indian population established in the 1950s. Forty years ago, Notting Hill was still dominated by slums, with richer residents living around the southern end of Ladbroke Grove. The proximity of wealth and poverty had always been a feature of Notting Hill, but the addition of inter-racial tensions led to riots in August 1958.

. . . Introduction

The world-famous **Notting Hill Carnival** (page 247) has its roots in this period, when West Indian community leaders decided a celebration was needed to restore the confidence of their people. Until the mid-1960s, the carnival remained a small Caribbean community jamboree. Since then, it has grown into the largest street festival outside South America. Held over three days in late August, the carnival wends its way along Ladbroke Grove and across Portobello Road.

Snaking northwards from Notting Hill Gate, **Portobello Road** is renowned for its colourful street market (page 183), held on Fridays, Saturdays and, to a lesser degree, on Sundays. The Portuguese and Moroccan communities, based around Golborne Road in the north of Notting Hill, add to the quirky mix of cultures which has made

Crowds at Notting Hill Carnival

INSIDER'S TIP

The middle day of the Notting Hill Carnival, a Sunday, has the best atmosphere.

Notting Hill the most fashionable place to live in London in the 1990s.

Even public housing is done in style in Notting Hill, with the country's tallest block of flats, Trellick Tower, declared an architectural masterpiece. The bulging head of the lift shaft, which is only connected to the main structure by high-level walkways, makes the 1973 building look like a strange long-necked monster.

Many young Londoners head for Notting Hill in the evenings to drink in lively Portobello Road pubs, like the Earl of Lonsdale or the Market Bar, or to eat at one of the dozens of exotic restaurants.

However, apart from Portobello Market, there are few tourist attractions in Bayswater or Notting Hill. It is not an area in which to

Portobello Market

sightsee, but to enjoy the blend of ethnic influences, the avant-garde shops and the general stylishness of the inhabitants.

London Toy & Model Museum

More than 7,000 toys and models are crammed into this small, but fascinating, museum.

Acquired in 1989 by the Japanese property company Fujita, the museum has been given a £4 million overhaul. Part of the redevelopment included purchasing the Mullion collection, renowned for its working models and antique slot machines. The

A member of the teddy bear collection

museum is devoted to commercially made toys and models, though this definition is broadly interpreted, with toys dating from AD1.

The 20 galleries on five floors have now been themed, with rooms devoted to model boats, board games and toy soldiers. Many of the toys are from private collections donated to the museum, including 300 teddy bears which belonged to the late Peter Bull, a distinguished British character actor.

ADDRESS

21-23 Craven Hill
☎ 0171-706-8000

GETTING THERE

Paddington, Lancaster Gate, Queensway or Bayswater tube stations

Model of an early double-decker bus

A 70-year-old working model coalmine, complete with toiling miners, pit ponies and clanking machinery, fills one gallery. The **Penny Arcade** contains a selection of working penny slot machines, several of which date from the Victorian period. You can win old pennies from one machine and have your palm read by another.

The elaborate Fleischmann **Model Railway** features ten trains and six tracks, including a mountain diesel line and a turntable. The **Aerodrome** room contains dozens of model planes on loan from British Airways. The airport control tower has interactive buttons which light up different runways.

HOURS

Mon-Sun: 9.30am-5.30pm
Last admission: 4.30pm

PRICES

Adult £4.95
Child £2.95
Senior £3.95
Student £3.95

In the **Whatever Next?!** gallery you can see the latest toy technology and get a sneak preview of the weird and wonderful toys being developed for 21st century children.

The museum ends with **Baywest**, an intricately detailed 6-metre model city, complete with skyscrapers and planes soaring overhead.

DISCOUNT

Adult, senior and student £1 off admission, child 50p off admission with your *London for less* card.

Baywest model city

Portobello Market

A Saturday stroll among the bustle, colour and street musicians of Portobello Market is one of the highlights of any trip to London.

Stretching more than a mile along the perennially trendy Portobello Road, the market offers everything from fine antiques (2,000 stalls) to bric-a-brac, with fruit, books, groovy clothing and trinkets galore in between. The stalls get seedier further north, but dotted along the road are specialist shops selling old LPs and comics. There is even a tattoo artist, who has

hundreds of photographs in his window showing the various parts of the anatomy which have been his canvas.

An antiques shop

A number of specialist bookshops, along with several of the area's growing number of avant-garde art galleries, can be found on Blenheim Crescent. **Portobello Green**, under the flyover, is an arcade of tiny shops in which innovative designers both make and sell their wares.

There are dozens of characterful eateries and bars, with a row of pavement cafés on the northern stretch of Kensington Park Road. Café Grove, on the corner of Lancaster Road, has a terrace from which you can observe the exotic and glamorous Portobello regulars.

At the far end of the market, on Golborne Road, there are a couple of very popular Portuguese cafés, the Lisboa and Porto patisseries.

Food shopping is a particular strength of the market. Applewood Farm Shop sells

An artist's stall

fresh farm produce, Garcia's offers Spanish food, and other shops sell game, fresh herbs and Caribbean fruits.

The market also operates on Friday and Sunday (when it is less lively). Many of the antique and specialist shops are open throughout the week.

GETTING THERE

Notting Hill Gate tube station for southern end, Ladbroke Grove tube station for northern end

HOURS

Sat: 8am-5pm. Fri -Sun: smaller markets 9am-5pm.

INSIDER'S TIP

Always try haggling on the stalls; prices inflate for foreign tourists.

Open Spaces

As many of the area's leafy squares are closed to non-residents, most locals head to Hyde Park and Kensington Gardens.

Little Venice

A short walk to the north-west, however, brings you to picturesque **Little Venice**. The Victorian poet Robert Browning coined the name for this triangular canal barge basin in the heart of an exclusive residential area. Many of the narrow-boats have been prettily painted, with hundreds of flower pots contributing to the colourful scene. It is a delightful place for a stroll, followed by a drink in one of the traditional, waterside pubs.

The **Puppet Theatre Barge**, on the Blomfield Road edge of the basin, performs weekend shows from October to May. The **London Waterbus Company** runs narrow-boat trips to Camden Lock, via Regent's Park and London Zoo. *(Little Venice, ☎ 0171-482-2550. Mon-Sun: 10am-5pm. Trips run hourly with a restricted out-of-season service. One way ticket: adult £3.70, child £2.30, senior £2.30, student £3.70. Return ticket: adult £4.80, child £2.90, senior £2.90, student £4.80.)*

Little Venice

Eating and Drinking

Queensway and Westbourne Grove are packed with restaurants. The northern end of Kensington Park Road has several fashionable cafés and bistros, most with pavement tables in summer.

There are lots of good value eateries around Notting Hill Gate, including **Malabar** *(27 Uxbridge Street)* for curries and **Manzara** *(24 Pembridge Road)* for Turkish food.

The third floor of **Whiteley's** *(Queensway, ☎ 0171-792-0406)* shopping mall is devoted to restaurants, several of which serve fast food.

Whiteleys

Perhaps the most unusual restaurant in the area is **Veronica's** (page 185), where the menu covers 500 years of British culinary history.

Beach Blanket Babylon *(45 Ledbury Road)* is a self-consciously trendy bar and restaurant near the Portobello Road. The **Windsor Castle** *(Campden Hill Road)*, probably the most up-market pub in west London, serves oysters and has a pleasant beer garden.

Several of the restaurants located close to Paddington Station are avoided by local residents because they offer poor value for money.

 # Veronica's

Historical English

3 Hereford Road
☎ 0171-229-5079

Average meal: £10-15
for less discount: 25%
AM/VS/MC/DC

Veronica's is small, beautifully furnished and serves historical English dishes. The award-winning food is light and healthy with robust flavours. Themes range from Georgian to Irish country home.

HOURS

Mon-Fri: 12noon-3pm,
7pm-12midnight
Sat: 7pm-12midnight
Sun: closed

 # Bombay Palace

Indian

50 Connaught Street
☎ 0171-723-8855

Average meal: £10-15
for less discount: 25%
AM/VS/MC/DC

This elegant restaurant, part of a distinguished chain with branches all over the world, offers fine Indian food in an impressive setting. The menu includes an extensive choice of vegetarian dishes.

HOURS

Mon-Sun: 12noon-3pm,
6pm-11.30pm

Chi-Chi's

Tex / Mex

**2nd Floor
Whiteleys Centre**
☎ 0171-792-8462

Average meal: £10-15
for less discount: 25%
AM/VS/MC

Chi-Chi's, located in Whiteleys shopping mall, is a lively restaurant specializing in Mexican food. A full range of typical Tex/Mex dishes is served and the fajitas are particularly recommended.

HOURS

Mon-Sun: 11.30am-10pm

HOURS

Mon-Sat: 9am-11pm
Sun: 9am-10.30pm

Ma Potter's Chargrill

International

2nd Floor
Whiteleys Centre
☎ 0171-792-2318

Average meal: £10-15
for less discount: 25%
AM/VS/MC/DC

Ma Potter's serves sizzling dishes straight from its chargrill. Try the chargrilled sirloin with melted cheese and salsa. The décor is rustic, with an authentic timber barn and a raised veranda.

HOURS

Mon-Sun: 9am-11pm

Bistro St. Orleans

American / French

2nd Floor
Whiteleys Centre
☎ 0171-229-5546

Average meal: £5-10
for less discount: 25%
AM/VS/MC

Bistro St. Orleans is located in the Whiteleys shopping mall. A good place for either lunch or dinner, the menu has something to suit every taste. Barbecue ribs are a speciality.

HOURS

Mon-Sun:
10.30am-12midnight

Bella Pasta

Italian

55 Queensway
☎ 0171-792-2880

Average meal: £5-10
for less discount: 25%
AM/VS/MC/DC

Bella Pasta serves a wide range of Italian dishes. Its restaurants in London have excellent locations and long opening times. In this area, there is another branch at 108 Queensway.

Royal Parks

Hyde Park

The vast green expanse of Hyde Park stretches over 350 acres, from Marble Arch in the north to Knightsbridge in the south. It is a favourite place for shoppers, office workers, tourists and residents to relax, play ball games, stroll among the trees and go boating on the Serpentine.

Speakers' Corner

HOURS

Mon-Sun:
5am-12midnight

INSIDER'S TIP

You can hire row boats and pedal boats on the Serpentine (Mar-Oct: 9am-7pm. £6 per hour.).

REFLECTIONS

'The parks are the lungs of London' - Prime Minister William Pitt (1808)

First cultivated by Benedictine monks in the medieval period, the area was one of Henry VIII's royal hunting parks. In the 17th century, it was a fashionable place for courtiers to drive

Hyde Park

their lavish carriages. Today, its association with horsemanship continues, as the barracks of the Household Cavalry lie along the south-western edge.

The park was fully opened to the public by Charles I in 1637. When the Great Plague of 1665 ravaged the City and Westminster, thousands of citizens camped in the park to escape the disease.

During the reign of William and Mary, a new royal court was established at Kensington Palace. The route through the park to the palace was known as 'Route du Roi' (King's Road), which was vulgarized to 'Rotten Row'. Horses are now exercised on **Rotten Row**, which runs along the park's southern flank.

The **Serpentine** lake was created during the 18th century. The self-service cafés are crowded and uninspiring, making a picnic an attractive alternative. Hyde Park has 10,000 deck chairs available for rental at a rate of 70p per chair for four hours.

The park's sculptures include Jacob Epstein's *Rima Monument*, whose naked goddess offended 1920s London and was twice covered in tar and feathers.

Riding in Hyde Park

There is a century-old tradition of public speaking in the park and soap-box orators still declaim, amid witty heckling, every Sunday morning at **Speakers' Corner**.

Major festivals, like the 1851 Great Exhibition, have been held in the park and the site is still used for massive outdoor concerts.

Apsley House

The magnificent home of the Duke of Wellington, who defeated Napoleon at Waterloo, is the last of London's great town houses to survive with its family still in residence and its art collection largely intact.

Apsley House stands in splendid isolation at Hyde Park Corner, one of the city's busiest traffic junctions. Its address is 'Number One London', because of its position just past a toll gate into the capital.

Apsley House

Built in the late 18th century by the architect Robert Adam, the house was later faced with Bath stone by the Duke of Wellington. In 1832 its windows were broken by an angry mob who rioted after the Duke tried to block an extension of the right to vote. To protect his home from further outrages, Wellington had iron shutters fitted to the windows. It is from this, not from his triumphs on the battlefield, that he acquired the nickname 'the Iron Duke'.

The 'Iron Duke'

Apsley House was presented to the nation in 1947 by the 7th Duke of Wellington. The 8th Duke of Wellington and his family still occupy the top floor and other areas, but the lower two floors are open to the public. These handsomely restored rooms have grand views of Hyde Park.

The art collection is small, but contains several important works, including Diego Velazquez's *Waterseller of Seville*, plus paintings by Franciso Goya, Sir Peter Paul Rubens and Pieter Brueghel. Canova's imposing nude statue of Napoleon stands at the foot of the mansion's ornate spiral staircase.

The most memorable exhibit is the eight-metre silver centrepiece of Wellington's Portuguese dinner service. It took two sculptors five years to make and adorned the table at the Duke's annual Waterloo Banquet for his loyal officers.

The Waterloo gallery

ADDRESS

Hyde Park Corner
☎ 0171-499-5676

GETTING THERE

Hyde Park Corner
tube station

HOURS

Tue-Sun: 11am-5pm
Last admission 4.30pm
Mon: closed

PRICES

Adult £3
Child £1.50
Senior £1.50
Student £1.50

DISCOUNT

Adult admission for the price of child admission with *London for less* card

Kensington Gardens

Originally part of Hyde Park, Kensington Gardens was established in the 18th century as the grounds of Kensington Palace. It is separated from Hyde Park by the north-south running West Carriage Drive.

Italian Gardens

One current palace resident, Diana, Princess of Wales, can occasionally be spotted on the **Broad Walk** among the rollerbladers. Despite the latter, Kensington Gardens are considerably more peaceful than Hyde Park, which bustles with activity.

HOURS

Mon-Sun: dawn - dusk

The Gardens were first opened to the public in the 18th century when the Royal Court moved to Buckingham Palace. Queen Victoria added the **Italian Gardens**, the four stone pools at the north-eastern corner, which make up perhaps the prettiest section of the park. She also commissioned the intricate 180-foot (54-metre) **Albert Memorial**, in memory of her beloved husband, Prince Albert, who died of cholera in 1861. The memorial, opposite the Royal Albert Hall on Kensington Gore, is currently being restored (page 118).

Italian Gardens

The **Flower Walk**, running from the Albert Memorial to the Palace Gate, is a haven for birds and butterflies in summer. Avenues of trees radiate out from the seven-acre **Round Pond**, where model boats are sailed. Radio-controlled boats are banned because they frighten the birds.

Other highlights of the park include Sir George Frampton's **Peter Pan** statue, in a wooded area near the **Long Water,** and the striking bronze figure entitled **Physical Energy**, which stands at a crossroads in the centre of the park. The **Elfin Oak**, carved in 1930 with fairies and elves, is outside the children's playground at the northern end of the Broad Walk.

Albert Memorial

A squirrel in Kensington Gardens

The **Serpentine Gallery** has a reputation for exhibiting controversial contemporary art. There was a public outcry when the artist Damien Hirst displayed a dead sheep suspended in formaldehyde. The gallery closed in 1996 for a major refurbishment and is due to reopen in October 1997. *(Beside West Carriage Drive, ☎ 0171-823-9727 for exhibition times. Admission is free.)*

Serpentine Gallery

 Kensington Palace

Kensington Palace, the home of Diana, Princess of Wales, has been a royal residence since 1689, when

William of Orange moved in because he feared living beside the river at Whitehall Palace would aggravate his asthma.

Originally a Jacobean mansion, Kensington Palace was substantially rebuilt by Sir Christopher Wren

Kensington Palace

and his assistant, Nicholas Hawksmoor. Wren added pavilions to each corner and re-oriented the building to create a courtyard on the west side.

Princess Victoria was born at the palace in 1819 and 18 years later was woken here at 5am to be told she was the new Queen of the British Empire.

Diana and several other royals, including the Queen's sister, Princess Margaret, have apartments on the west side of the Palace. Prince Charles now lives in St. James's Palace.

You can visit the east side, where the tour is divided into two sections: the **State Apartments** and the **Court Dress Collection**, both recently re-opened following a £2.8 million refurbishment.

Decorative paintings by William Kent, especially the *trompe l'oeil* murals on the **King's Grand Staircase**, are the main appeal of the royal apartments. The optical trickery of the painted ceiling in the **Cupola Room** makes you think it is capped by a dome.

The 96-foot (29-metre) long **King's Gallery** has ceiling paintings by Kent depicting scenes from the story of Ulysses. Of the canvases on display, Rubens's *Satyrs and Sleeping Nymphs* is perhaps the finest. The elaborate wind-dial above the fireplace, made for William III by Robert Morden in 1694, is operated by rods connected to a wind-vane on the roof.

The Dress Collection charts the changing fashion in coronation robes and other ceremonial attire. Its most famous exhibit, the wedding dress of Diana, Princess of Wales, has now been removed.

In the palace grounds, the **Sunken Garden** contains a pretty, rectangular pond surrounded by flower beds.

Bed inside Kensington Palace

ADDRESS

The Broad Walk
☎ 0171-937-9561

GETTING THERE

High Street Kensington, Queensway or Bayswater tube stations

HOURS

May-Sep: Check opening times by calling
☎ 0171-376-2452

PRICES

Adult £6
Child £4
Senior £4.50
Student £4.50

DISCOUNT

10% off admission per person with voucher on page 281.

Open Air Theatre

HOURS

Mon-Sun: 5am - dusk

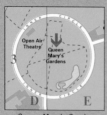
Queen Mary's Garden

Central Mosque

The Boating Lake

Regent's Park

Regent's Park is the second largest open space in central London after Hyde Park/Kensington Gardens. It draws tens of thousands of people every day: office workers playing ball games, visitors to the **Open Air Theatre** *(Box Office ☎ 0171-486-2431)* or the **Zoo**, families boating on the lake and couples wandering the paths that criss-cross the park.

Regent's Park

The park was laid out between 1817 and 1828 by **John Nash** for the Prince Regent, hence the title Regent's Park. Nash's original grand plan for 56 villas and a royal residence for the prince was significantly scaled down. Only eight villas and several palatial terraces were built. However, the double-circle framework has remained, preserving the boundaries of this spacious park.

Initially, access to the park was restricted to people living in the surrounding mansions and those rich enough to have carriages. In 1845, however, the public was allowed into the park on two days of the week for a small entrance fee. The park suffered severe damage in the Second World War, when troops encamped there were targeted by V2 rockets. A huge amount of bomb rubble was dumped in the park, levelling off previously undulating grassland.

The park has several beautiful formal gardens and well-manicured flower beds stretch along the main north-south avenue. There are over 6,000 forest trees and, in **Queen Mary's Garden** in the Inner Circle, 400 varieties of rose. The main lake, shaped like a curved 'Y', has six wooded islands. The **Heronry**, with 25 breeding pairs, is on the island closest to the fork of the 'Y'. From all round the lake, you can see the golden dome of the **London Central Mosque** beside Hanover Gate.

There is a separate children's pool west of the main lake, with row, canoe and pedal boats for hire.

🏛 London Zoo

Located at the northern end of Regent's Park, the 170-year-old London Zoo has for many years been concerned with the conservation of endangered species. Of particular note is its breeding programme for Sumatran tigers, of which there are only 800 left in the world.

In addition, the Zoo is home to more than

Golden Lion Tavarin twins

12,000 creatures, not counting the ants in the ant colony. There are almost 100 rare species, like the Arabian oryx and Persian leopard. As well as giraffes, gorillas, and rhinos, there are three Asian elephants, Dilberta, Layang-Layang and Mya, who are brought out for a daily weigh-in.

The **Aquarium** has several tanks including separate ones for sharks and piranhas. One of the biggest crowd-pullers is penguin feeding time, which takes place at the famous **Penguin Pool**, designed in 1934 by Bertholdt Lubetkin.

Moonlight World is devoted to nocturnal creatures, revealed by special lighting. The **Invertebrate House** has a trio of Mexican Red-kneed Bird-eating Spiders, called Sharon, Tracey and Frieda.

The Zoo remains very popular with children, partly due to the **Touch Paddock** where they can stroke sheep, goats and wallabies. When you arrive, ask for details of the daily events programme, which includes feeding times.

A Rhinoceros

The Zoo's future had been uncertain for several years, but it was saved from possible closure in the early 1990s with help from the Kuwaiti government, grateful for Britain's help in the Gulf War.

The Zoo has several Grade One listed buildings. There is also a huge netted **Aviary**, designed by Lord Snowdon, on the north side of Regent's Canal, which bisects the zoo.

A Sumatran tiger

New: The Mappin, London's only 'mountain terraces' re-opened in 1997 after being closed for 11 years.

ADDRESS

Regents Park North
☎ 0171-722-3333

GETTING THERE

Camden Town or
Regent's Park
tube stations

HOURS

Mon-Sun: 10am-4pm
Last admission 3pm

PRICES

Adult £8
Child (4-14) £6
Senior £7
Student £7

DISCOUNT

Adult £2 off admission,
child, senior and student
£1 off admission with
voucher on page 281.

Green Park and St. James's Park

St. James's Park and Green Park well deserve their 'royal' epithet, as Buckingham Palace overlooks the tree-lined walkways of both.

Duck Island

HOURS

Mon–Sun: 24 hours a day

INSIDER'S TIP

The pelicans are fed with whole fish at 4pm daily on the lawn near Duck Island.

Constitution Arch

St. James's Park began its long royal association in 1532, when Henry VIII had it enclosed for deer hunting and built the Palace of St. James's.

James I introduced exotic animals, such as an elephant and crocodiles, given to him by foreign princes.

Pelicans in St. James's Park

Charles II, who had been captivated by the gardens of Versailles, created the first formal gardens and a half-mile ornamental canal was dug down the middle of the park.

In the late 18th century, the architect John Nash re-landscaped the park. Adopting a more romantic style, he created winding paths and a natural-looking lake. Today, it remains much how he left it.

The view from the bridge in the centre of the lake, with Buckingham Palace in one direction and Westminster in the other, is one of the finest in London. Bahama pintails, chiloe wigeon and pelicans inhabit the lake and the **Duck Island** sanctuary, east of the bridge. In summer, brass bands give lunchtime and evening concerts on the bandstand north of the bridge.

Green Park is more peaceful than its neighbour, St. James's. The benches on the long, leafy avenues are rarely full.

At the western tip of the park is the spectacular **Constitution Arch**, marooned on the traffic island known as Hyde Park Corner.

The arch is topped by the immense bronze statue *Quadriga*, depicting Peace riding a chariot drawn by four rearing horses. The size of the statue can be gauged from the fact that the sculptor, Adrian Jones, held a dinner for eight people inside one of the horses shortly before it was completed in 1912.

Constitution Arch

London by Night

Introduction

Whether you want to see a show, listen to some live jazz, watch a film at a big-screen cinema, eat at an exotic restaurant or go nightclubbing, the choice in London is huge and bewildering.

Each of the eight areas in this guide has restaurants, cinemas and clubs, but the West End is the principal entertainment district. Tens of thousands of people head to the West End every night of the week. On Fridays and Saturdays, the busiest nights, the area is overrun, and queues form outside some pubs and restaurants. Simply wandering through the streets among the crowds is an experience in itself.

Her Majesty's Theatre

The West End is a remarkably compact area, with entertainment venues of all kinds packed tightly together. Whether you have tickets for a theatre on Shaftesbury Avenue, the Strand or in Covent Garden, you will have a choice of several dozen restaurants within two minutes walk.

Legal restrictions on serving alcohol after 11pm have recently been relaxed and now many West End bars stay open later. Soho and Mayfair have the most late-night bars, though they can be difficult to get into after 11pm: try the Atlantic Bar *(20 Glasshouse Street)* or Café Boheme *(13 Old Compton Street)*. In Soho, several cafés stay open until the early hours serving food and non-alcoholic drinks, including Bar Italia *(22 Frith Street)*.

Café de Paris

Although the tube system closes shortly after midnight, night buses run at roughly hourly intervals throughout the night, starting in Trafalgar Square.

Beware of the rip-off 'strip' clubs around Wardour Street in Soho. You may pay only a modest entry fee, but compulsory drinks can boost the bill per person to well in excess of £100, with bouncers adopting aggressive tactics to extract your cash. Westminster City Council is trying to clamp down on the con-men, so inquire if the club has a current council licence.

Theatres

London's renowned theatre scene is a major visitor attraction. There are clusters of theatres in three main areas: Shaftesbury Avenue/Haymarket, St. Martin's Lane/Charing Cross Road and Covent Garden/the Strand.

The Garrick

Many of the theatres have colourful histories. The interiors are often richly decorated with painted ceilings and wooden carvings. Some are reputed to have ghosts. It is claimed that the **Garrick** *(Charing Cross Road, ☎ 0171-494-5085)* , for example, is haunted by Arthur Bourchier, the theatre's manager 100 years ago, who hated critics and is said to be trying to scare them off. The most famous theatre of all, the **Theatre Royal, Drury Lane** (page 78), is nearly 200 years old. There has been a theatre on the site since the 1660s, when Charles II's mistress, Nell Gwyn, performed comic roles.

In addition to the dozens of independent theatres, there are two main national companies: the **Royal National Theatre** *(South Bank, ☎ 0171-928-2252)* and the **Royal Shakespeare Company** (page 202).

The West End hit musical "Miss Saigon"

From December to February, several theatres stage **pantomimes**, musical comedies with lots of audience participation and absurd costumes. A trip to the pantomime is a well-loved British family tradition.

INSIDER'S TIP

In the summer months, open-air theatre is performed in Regent's Park *(☎ 0171-486-2431)* and Holland Park *(☎ 0171-602-7856)*. Take a picnic and rugs to keep you warm.

If you feel like experimenting, London is richly endowed with innovative fringe theatre. Productions are usually staged in rooms over pubs, such as the **Gate Theatre** *(11 Pembridge Road, ☎ 0171-229-5387)* above Notting Hill's Prince Albert, the **Grace** *(503 Battersea Park Road, ☎ 0171-223-5349)* above Battersea's Latchmere, and the theatre at Islington's **King's Head** *(115 Upper Street, ☎ 0171-226-1916)*.

The Royal National Theatre

A new production of the smash-hit musical *Jesus Christ Superstar* opened at the end of 1996 at the **Lyceum Theatre** *(Wellington Street, ☎ 0171-656-1803)* , which lay derelict for eight years but has undergone a £14.5 million restoration. Disney's *Beauty and the Beast*, at £10 million the most expensive musical ever staged in London, opened in Spring 1997 at the **Dominion** *(Tottenham Court Road, ☎ 0171-416-6060)*.

Lyceum Theatre

Opera, Ballet and Classical Concerts

Huge subsidies and grants ensure devotees of classical music and opera have much to celebrate in London.

There are five orchestras and two permanent opera companies, as well as a host of smaller ensembles and touring companies. Below is a brief guide to London's leading opera houses and concert halls. Also, see pages 202-204 to see where you can obtain discounts with you *London for less* card.

The Royal Opera House

The Royal Opera House (page 203) is undergoing major refurbishment, partially paid for by an enormous National Lottery grant (the size of which delighted British opera lovers, but outraged just about everyone else).

London Coliseum

Sadler's Wells (*Rosebery Avenue,* ☎ *0171-278-8916*) is renowned for its daring ballet productions, including a recent version of *Swan Lake* in which men were cast as swans. It plays host to several excellent touring companies, including the Gilbert and Sullivan specialists D'Oyly Carte in April and May.

The **London Coliseum** is the home of the **English National Opera** (page 202), which pulls in younger crowds with audacious productions sung in English.

Royal Albert Hall

The **Royal Albert Hall** (*Kensington Gore,* ☎ *0171-589-8212*) hosts the Promenade Concerts from mid-July to mid-September . The 'Proms', are very British events, which end with an outpouring of national sentiment during the televised 'Last Night of the Proms'. Tickets can be bought on the day of a performance, though queues form early. Other concerts and special events take place throughout the year at this historic venue (page 118).

The English National Ballet

Royal Festival Hall

The **Royal Festival Hall** (*South Bank,* ☎ *0171-960-4242*) at the South Bank Centre hosts seasons by the English National Ballet and regular classical concerts. The RFH was built to mark the 1951 Festival of Britain.

The **Barbican Centre** (*Silk Street,* ☎ *0171-638-8891*) is the home of the London Symphony Orchestra and is renowned for its performances of contemporary music. There are frequent free foyer concerts.

Cinemas

With more than 200 screens in central London alone, finding a film to suit your taste should not be a problem.

Several of the biggest screens are to be found in the cinemas around Leicester Square. This is where most films tend to be premièred in Britain, where film launches lag weeks or months behind the US.

The Warner Village West End

Empire Leicester Square

On the north side, is the **Empire**, proud of being Britain's most expensive cinema (£9 a seat). It has 1,200 plush seats, a massive screen, Digital Dolby Surround Sound and an opening laser show. *(Leicester Square, ☎ 0171-437-1234)*

The other big screens on Leicester Square are the **Odeon** *(☎ 0181-315-4221)* to the East and the **Warner Village West End** *(☎ 0171-437-3484)* in the North East corner.

Expect to pay £7-9 for a seat in the West End, with a soft drink and tub of popcorn adding another £3-4. Most of the large cinemas accept credit card telephone bookings.

Film are given certificates (ratings) according to minimum age limits, i.e. 18, 15 and 12, while others are PG (meaning 'parental guidance' but no age restriction) and U for 'universal' (acceptable for young children).

National Film Theatre

INSIDER'S TIP

For a luxurious cinematic experience, try the more intimate surroundings of the **Curzon Mayfair**, London's smartest cinema.

London has several independent art-house cinemas, which generally spurn Hollywood blockbusters and specialize instead in off-beat, cult and foreign language movies. Below is a list of the best art-house cinemas.

Barbican *(Silk Street, ☎ 0171-638-8891)*; **Electric** *(191 Portobello Road, ☎ 0171-792-2020)*; **ICA Cinematheque** *(The Mall, ☎ 0171-930-3647)*; **Lumière** *(42-49 St. Martin's Lane, ☎ 0171-836-0691)*; **Minema** *(45 Knightsbridge, ☎ 0171-369-1723)*; **National Film Theatre** *(South Bank, ☎ 0171 928 3232)*; and **Renoir** *(Brunswick Square, ☎ 0171-837-8402)*.

The **London Film Festival** in November screens at least 100 of the world's best films from that year. There are various venues, but the National Film Theatre is the principal host.

The Odeon Leicester Square

Nightclubs

Staying abreast of the latest trends in London's ever-changing nightclub scene is a full-time job. A certain club can be wildly popular one night of the week, while the next night it is deserted.

A night on the town

However, amid all the breathless variety and glamour, there are a few stalwarts that consistently pull in the crowds.

The dress code varies, though most places frown on jeans, T-shirts and trainers (sneakers). Most places open around 10pm and keep going until at least 3am (later at Legends, Ministry of Sound and Wag). Expect to pay an entry charge of at least £10 on Friday and Saturday nights, and considerably more at the top spots. The clubs section of *Time Out* (a London magazine with extensive listings) gives details of 200 different clubs and one-nighters.

Listed below are a few recommended dance clubs.

Hippodrome

Hippodrome *(Charing Cross Road, ☎ 0171-437-4311)*, one of London's biggest clubs, has a brilliant light show, but the décor is a little dated. It also stages a top-notch floor show that regularly springs surprises.

Hippodrome nightclub

Ministry of Sound *103 Gaunt Street, ☎ 0171-378-6528)* is well outside the city centre, but it is worth the trek for the astonishing energy of the young clubbers.

Stringfellows *(16 Upper St. Martin's Lane, ☎ 0171-240-5534)* has more limousines parked outside it than any other club in London. Always ahead of its time, it was the first club to introduce table dancers.

Stringfellows

Heaven *(Underneath the Arches, Villiers Street, ☎ 0171-930-2020)*, London's legendary gay club, is practically a village with its maze of bars, dance floors, shops and refreshment kiosks that are located in the cavernous vaults beneath Charing Cross Station.

Jazz Clubs

The **Jazz Café** *(5 Parkway, Camden Town tube station, ☎ 0171-916-6060)* features some of the biggest names in jazz, Latin and hip hop. Booking a table is highly recommended.

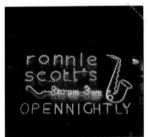

Ronnie Scott's

Ronnie Scott's *(47 Frith Street, ☎ 0171-439-0747)* is the legendary Soho jazz club founded by the British saxophonist Ronnie Scott, who died tragically in late 1996. Book a table close to the stage for the best views.

100 Club

Upstairs you can dance to Jazz, Funk and Soul on Wednesdays and Thursdays and Salsa Music on Fridays and Saturdays

The **100 Club** *(100 Oxford Street, ☎ 0171-636-0933)* hosted The Who and the Rolling Stones in the 1960s, then the Sex Pistols and the Clash in the 1970s. It has now reverted to its former identity as a club for jazz and blues enthusiasts.

Comedy Clubs

The Comedy Store *(1a Oxendon Street, ☎ 0171-344-4444),* the most famous comedy club in Britain, is where all the best stand-up comedians appear. Tickets are gold dust for the Comedy Store Players' superb improvisation shows on Wednesdays and Sundays.

The Comedy Store

A night of comedy at **Jongleurs** *(☎ 01426-944346)* involves a trip out of the centre to one of this famous club's two venues at either Battersea *(The Cornet, 49 Lavender Gardens)* or Camden Lock *(Dingwalls Building, Chalk Farm Road).*

Oranje Boom Boom *(Macclesfield Street ☎ 0171-737-6204)* is one London's more intimate comedy spots, with highly original acts playing Wednesday nights in a crowded room over De Hems pub near Chinatown.

The Comedy Café *(Rivington Street ☎ 0171-739-5706),* based in the City, Has some of the most talented emerging stand-up comedians. The club also has the advantage of a late alcohol license until 1am on certain nights.

DISCOUNT

Discounts vary but are typically 20% to 50% off. Discounts are subject to availability.

DISCOUNT

20% off tickets Mon-Thu and Sat matinées with your *London for less* card. Discounts are subject to availability.

DISCOUNT

Tickets £23 reduced to £6 with *London for less* card. Discounts are subject to availability.

West End Shows

Ticketmaster-London for less
☎ 0171-413-1436

(Telephone 24-hours a day and ask what discounts are available with London for less. AM/VS/MC. c.£10-50.)

Ticketmaster offers discounts off West End shows to *London for less* cardholders. Discounts vary from show-to-show and from time-to-time. You can also book non-discounted tickets but a booking fee might be charged.

English National Opera

London Coliseum, St. Martin's Lane
☎ 0171-632-8300

(Visit Box Office or order tickets by phone Mon-Sat 10am-8pm. AM/VS/MC/DC. £6.50-£45)

The ENO performs from September to July at the magnificent Coliseum. Formed in 1931, the ENO aims to make opera accessible to everyone. Its spectacular and innovative performances are always in English.

Royal Shakespeare Company

Barbican Box Office Barbican Centre
☎ 0171-638-8891

(Buy tickets by telephone on day of performance. No advance bookings. Telephone for information on performances. AM/VS/MC.)

The RSC is renowned worldwide for its performances of Shakespeare. Its repertoire also includes modern and ancient classics, new plays and musicals. It plays at both the Barbican Theatre and the Pit.

The Royal Opera House

Bow Street
☎ 0171-304-4000

(Call above number and press 5 for standby information. Buy ticket at foyer Box Office 90 minutes before performance. No advance bookings. AM/VS/MC/DC. £12-120)

DISCOUNT

Up to 80% off with *London for less* card. Discounts are subject to availability.

See The Royal Opera and The Royal Ballet perform this season. In July 1997 the Royal Opera House will be closed for redevelopment. When redevelopment commences on 15 July 1997, this offer will expire.

Almeida

Almeida Street, Islington
☎ 0171-359-4404

(Call the Box Office for performance times and prices. AM/VS/MC/DC. £6.50-19.50.)

DISCOUNT

2 tickets for the price of 1 on day of performance only. Discounts are subject to availability.

The Almeida is one of Britain's most exciting and innovative theatres. It produces an ambitious programme of classical and contemporary plays, providing epic theatre in an intimate space.

Royal Court Theatre

Duke of York's, St. Martin's Lane
☎ 0171-565-5000

(Call the Box Office for performance times and prices. AM/VS/MC/DC. £4-18.)

DISCOUNT

25% off all tickets Tue-Fri and Sat matinées. Discounts are subject to availability.

The Royal Court has played a major part in English drama for over a century. During the two year refurbishment of its theatre it will have a temporary home. It continues to present the best in new writing.

The London Philharmonic

Royal Festival Hall
☎ 0171-960-4242

(Call the Royal Festival Hall for performance times and prices. AM/VS/MC/DC. £5-32.)

DISCOUNT

25% off all tickets

The London Philharmonic's repertoire ranges from traditional classical music to world premières. The orchestra is resident at the Royal Festival Hall from September to May.

The Philharmonia

Royal Festival Hall
☎ 0171-960-4242

(Call the Royal Festival Hall for performance times and prices. AM/VS/MC/DC. £5-30.)

DISCOUNT

25% off all tickets

The Philharmonia is world renowned for the quality of its playing. Approximately 30 concerts are held at the Royal Festival Hall throughout the year except during July and August.

BBC Symphony Orchestra

Royal Festival Hall
☎ 0171-960-4242

(Call the Royal Festival Hall for performance times and prices. AM/VS/MC/DC. £11.)

DISCOUNT

25% off all tickets

The BBC Symphony Orchestra was London's first permanent orchestra. It has always had a special commitment to 20th century music. Seats for concerts at the Royal Festival Hall are unreserved, so arrive early.

Greater London

Hampstead and Highgate

GETTING THERE

Hampstead: Hampstead
tube station

Hampstead & Highgate . . .

One of the most fashionable of London's boroughs,
Hampstead breathes an air of superiority stemming
partly from its
location on a
high ridge
overlooking
central London.

A Hampstead Garden

For two
centuries,
Hampstead has
been popular
with artists,
scholars and
writers. Among those who lived here were the
Romantic poet John Keats, whose house you can visit
(Wentworth Place, Keats Grove, ☎ *0171 435 2062)*, the
painter John Constable and the writers H.G. Wells,
D.H. Lawrence and Katherine Mansfield.

Kenwood House

The well-preserved Georgian village is
now bristling with stylish bars,
restaurants and boutiques. Yet for most
Londoners, Hampstead means one thing:
the glorious 800-acre wooded expanse of
Hampstead Heath. There is an
unparalleled view of London from the top
of **Parliament Hill**, on the southern
stretch of the Heath. A network of pretty
streets runs between the Heath and
Hampstead High Street, with interesting
specialist shops lining **Flask Walk** and
Well Walk. Around the corner from the
tube station is **Church Row**, one of
London's finest Georgian streets.

REFLECTIONS

'I have hated Hampstead
for her Left-wingery, but I
have loved her for her
strange, secret, leafy soul.
Nowhere in London are
green thoughts so green,
especially in rainy June,
when grass grows high in
her innumerable gardens
tamed or wild.' – *The
Stretchford Chronicles*,
Peter Simple (1980)

Kenwood House, at the northern tip of the Heath
beside Hampstead Lane, sits majestically atop a steep
bank. The original 17th-century mansion was
redesigned in the 1760s by Robert Adam for the Earl
of Mansfield. As Lord Chief Justice, Mansfield sent
more than 100 people to the gallows and was one of
the most hated men of his day. Kenwood's last private
owner, the Earl of Iveagh of the Guinness dynasty,
bequeathed the house and his superb art collection to
the nation in 1927. The **Iveagh Bequest** includes
important works by Van Dyck, Gainsborough and
Reynolds as well as a Rembrandt self-portrait. Adam's
blue and gold library, with its richly decorated tunnel-
vaulted ceiling, is the principal feature of the interior.
(8 Hampstead Lane, ☎ *0181-348-1286. Apr-Sep: Mon-Sun:
10am-6pm. Oct-Mar: Mon-Sun: 10am-4pm. Admission is
free.)*

. . . Hampstead & Highgate

Classical concerts are held on summer evenings in the huge, grassy amphitheatre below Kenwood House. The orchestra plays under a canopy across the lake from the audience. The highlight of the season is Handel's *Fireworks Music*, played on July 4 and accompanied by a fireworks show to celebrate America's Independence Day. *(Kenwood Lakeside Concerts, Jun-Sep: Saturdays only, ☎ 0181-348-1286.)*

Hampstead High Street

The Spaniard's Inn *(Spaniard's Road)*, opposite the heath on Spaniard's Road, is a 16th-century weatherboarded house. The infamous highwayman Dick Turpin stabled his horse, Black Bess, at the inn and Shelley, Keats and Byron all frequented it. Dickens used the inn for the scene in *The Pickwick Papers* where Mrs Bardell plots the downfall of Mr Pickwick. There are real fires in winter and a beautiful garden with rose bushes and plenty of picnic tables.

On the other side of the Heath, to the east, lies the equally exclusive **Highgate**. While the literati preferred Hampstead, Highgate has maintained its own prestige largely through its famous cemetery, where **Karl Marx** is buried. Most people head for the **East Cemetery**, where Marx lies beneath an enormous black bust. However, the wilder and spookier **West Cemetery**, which inspired Bram Stocker to write *Dracula*, is much the more memorable. Tours of the West Cemetery are run by the Friends of Highgate Cemetery, who have restored the grand tombs, including the **Egyptian Avenue** and a group of incredibly ostentatious mausoleums built for rich Victorian families. *(East Cemetery: ☎ 0181-340-1834, Apr-Oct: 10am-5pm, Nov-Mar: 10am-4pm. Admission £1; West Cemetery entry by tour only: Mar-Nov: Mon-Fri: 12noon, 2pm and 4pm, Sat-Sun: 11am, 12noon, 1pm, 2pm, 3pm, 4pm. Tour £3.)*

Holly Walk

GETTING THERE

Highgate: Archway tube station

REFLECTIONS

'Coleridge sat on the brow of Highgate Hill, in those years, looking down on London and its smoke-tumult, like a sage escaped from the inanity of life's battle.' – *The Life of John Sterling*, Thomas Carlyle (1851)

Docklands . . .

Docklands

The best place to view the startling modern architecture of this rejuvenated former industrial wasteland is from the driverless **Docklands Light Railway** (DLR).

Departing from Bank tube station in the City or Tower Gateway close to Tower Bridge, the DLR runs on an elevated track down through the Isle of Dogs. It passes **One Canada Square,** the 800-foot (240-metre) stainless steel-clad tower at Canary Wharf designed by Cesar Pelli. The tower symbolises the 1980s and 90s rebirth of the old docks which lie immediately to the east of the City.

Docklands' skyline

For 300 years, until the middle of this century, the Port of London was the key to the city's wealth. Thousands of ships would queue to unload their wares at the vast docks. In 1981, two decades after the port had moved to Tilbury, the London Docklands Development Corporation began redeveloping the area. Canadian property giant Olympia & York invested most of the money, and, after huge losses, went bust in the recession of the early 1990s.

GETTING THERE

DLR connects with the London Underground at Tower Hill and Bank tube stations. The Jubilee line is being extended to Docklands and is expected to open in 1998.

REFLECTIONS

'The new Docklands of the 1980s show the triumph of commercial expediency over civic values. Too many mediocre buildings, and a railway suitable only for Toytown represent a feeble contribution to the rebuilding of the capital.' – HRH Charles, Prince of Wales (1989)

The **London Docklands Visitor Centre**, close to Crossharbour DLR station, has a free exhibition and video presentation exploring the area's past, present and future. Close to the visitor centre is **Mudchute City Farm**, the largest urban farm in London. It has all the usual farm animals plus a llama called Gaza.

The easiest part of Docklands to explore is **Wapping**, around the corner from the Tower of London. **St. Katherine's Dock**, built in the 1820s to handle luxury goods like ivory and live turtles, is now a yachting marina with authentic swing bridges. The huge timber-framed **Dickens Inn** *(St. Katherine's Way)*, though it has no connection with Charles Dickens,

Gaza the llama at Mudchute City Farm

has attractive terraces and a fish restaurant. The building dates from the 1790s, when it was a brewery. For a real Dickens pub, try the **Grapes** at Limehouse *(76 Narrow Street)* which is believed to be the model for the Six Jolly Fellowship Porters in *Our Mutual Friend*.

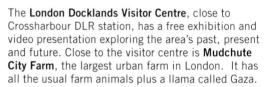

. . . Docklands

Purists scoff at the hotch-potch of high-rise architecture that makes up Docklands, but there are several stunning buildings. **Cascades**, on Westferry Road, is a peculiar, stepped pyramid of apartments overlooking the river.

By far the most impressive building in Docklands is **One Canada Square**, the 60-floor tower that is the centrepiece of the Canary Wharf development. The tallest building in Europe after Frankfurt's Messerturm, the tower is capped by a glass pyramid which is illuminated at

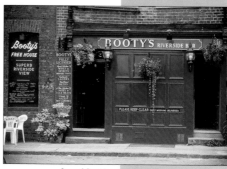

One of Docklands' historic pubs

Christmas with red and green lights. Two similar towers were part of the original design but were never built. For several years the existing tower remained mostly empty. Its fortunes changed in the mid-1990s,

Millwall Dock

however, when the national press decamped to it from Fleet Street. The building has become a vertical Fleet Street, accommodating the *Mirror*, the *Independent*, the *Daily Telegraph* and

several Sunday newspapers. Unfortunately, the tower was closed to the public after the Irish Republican Army detonated a huge bomb at nearby South Quay station in February 1996, killing two people.

Cabot Square, in front of the tower, is a plush shopping mall with designer boutiques. Several local pubs have pleasant waterside terraces, including the **Cat and the Canary** *(1-24 Fisherman's Walk)*. The latter has pews and a pulpit recycled from old churches and is popular with journalists from One Canada Square.

Island Gardens is the final stop on the DLR at the southern-most tip of the Isle of Dogs. The view from here across the Thames to the Royal Naval College at Greenwich was painted in 1755 by Canaletto. The scene has changed little since then.

INSIDER'S TIP

The Thames Barrier, the largest moveable flood barrier in the world, is one of London's modern engineering wonders. It is a couple of miles downriver from Canary Wharf. ☎ 0181-305-4188

One Canada Square

Greenwich . . .

A day trip to Greenwich, by boat along the Thames, has been enjoyed by generations of Londoners. The excursion combines fine views of London with Greenwich's superb museums and historic buildings, most of which are associated with Britain's maritime history.

Greenwich and the Cutty Sark

GETTING THERE

Take the DLR (which connects with the London Underground at Tower Hill) to Island Gardens and cross the river to the Cutty Sark via the Greenwich Foot Tunnel. Return to central London by boat from Greenwich.

Alternatively, take the river cruise on page 237 and receive 20% off ticket prices with your *London for less* card.

The **Cutty Sark** is the world's last surviving tea clipper – an exceptionally fast tall sailing ship which catered for the Victorian fashion for the freshest tea from China. This fully rigged ship, open to visitors in its dry dock, was considered a modern marvel in the 1870s because it could sail between China and London in as few as 107 days. Several cabins, including the cramped but elegant officers' saloon, are open for viewing. The main hold contains an historical display, with a collection of ships' figureheads. *(King William Walk, ☎ 0181-858-3445. Jun-Sep: Mon-Sat: 10am-6pm. Sun: 12noon-6pm. Oct-May: Mon-Sat: 10am-5pm. Sun: 12noon-5pm. Adult £3.50, child £2.50, senior £2.50, student £2.50. £1 off admission with voucher on page 283.)*

The Cutty Sark

Beside the Cutty Sark is the much smaller **Gipsy Moth IV**, in which Sir Francis Chichester broke the record for solo world circumnavigation in 1966/7. It is likely to be closed throughout 1997 for restoration.

The **Royal Naval College**, around the corner from the Cutty Sark, is best viewed from the river. The view of the buildings stretching out towards the old observatory on the hill hasn't changed since Canaletto painted the scene in the 18th century.

Flamsteed house and the courtyard of the Old Royal Observatory

Begun as a palace for Charles II in the 1660s, the building was later completed by Sir Christopher Wren as a hospital for disabled seamen. The college contains two impressive buildings open to the public. Lord Nelson lay in state in 1806 in the grand **Painted Hall**. Across the courtyard, the **RNC Chapel** is decorated with intricate pastel-shaded plasterwork.

. . . Greenwich

(King William Walk, ☎ 0181-858-2154. Mon-Wed and Fri-Sun: 2.30pm-4.45pm. Thu: closed. Admission is free.)

The **National Maritime Museum** celebrates Britain's long and glorious naval history, with collections of model ships, navigational instruments and paintings of sea battles.

Royal Naval College

The highlight of this, the world's largest nautical museum, is the new **Nelson Gallery**, where you can see the musket ball that killed the admiral at the Battle of Trafalgar. His 'undress coat', with a hole in the shoulder where the bullet struck, is also on display. Turner's huge *Battle of Trafalgar* is the prize painting in the collection. Other striking exhibits include the 63-foot Royal Barge in the **Barge House** and a steam-powered paddle tug in the **Neptune Hall**.

Inigo Jones's **Queen's House** is a mini royal palace containing the beautiful **Tulip Staircase**, restored

The Great Hall in the Queen's House

Royal Apartments and an exquisite 17th-century ceiling decoration in the **Queen's Presence Chamber**.

The **Old Royal Observatory** has displays on astronomy and regular shows in the Planetarium. You can stand on the Greenwich Meridian, with one foot in each of the eastern and western hemispheres. There is a magnificent view across London from the top of the royal park's steep hill. The world sets its clocks according to Greenwich Mean Time (GMT), established in 1884 in recognition of the observatory's success in first calibrating longitude.

The **Telescope Dome** contains a huge Victorian telescope weighing over one and a half tons. The adjoining **Planetarium** runs presentations. The red Timeball on top of the observatory dates from 1833, when ships on the Thames adjusted their clocks by it. The ball climbs the mast at 12.58pm and drops at 1pm precisely. *(National Maritime Museum, Romney Road, ☎ 0181-858-4422. Mar-Oct: Mon-Sat: 10am-6pm. Sun: 2pm-6pm. Nov-Feb: Mon-Sat: 10am-5pm. Sun: 2pm-5pm. Combined ticket includes admission to the museum, the Queen's House and the Royal Observatory: Adult £5.50, child £3, senior £4.50, student £4.50, family £16.)*

INSIDER'S TIP

Children will enjoy the **All Hands Gallery**, where they can try out sailors' skills.

DON'T MISS

The Millennium Countdown Clock, accurate to the nearest millionth of a second, is positioned on the meridian line – the exact point from which world time is measured. Linked to eight satellites, this 'atomic' clock started the 1,000 day countdown to the year 2000 on April 4, 1997.

ADDRESS

Hampton Court
☎ 0181-781-9500

GETTING THERE

Train from Waterloo
Station takes 30 minutes

HOURS

Mar-Oct:
Mon: 10.15am-6pm
Tue-Sun: 9.30am-6pm

Nov-Feb:
Mon: 10.15am-4.30pm
Tue-Sun: 9.30am-4.30pm

 # Hampton Court Palace . . .

The sumptuous interiors and beautiful gardens of Hampton Court, a few miles up the Thames from the centre of London, make it one of the most popular day-trip destinations for tourists and Londoners alike.

Cardinal Wolsey, Henry VIII's Lord Chancellor, built Hampton Court as his own palace in 1516. The extravagance of the buildings annoyed Henry, and

Wolsey attempted to win back royal favour by handing over the keys to his king.

Henry made substantial changes, rebuilding the chapel and extending the kitchens. Many

Hampton Court Palace

of the great events of his reign took place at Hampton Court, including the birth of the future King Edward VI and the deaths of Edward's mother and Henry's third wife, Jane Seymour. It was here that Henry, while at mass, was told that his fifth wife, Catherine Howard, had been unfaithful to him.

During the reigns of Elizabeth I and James I, Hampton Court was the centre of the royal court's cultural life, hosting many plays and masques. Charles I was

imprisoned here during the Civil War, after which the Lord Protector, **Oliver Cromwell**, made the palace his home.

William III and Mary II commissioned **Sir Christopher Wren** to remodel the buildings and design the new Banqueting House on the river. George III decided to turn the place over

The Tudor kitchens

to members of the royal household and some parts still serve as 'grace and favour' residences for retired royal employees and courtiers.

A devastating fire in 1986 destroyed part of William III's **King's Apartments**. It was accidentally started by the bedside candle of an elderly resident, Lady Gale, who died in the blaze. Elizabeth II reopened the restored King's Apartments in 1992. The marvellous wall and ceiling paintings above the **King's Staircase**

. . . Hampton Court Palace

are by Antonio Verrio. The paintings represent a political allegory praising William III.

The King's Apartments are one of the palace's six thematic walking routes for visitors. Starting in Base Court, Clock Court or Fountain Court, the routes explore the public and private lives of the monarchs who lived at Hampton Court. One route explores the **Tudor Kitchens**, laid out as if a royal banquet was being prepared, while another proceeds through the magnificent Great Hall and Chapel of **Henry VIII's State Apartments**.

An aerial view of the Palace

Hanging from the walls of the **Great Hall** are priceless Flemish tapestries of the Story of Abraham, commissioned by Henry VIII in the late 1520s.

Shakespeare's *Hamlet* and *Henry VIII* were performed in the Great Hall before George I in 1718.

The **Haunted Gallery**, said to be haunted by the ghost of Catherine Howard, leads into the **Chapel**. The timber-vaulted Chapel ceiling, with its glorious blue and gold design, is the most important Tudor ceiling in the country. The great oak panel behind the altar, flanked by double columns, was carved by Grinling Gibbons in the reign of Queen Anne.

An historical guide

The **Renaissance Picture Gallery** contains the finest Renaissance works from Elizabeth II's collection, including Pieter Breugel the Elder's *The Massacre of the Innocents*.

The **Palace Gardens,** which cover 60 acres, include the famous **Maze** which dates from the 1690s. The **Great Vine**, planted in 1768, still produces an annual crop of delicious grapes. The serenely beautiful **Pond Gardens** were built by Henry VIII in 1536 as ornamental fishponds to breed edible fish for the royal table.

The maze

Windsor . . .

ADDRESS

Windsor Castle
☎ 01753-868-286.

GETTING THERE

Direct train from Waterloo
Station to Windsor
Riverside (50 minutes) or
train from Paddington
Station to Windsor Central
changing at Slough
(35 minutes).

St. George's Chapel

HOURS

Mar-Sep: Mon-Sun:
10am-4pm.
Oct-Feb: Mon-Sun:
10am-3pm.

State Apartments will be
closed from June 8-20,
1997 and between Oct 6-
Dec 31, 1997.

Windsor Castle, with its mighty medieval turrets and towers, is the oldest royal residence to have remained in continuous use by British monarchs.

Founded as a fortress by William the Conqueror in 1080, the castle occupies a naturally defendable chalk ridge 100 feet (30 metres) above the Thames. The proximity of the fortress to royal hunting grounds (now **Windsor Great Park**), encouraged Henry II to convert it into a palace in the 12th century. The greatest medieval expansion of Windsor took place during the reign of Edward III, who spent the proceeds from his military triumphs on creating a palace of chivalric splendour.

Windsor Castle

During the **English Civil War** in the 1640s, Parliamentary forces seized the castle and used it as a prison for royalists. Charles I was buried in the vaults beneath St. George's Chapel after he was beheaded at Whitehall in 1649. After the Restoration of the Monarchy in 1660, the new king, Charles II, initiated a grand refurbishment of the castle to assert his royal glory. Ceiling paintings by Antonio Verrio and a magnificent sequence of baroque state apartments were added.

Windsor Castle enjoyed its heyday under **Queen Victoria**, who made it her principal palace. Her husband, Prince Albert, died here on December 14, 1861. A disused 13th-century chapel was lined with gold mosaics and inlaid marble to create the Albert Memorial Chapel.

The present queen, Elizabeth II, spent much of her childhood at Windsor. She still stays at the castle most weekends, for the whole of April and during Ascot week in June. The flagpole of the Round Tower flies the Royal Standard when the Queen is at home.

On November 20, 1992, a devastating fire broke out in the **Queen's Private Chapel**, destroying the ceilings of **St. George's Hall** and the **State Dining Room**. Fortunately, few artistic treasures were destroyed as the rooms had been emptied for rewiring. The £50 million restoration programme is to be completed in 1998.

. . . Windsor

The visitors' entrance is on Castle Hill. The State Apartments are accessed from the north terrace. To the east of the entrance hall is **Queen Mary's Dolls' House**, with working water and electricity systems, and miniature books hand-written by leading authors of the 1920s. More than 1,000 craftsmen contributed to the 1:12 scale dolls house.

The **Grand Staircase**, lined with arms and armour, leads to the **Grand Vestibule**, where there are more war trophies. The tour continues into the **Waterloo Chamber**, where the Queen holds an annual luncheon in June for the Knights of the Garter.

After passing through several sumptuous drawing rooms and bedrooms, you come to the **Queen's Ballroom**, with its three glorious chandeliers and

collection of portraits by Sir Anthony Van Dyck. The **Queen's Presence Chamber** has perhaps the finest of the surviving Verrio ceilings, framed by exquisite 17th-century wood carvings.

St. George's Chapel is the resting place of ten sovereigns. Completed in 1528, it is dedicated to St. George, the patron saint of the Most Noble Order of the

The Queen's Presence Chamber

Garter, Britain's highest order of chivalry.

Make sure you save some time to explore **Windsor Great Park**, with its three-mile **Long Walk**. At the far end of the Long Walk is the huge equestrian statue of George III known as the Copper Horse.

In **Windsor Home Park**, to the south-east of the castle, is **Frogmore House**, which dates from the 1680s. It was a favoured retreat of Queen Victoria, who built an elaborate mausoleum in the picturesque gardens.

Across the river from Windsor Castle is the one street village of **Eton**, famous as the home of **Eton College**, where Britain's 'ruling class' has traditionally been educated. Charles and Diana's son, Prince William, is a pupil at the school. The highlight for visitors is the **College Chapel** (1482) with its fan vaulting and medieval wall paintings.

The Grand Vestibule

ADDRESS

Kew, Richmond
☎ 0181-940-1171

GETTING THERE

Kew tube station

HOURS

Mon-Fri: 9.30am- 6pm
Sat-Sun: 9.30am-7pm

PRICES

Adult £4.50
Child £2.50
Senior £3
Student £3
Includes entry to all places
highlighted in text except
Kew Palace.

DISCOUNT

£1 off admission with
voucher on page 283.

Kew Gardens

The world-renowned **Royal Botanic Gardens** never fail
to bewitch visitors with their tranquil beauty and year-
round profusion of the colourful glories of nature.

Kew grows more species of flowers and plants in its
300 acres than any
other garden in the
world: more than
40,000, many
extinct in the wild,
are displayed in
glasshouses,
plantations and in
its vast lawns.

The Palm House

As well as being a
major attraction for
garden-lovers, Kew is a global scientific resource
which has played a key role in plant conservation for
over 200 years. Captain Cook brought back some of
the earliest specimens.

The **Palm House** is the most magnificent of Kew's
many glasshouses. Built in the 1840s, it accommo-
dates every main species of palm on the planet in
tropical humidity. Dating from the same period is the
massive **Temperate House**, with plants from every
continent. It boasts the impressive Chilean Wine
Palm, probably the tallest indoor palm in the world.

One of Kew's most famous vistas looks upon the 18th-
century, ten-storey **Pagoda**. Kew's tallest structure,
however, is the 225-foot (67-metre) flagpole hewn
from a single Canadian fir tree in 1959.

The **Princess of Wales Conservatory**, opened in 1987,
has ten climatic zones and includes a large collection
of cacti.

Inside a glasshouse

The south-western section of Kew Gardens
is the least visited and contains the
thatched **Queen Charlotte's Cottage**, built
as a royal picnic spot. The tiny **Kew
Palace,** which is currently closed for
restoration, is the most humble of the
royal residences. It is notable for being
the place where King George III was
confined during his 'madness' in 1802.

There are two art galleries on the eastern
edge of the gardens. The **Kew Gardens
Gallery** has exhibitions with horticultural
themes. The smaller gallery contains the work of
flower painter Marianne North (1830-90).

The Freud Museum

**20 Maresfield Gardens,
Hampstead
☎ 0171-495-2002**

(Wed-Sun: 12noon-5pm. Mon-Tue: closed. Adult £3, child £1.50, senior £1.50, student £1.50.)

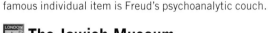

Sigmund Freud lived here from the time that he fled Vienna until his death. The centrepiece of the museum is Freud's study, which is preserved intact. The most famous individual item is Freud's psychoanalytic couch.

DISCOUNT

Adult admission at £1.50 with your *London for less* card.

The Jewish Museum

**129 Albert Street,
Camden Town
☎ 0171-284-1997**

(Sun-Thu: 10am-4pm. Fri-Sat: closed. Adult £3, child £1.50, senior £2, student £1.50.)

This museum has one of the finest collections of Jewish ceremonial art. Highlights include a 16th-century Italian synagogue ark. There are also temporary exhibitions, cultural events and a history gallery.

DISCOUNT

Adult £1 off admission, child, senior and student 50p off admission with your *London for less* card

Ranger's House

**Chesterfield Walk,
Blackheath
☎ 0181-853-0035**

(Apr-Sep: Mon-Sun: 10am-6pm. Oct-Mar: Mon-Sun: 10am-4pm. Adult £2.50, student £1.90, senior £1.90, child £1.30.)

This handsome red-brick villa, built c.1700, overlooks Greenwich Park. It is best known for housing the Suffolk Painting Collection. There is a fascinating Architectural Study Collection in the Coach House.

DISCOUNT

2 admissions for the price of 1 with your *London for less* card

Chiswick House

Burlington Lane
☎ 0181-995-0508

(Apr-Sep: Mon-Sun: 10am-6pm. Oct-Mar: Mon-Sun: 10am-4pm. Adult £2.50, child £1.30, senior £1.90, student £1.90.)

Chiswick House is a Palladian villa built c.1728 for Lord Burlington who was the architect of the house. Highlights are the lavish blue velvet room and the perfectly symmetrical Italianate gardens.

Dulwich Picture Gallery

College Road, Dulwich
☎ 0181-693-5254

(Tue-Fri: 10am-5pm. Sat: 11am-5pm. Sun: 2pm-5pm. Mon: closed. Adult £2, student £1, senior £1, child free)

Dulwich Picture Gallery is Britain's oldest public gallery. The collection includes paintings by Rembrandt, Rubens, Poussin, Van Dyck, Canaletto, Gainsborough, Reynolds and Watteau.

Wimbledon Tennis Museum

Church Road, Wimbledon
☎ 0181-946-6131

(Tue-Sat: 10.30am-5pm. Sun: 2pm-5pm. Mon: closed. VS/MC. Adult £2.50, child £1.50, senior £1.50, student £1.50.)

This museum tells the story of the history of lawn tennis. The collection includes rackets, equipment and costumes. You can stand and look out over the famous Centre Court.

DISCOUNT

2 admissions for the price of 1 with your *London for less* card.

DISCOUNT

50% off admission with your *London for less* card

DISCOUNT

£1 off admission per person with your *London for less* card

Beyond London

Introduction

You could spend a month in London and hardly scratch the surface of what it has to offer. Yet it would be a shame to visit England without exploring beyond the capital. To get a true flavour of traditional English life, you must travel beyond the multicultural melting pot of London.

Victoria Station

This is a remarkably compact country and dozens of cities, towns and villages can easily be visited on day trips from London. The following pages contain a selection of the most interesting and popular places: the beautiful Georgian city of Bath, with its Roman spa, the ancient university of Oxford, with its fine college buildings, the famous cathedrals of Canterbury, Salisbury and York and several other outstanding places.

The cities, towns and historic sites featured in this chapter have been grouped according to their proximity to each other, to help you plan your trip. For example, an outing to Stonehenge could easily be extended to include a few hours in Salisbury or Shaftesbury. Each of the places listed, except Edinburgh, could comfortably be visited on a day trip.

Internal flights *(British Airways ☎ 0345-222111, British Midland ☎ 0345-554554)* are expensive and only really likely to be useful for getting to Scotland.

Trains *(☎ 0345-484950)* are often the best alternative. Although they can be expensive, day-return tickets are usually cheaper.

Coaches *(National Express, ☎ 0990-808080)* are much cheaper, but also much slower.

Longleat House, near to Bath

Renting a car (see opposite) can be an economical way to travel, especially for a group. However, at peak times the motorways into and out of London can be severely congested. Parking is also a nightmare in some cities, especially Oxford, Cambridge and Bath.

Taking a **coach tour** is the most convenient way to cover a number of sites while learning about their history from experienced guides (see pages 238-244).

INSIDER'S TIP

If you are travelling by train on Saturday or Sunday, buy a Second Class ticket but sit in the First Class carriage. Ask the conductor for a 'Weekend First' upgrade which costs £5-7 and enjoy the luxury of First Class seating at cut-priced rates. The ticket is a flat fee so it makes more sense the longer your journey.

Kenning Car Rental

The United Kenning Group is the largest Car and Van Rental Company in Britain. It has more branches and more vehicles than any other company and can therefore offer you the flexibility to pick-up and drop-

off at branches all over the country.

Kenning offers tariffs to holders of valid *London for less* cards that represent an average discount of over 30% off its standard rates.

Fiat Cinquecento

You can book your car in advance by telephone or fax by simply quoting your *London for less* card number. Alternatively, go to one of Kenning's rental desks and present your card.

Drivers must be aged between 21 and 75 and have a full driving licence for at least a year (it can be your own national licence). There is a charge of £2 per day for each extra driver.

ADDRESS

London branches:
88/90 Holland Park Avenue, 1 York Way (Kings Cross), Heathrow Airport and Gatwick Airport
☎ 01246-208888

Ford Mondeo Estate

London for less daily rates:	1-6 days	7-20 days	21+ days
Manuals			
Fiat Cinquecento 1.0	N/A	£17	£16
Ford Fiesta 1.1	£24	£19	£18
Ford Escort 1.4 LX	£26	£23	£21
Ford Escort 1.6 LX	£29	£25	£23
Ford Mondeo 1.8 LX	£31	£27	£25
Ford Mondeo 2.0 GLX	£33	£29	£27
Rover 620 Si	£35	£31	£29
Automatics			
Ford Fiesta 1.3 LX (Auto)	£29	£25	£23
Rover 416S Li (Auto)	£34	£29	£27
Rover 620 Si (Auto)	£37	£33	£31
Rover 820 Si (Auto)	£47	£43	£41
Estates			
For Escort 1.6 L	£29	£25	£23
Ford Mondeo 1.8 LX Estate	£35	£31	£29
Multi-seater			
Nissan Serena 7 seats	£41	£36	£33
VW Caravelle 7 seats (Auto)	£73	£63	£57
Ford Minibus 12 seats	£69	£59	£54
L.D.V Minibus 15 seats	£73	£63	£57

PRICES

Rates include rental, unlimited mileage, Loss and Damage Waiver and VAT.

Prices do not include an insurance excess of £90 for which the renter is responsible and which can be waived for £4.10 per day or £21 per week.

Personal Accident Insurance (PAI) is an optional extra at £2.75 a day, except on multi-seaters when it is £7.50 per day.

Cars taken to continental Europe require a 40% surcharge.

Edinburgh . . .

Edinburgh Castle

No other British city apart from London exudes as much national pride and sense of its own grandeur as Edinburgh, the capital of Scotland.

The city is split into the **Old Town**, the tenements and medieval alleys to the south of the castle, and the grand terraces and crescents of the **New Town**, north of **Princes Street**. A testament to the excellence of Georgian town-planning, the New Town was laid out in the 18th century.

There's no escaping **Edinburgh Castle**, perched high on a volcanic promontory above the bustling main shopping thoroughfare, Princes Street. The rock has been a fortification for 1,500 years, but the first castle-like structure was built on it in the 11th century.

Inside the castle, the tiny **St. Margaret's Chapel** survives from this period. National treasures on display include **Scotland's Crown Jewels** and, recently transferred from London's Westminster Abbey, the **Stone of Scone**. The tartan-clad castle guides give informative and entertaining tours, telling the colourful tale of the giant siege gun **Mons Meg**. A more modern field gun is fired from the battlements at 1pm each day. *(Edinburgh Castle, ☎ 0131-225-1012. Apr-Sep: Mon-Sun: 9.30am-6pm. Oct-Mar: Mon-Sun: 9.30am-5pm. Last admission 45 minutes before closing. Adult £5.50, child £1.50, senior £3.50, student £3.50.)*

Gladstone's Land

Running downhill from the castle is the famous **Royal Mile**, which has a number of interesting buildings such as **Gladstone's Land**, a 17th-century merchant's tenement building. The Royal Mile ends at the Queen's official residence in Scotland, the **Palace of Holyrood House**. This is where Mary Queen of Scots spent six years of her reign and where her secretary, David Rizzio, was murdered. A few decades later, Bonnie Prince Charlie held court in the palace before the last, ill-fated invasion of England. Visitors can tour the royal apartments.

The Royal Mile contains many other historic buildings, including **John Knox House**, a medieval house associated with Scotland's religious reformer. After a stern, recorded Presbyterian lecture from John Knox,

VISITOR INFORMATION

Edinburgh & Scotland Tourist Information Centre
3 Princes Street
Edinburgh EH2 2QP
☎ 0131-557-1700

GETTING THERE

By train from London King's Cross. Trains approximately every hour, the fastest trains take four hours.

By plane from Heathrow (takes one hour).

REFLECTIONS

'And so I went to Edinburgh. Can there anywhere be a more beautiful and beguiling city to arrive at by train early on a crisp, dark Novembery evening?'
– *Notes from a Small Island*, Bill Bryson (1995)

. . . Edinburgh

many visitors head for the **Scottish Whisky Heritage Centre** further along the Royal Mile.

The city skyline

Just off the Royal Mile, in Lady Stairs Close, is the **Writers Museum**, commemorating Scotland's national poet, **Robert Burns** and two great novelists, **Sir Walter Scott** and **Robert Louis Stevenson**. This spirit of intellectual excellence, which also produced the philosopher **David Hume** and the economist **Adam Smith**, is still apparent in Edinburgh, which has more bookshops per capita than any other British city.

The National Gallery of Scotland, on Princes Street, has a small but well-presented collection. The most famous exhibit is Canova's *Three Graces*, set prominently in the second of the two main aisles.

Behind Princes Street, at 7 Charlotte Square, is the **Georgian House**, a fine example of 18th century New Town architecture and one of Robert Adam's finest urban architectural achievements.

At the northern edge of the New Town lies the **Royal Botanic Garden**, 70 acres of exotic plants and perfectly manicured flower beds and lawns. Don't miss the elegant, lofty Palm House. A couple of miles west of the centre is **Edinburgh Zoo,** which houses more than 1,000 animals. The highlights are the enormous penguin pool and the well-designed chimpanzee enclosure.

The **Edinburgh International Festival,** Britain's biggest cultural extravaganza, takes place over three hectic weeks in late August and early September. Now 50 years old, the festival incorporates experimental performances in the Festival Fringe, which often threatens to eclipse the main events. Not to be outdone, the armed forces put on an impressive display in the **Edinburgh Military Tattoo** beside the castle.

The Georgian House

Edinburgh's **Hogmanay** claims to be Europe's biggest New Year's Party. It is certainly spectacular, with fireworks cascading down the castle rock, but has begun to be overwhelmed by sheer weight of numbers.

Bath . . .

With its graceful, honey-coloured Regency buildings and surrounding wooded hills, Bath is one of Europe's most beautiful cities.

The Royal Crescent in snow

In recognition of its historical and architectural importance, UNESCO designated Bath a World Heritage Site in 1987, placing it on a par with Florence and Rome.

The city owes its existence to the hot springs, around which it is built. According to legend, the healing properties of the springs were first discovered 2,500 years ago when a prince bathed in the waters and was cured of leprosy.

In Roman times, Bath was known as Aquae Sulis, after the goddess Sulis Minerva. The Roman city was centred on a hot spring from which more than a quarter of a million gallons of water still flow each day. The Roman remains are buried some 30 feet below the present streets.

In the Norman period, Bath prospered as a wool town, though its reputation as a healing spa once again began to attract thousands of visitors.

The layout of Bath as seen today is a legacy of Georgian times, when Britain's landed gentry took houses for the 'Season'. They came initially for the healing waters, but Bath soon boasted a social whirl to rival London and, as the novelist Jane Austen described in *Persuasion* and *Northanger Abbey*, young women were brought here to find husbands. Austen herself lived in Bath at 4 Sydney Place between 1801 and 1804.

The Roman Baths

The architect John Wood created the Palladian designs of the **Circus** and **Queen Square**, while his son, John Wood the Younger, built the majestic **Royal Crescent**. The longest crescent in Europe, this colonnaded terrace faces a grassy slope with stunning views across the city.

VISITOR INFORMATION

Bath Tourist Information Centre
Abbey Chambers
Abbey Church Yard
Bath BA1 1LY
☎ 01225 477101

GETTING THERE

By train from Paddington station. Services run about every half an hour and the journey takes about 1½ hours.

INSIDER'S TIP

During August, the Roman Baths open in the evenings for tours by torchlight.

. . . Bath

There are breathtaking views from the banks of the River Avon of **Pulteney Bridge**, which houses small shops in its stone buildings. The bridge leads to the very grand **Great Pulteney Street**.

The interior of **Bath Abbey**, which dates from 1500, has recently been cleaned. Carved stones and pieces of sculpture from the earlier Norman church on this

Guide Friday city tours

site are displayed in the **Heritage Vaults**.

There are 16 museums in Bath, the most important of which is the **Roman Baths Museum**. Set around the excavated Temple of Sulis Minerva, the museum

displays Roman mosaics, sculpture, coins, jewellery and the gilt bronze head of a goddess, which was found in 1727 by workmen in Stall Street. The Great Bath was only discovered in 1878, but the site had been the city's social centre since the 18th century, when the **Pump Room** was opened. The Pump Room now serves traditional teas and warm spa water from the fountain. *(Abbey Churchyard, ☎ 01225-477785. Apr-Sep: Mon-Sun: 9am-6pm. Aug: Mon-Sun: 9am-6pm, 8pm-10pm. Oct-Mar: Mon-Sat: 9.30am-5pm. Sun: 10.30am-5pm. Adult £6, child (under 19) £3.60, senior £5.60, student £6.)*

A couple of Bath's smaller museums are well worth visiting. The **Museum of Costume**, located in the splendid **Assembly Rooms**, is the premier collection of costume in the country. It follows the history of fashion from the late 16th century to the present day.

The **Victoria Art Gallery** *(opposite Pulteney Bridge)* houses Bath's collection of post-17th-century British and European art, including paintings by Gainsborough and Turner.

Rowing on the River Avon

The 500 treasures in the **Museum of East Asian Art** *(12 Bennett Street)* span 7,000 years. Purchased over a 35-year period by a wealthy Hong Kong lawyer, the collection includes jade, bronze and ceramic works.

REFLECTIONS

'I really believe I shall always be talking of Bath, when I am home again [said Catherine] – I *do* like it so very much... Oh! Who can ever be tired of Bath?' – *Northanger Abbey*, Jane Austen, (1818)

York . . .

The ancient walled city of York is remarkably unscathed by the huge influx of tourists who come to see the majestic cathedral, wander the medieval alley and enjoy the colourful street entertainers.

York Minster

The Romans established the first major settlement at York, at the confluence of the River Ouse and River Foss. Initially, the Viking came to pillage and then, more than 1,000 years ago, founded 'Jorvik', the remains of which have now been excavated.

The best way to see York is from the **Bar Walls** which ring the city. The full circuit takes two hours at a leisurely pace, though there are plenty of access points for a shorter walk. The walls are punctuated by bars, or gate towers, including **Bootham Bar,** at the city's northern entrance, which dates from the 12th century. Only a public outcry saved the bars from demolition in 1832. The tallest gateway is **Monk Bar**, which has a working portcullis. **Walmgate** is the best preserved of the bars, despite being damaged in the English Civil War. Bullet holes inflicted by Oliver Cromwell's troops after the Battle of Marston Moor in 1644 can still be seen in the stonework. **Micklegate Bar**, marking the approach from London, was the mos important of the four main gates. The decapitated heads of traitors used to be displayed over the gate as a warning to others.

Perhaps the best section of the walls runs behind the 800-year-old **York Minster**, the largest Gothic cathedral in northern Europe. Built on the site of a Roman fortress, the minster is renowned for its magnificent stained glass windows. The **Great West Window** is known as the 'Heart of Yorkshire' because of its decorative heart-like shapes. The top of the **Central Tower** offers an unrivalled view and the remains of previous Roman and Norman buildings can be seen in the minster's foundations. In

Clifford's Tower

the late 1960s, huge concrete collars were installed after surveyors realised that the minster's central tower was on the verge of collapse. However, disaster

VISITOR INFORMATION

York Tourism Bureau
The Travel Office
6 Rougier Street
York YO1 1JA
☎ 01904-620576

GETTING THERE

By train from London Kings Cross. Services run approximately every hour and the journey takes just under 2½ hours.

INSIDER'S TIP

The Jorvik Viking Festival, which includes a longship regatta, boat burning and other Viking-themed events, takes place in mid-February.

. . . York

of a different sort struck in 1984, when lightning sparked a fire in the roof. The **Rose Window** shattered into thousands of fragments but it has now been painstakingly restored. *(Minster Yard ☎ 01904-624426. Nov-May: Mon-Sun: 8am-6pm. Jun-Oct: Mon-Sun: 8am-8.30pm. Admission is free.)*

Micklegate Bar

The **Treasurer's House** behind the minster has an intriguing confusion of architectural styles, ranging from Roman to Victorian.

Another fascinating historic building is the **Merchant Adventurers' Hall** on Piccadilly/Fossgate, the finest surviving medieval guild hall in Europe. This 600-year-old timbered structure contains a collection of Elizabethan portraits, silver and furniture.

At the southern end of the walled city, on a high mound, stands **Clifford's Tower**. Originally a Norman tower constructed to help overawe the northern tribes, it was rebuilt in the 13th century by Henry III. Beside the tower is the **York Castle Museum**, which recreates Victorian and Edwardian interiors and street scenes.

Shambles and **Stonegate** are two of the prettiest shopping streets in York. Shambles, reckoned to be Britain's best-preserved medieval street, is still lined with craftsmen's shops which lean precariously towards each other. Stonegate, originally the Via Pretoria of Roman York, abounds with modern gift shops and ancient pubs like Ye Olde Starre Inne. The narrow medieval passages running between the streets are known as snickelways.

The **Jorvik Viking Centre** is built over the Coppergate archaeological dig. It contains a reconstructed Viking settlement, with a busy market, a wharf and dark, smoky houses. Visitors travel around in 'time capsules'.

Merchant Adventurers' Hall

Graphic representations of torture and execution are the big draws of **York Dungeon** on Clifford Street. The final exhibit recreates the Gunpowder Plot of 1605, when York native Guy Fawkes tried to blow up Parliament.

REFLECTIONS

The history of York 'is the history of England' – King George VI (1895-1952)

Oxford & Blenheim Palace . . .

Oxford is an enticing mixture of old and new, with ancient colleges scattered across the bustling modern university town. Wandering around the colleges, punting on one of the rivers, having a pint of beer in one of the old pubs – all of these are essential Oxford experiences.

Once a royal city under the 'Scholar King' Henry I, Oxford again became the monarch's headquarters during the English Civil War. Charles I made the city the Royalist capital of England. He was supported by Oxford's colleges, which were then essentially ecclesiastical institutions. The city, however, sided with the Parliamentarians, reviving the old medieval conflict between 'Town' and 'Gown'. Nowadays the tension has all but disappeared, although students and 'townies' tend to keep themselves apart, going to different pubs and clubs.

VISITOR INFORMATION

Oxford Tourist
Information Centre
Old School Building
Gloucester Green
Oxford OX1 2DA
☎ 01865-726871

Oxford, city of dreaming spires

There are about 30 colleges, ranging from the medieval **St. Edmund Hall** to the modernist **St. Catherine's**. Each college is unique in character, some small and intimate like **Exeter**, others vast and impressive like **Christ Church**. The latter contains the city's **Cathedral** and has a grand main gateway designed by Sir Christopher Wren and known as **Tom Tower**. The **Christ Church Picture Gallery** has a fine collection of paintings and drawings, including some by Leonardo da Vinci and Michelangelo. Unlike most of the other colleges, Christ Church charges an entrance fee.

Perhaps the most impressive colleges are **Keble**, for the glorious Victorian Gothic Liddon Quad, **Magdalen** for the deerpark and cloisters and **New College**, for the fine chapel and walled gardens.

At the centre of Radcliffe Square is the magnificent domed **Radcliffe Camera**, part of the prestigious **Bodleian Library**. It is surrounded by **Brasenose** and **All Soul's** Colleges and **St. Mary's Church**. Close by is the **Sheldonian Theatre**, designed by Wren in the 1660s and used for university graduations.

The **Ashmolean Museum** on Beaumont Street is Britain's oldest public museum. There are collections

GETTING THERE

By train from Paddington station at least once every hour and the journey takes about an 1 hour.

By coach from Victoria or Marble Arch – take the Oxford Tube or Oxford Citylink buses. Journey time is approximately 90 minutes.

Frames Rickards' guided coach tours to Oxford (pages 242-243).

. . . Oxford & Blenheim Palace

of European and Oriental paintings, silver and ceramics and a bizarre collection of curiosities that includes Guy Fawkes's lantern and Oliver Cromwell's death mask. The **University Museum**, housed in an impressive Victorian Gothic building on Parks Road, has natural history displays. The dinosaur skeletons and dodo relics are the most popular exhibits. The **Pitt Rivers Museum**, entered from the University Museum, has one of the world's finest ethnographic collections. Gaze, if you dare, at the group of shrunken human heads from Ecuador.

Keble College

Aside from the university and its history, Oxford is also a highly popular place to shop. Hundreds of independent shops specialise in books, antiques, crafts and other, more exotic wares. **Gloucester Green**, a new but remarkably traditional-looking development based around a lively piazza, has a general market on Wednesdays and an antiques market on Thursdays. The **Covered Market**, created in 1772 behind the High Street, contains many small shops and colourful stalls selling fresh fruit and meat.

The most convenient place for hiring a punt is beside **Magdalen Bridge**. Boats can also be hired from Folly Bridge. These places can get very busy, however, and an alternative is the Cherwell Boat House in north Oxford off Banbury Road.

Blenheim Palace

Eight miles north of Oxford stands **Blenheim Palace**. One of the finest examples of English baroque architecture, it is set in 2,100 acres of parkland landscaped by 'Capability' Brown to represent the battlefield at Blenheim, the Bavarian village where the 1st Duke of Marlborough defeated Louis XIV in 1704. It has recently become familiar to many as Elsinore in Kenneth Branagh's *Hamlet*. It has the world's largest symbolic hedge maze, beautiful formal gardens, gilded state rooms and an exhibition devoted to Sir Winston Churchill, who was born at the palace. *(Blenheim Palace, ☎ 01993-811325. Mar 17 -Oct 31: Mon-Sun: 10.30am-5.30pm, last admission: 4.45pm. Adult £7.80, child £3.80, senior £5.80, student £5.80.)*

INSIDER'S TIP

Climb the 125 steps to the top of St. Mary's Church tower for the finest views across the city.

REFLECTIONS

'That sweet city with her dreaming spires, / She needs not June for beauty's heightening' – *Thyrsis*, Matthew Arnold (1866)

'I was not unpopular [at school]...It is Oxford that has made me insufferable' – Sir Max Beerbohm (1899)

Stonehenge, Salisbury & Shaftesbury . . .

VISITOR INFORMATION

Salisbury Tourist
Information Centre
Fish Row
Salisbury
Wiltshire SP1 1EJ
☎ 01722-334956

As you cross **Salisbury Plain**, the great stone circle of **Stonehenge** is majestically silhouetted against the sky. It is a sight which has inspired awe in visitors since Roman times and, even when it is crowded with daytrippers, you will marvel at the mystery of how it was built more than 4,000 years ago.

Some of the colossal bluestones were probably brought from South Wales before being placed upright, with other huge stones positioned, like lintels, on top. This was no mean feat, for the biggest stones are 25-feet (7.5-metres) high and weigh 40 tons.

Stonehenge

The orientation of the concentric stone circles would suggest that the secret of Stonehenge is linked to the cycle of the moon and sun. Scholars, however, cannot agree whether the builders were part of a sun-worshipping culture or created Stonehenge as some kind of giant astronomical calendar. The association of Stonehenge with druids is a myth which gained currency in the 18th century.

In recent years, Stonehenge has been the scene of clashes between police and groups of travelling people who congregate there to celebrate the summer solstice, the longest day of the year.

You can see the stones from the road or pay to walk a little closer. Visitors receive headsets with a soundtrack giving information about the site. There is a visitor centre a mile and half from the stones. *(Stonehenge, ☎ 01980-624715. Mar 15-May 31 and Sep 1-Oct 14: Mon-Sun: 9.30am-6pm. Oct 15-Mar 14: Mon-Sun: 9.30am-4pm. Jun 1-Aug 31: Mon-Sun: 9am-7pm. Adult £3.70, child £1.90, senior £2.80, student £2.80.)*

GETTING THERE

By train from Waterloo station to Salisbury. Trains run once an hour and the journey takes 1½ hours. (Nearest station to Stonehenge is Salisbury)

Nearest train station to Shaftesbury is Gillingham, Dorset. Trains from Waterloo station to Gillingham run about once every hour and the journey time takes 2 hours.

Frames Rickards' guided coach tour to Stonehenge, Salisbury and Bath (page 241).

A few miles south lies **Salisbury**, dominated by **Salisbury Cathedral**, which has the tallest spire in England (404 feet, 123 metres). Constructed between 1220 and 1258, it is the only medieval cathedral in the country to be built throughout in the same early-English style. The **Chapter House** contains one of the four surviving originals of the **Magna Carta**, which defined the limitations of royal power and was sealed by King John in 1215.

The **Salisbury Festival** usually takes place during the

... Stonehenge, Salisbury & Shaftesbury

last week of May and the first week of June, with street theatre and jazz as well as classical concerts in the cathedral. There is a two-day medieval pageant in

mid-April based on the dragon-slayer, St. George. Another two-day event takes place in early September and celebrates the city's past and present. The 700-year-old Salisbury charter market takes place on

Salisbury Cathedral

Tuesdays and Thursdays in the Market Square.

Just to the north of the town is **Old Sarum Castle**, a massive Iron Age hill-fort which was successively occupied by the Romans, Saxons and Normans before becoming a major medieval settlement. There are sweeping views across south Wiltshire from the ramparts. *(Old Sarum Castle ☎ 01722-335398. Apr-Sep: Mon-Sun: 10am-6pm. Oct: Mon-Sun: 10am-dusk. Nov-Mar: Mon-Sun: 10am-4pm. Adult £1.90, child £1, senior £1.40, student £1.40.)*

Twenty miles west of Salisbury lies the picturesque hill-top town of **Shaftesbury**. This is the northern tip of Dorset, the beautiful green county in which Victorian novelist Thomas Hardy lived and where he set most of his books.

Shaftesbury, known as 'Shaston' in Hardy's Wessex, is best known for the amazingly steep, pretty cobbled street Gold Hill.

Gold Hill - Shaftesbury

King Alfred the Great recognised the strategic value of Shaftesbury's location on a 700-foot (210-metre) promontory, and it was here in the 9th century that he founded an abbey for his daughter. She was its first abbess and it became the wealthiest Benedictine nunnery in England. The abbey ruins and a museum with Saxon and Norman artefacts can be visited on Park Walk. There are splendid views across Blackmore Vale from Park Walk and Castle Hill.

VISITOR INFORMATION

Shaftesbury Tourist Information Centre
8 Bell Street
Shaftesbury
Dorset SP7 8AE
☎ 01747-853514

Cambridge

The majestic colleges of Cambridge University line the banks of the River Cam, creating the famous **'backs'**.

The city is largely turned over to tourism in July and August, but during term time the presence of thousands of students creates an atmosphere of youthful energy and intellectual endeavour.

The origins of Cambridge date back to the Iron Age, when a Belgic tribe settled in the area, because it was the most reliable place to ford the Cam. The Romans, Saxons and Normans all built settlements prior to the first scholars arriving in 1209. The oldest surviving college, Peterhouse, was founded by the Bishop of Ely in 1284.

Trinity College

Henry VI founded the grandest of the colleges, **King's College**, with its world-famous chapel containing Rubens' *Adoration of the Magi*, in 1441. The college occupied nearly a quarter of the medieval city. Henry VIII combined two colleges to form **Trinity**, which has the largest court and a magnificent library by Sir Christopher Wren. Other Wren buildings include the chapels of **Pembroke College** and **Emmanuel College**. The latter contains a plaque commemorating John Harvard, a former student who sailed to America on the *Mayflower* in 1636 and gave his name to Harvard University.

The colleges are private, but they allow visitors to walk through the courts, visit the chapels and, in some cases, the libraries and halls. Walking on lawns is not allowed. Some colleges, including King's and Queens', charge an admission fee. Most colleges are closed for examinations from mid-April to late June.

GETTING THERE

By train from King's Cross. Services run three times every hour and the journey takes about 1 hour.

REFLECTIONS

'Oxford is on the whole more attractive than Cambridge to the ordinary visitor; and the traveller is therefore recommended to visit Cambridge first, or to omit it altogether if he cannot visit both.' – *Great Britain*, Karl Baedeker (1887)

Punting on the Cam

There are plenty of pretty towns and villages and interesting places to visit near Cambridge. They include **Ely Cathedral**, **Bury St. Edmunds**, and the stately homes of **Audley End**, **Anglesey Abbey** and **Wimpole Hall**. The surrounding, amazingly flat countryside, known as **the Fens**, often has spectacular skies and sunsets.

Canterbury

Every day, thousands of tourists follow in the footsteps of Chaucer's pilgrims to the quaint cathedral city of Canterbury.

Canterbury Cathedral

St. Augustine and a band of 40 missionary monks arrived in Canterbury in the spring of 597, sent from Rome to bring Christianity to the British. By Christmas, Augustine had converted King Ethelbert and 10,000 of his subjects. Their first church, **St. Martin's**, is still in use and is England's oldest parish church.

Within the city's surviving Roman walls is the Norman **Cathedral**, built on the foundations of an earlier cathedral established by St. Augustine. The present cathedral has a shrine to the 12th-century Archbishop of Canterbury, Thomas à Becket. He was murdered in 1170 in the north-west transept. The killers were responding to Henry II's impetuously voiced wish to be rid of "this turbulent priest". Becket was canonised three years later and Henry did public penance at his tomb. *(Canterbury Cathedral, ☎ 01227-762862. Easter-Sep: Mon-Fri: 9am-7pm. Oct-Easter: Mon-Sun: 9am-5pm. The Crypt: Mon-Sat: 10am-4.30pm. Sun: 12.30pm-2.30pm, 4.30pm-5.30pm. Adult £2.50, child £1.50 (under school age free), senior £1.50, student £1.50.)*

Al fresco dining in Canterbury

Augustine also established a monastery, which became the country's most important seat of learning and was renamed St. Augustine's Abbey in 978. The oldest public school in England, **King's School**, grew out of the Abbey and still occupies part of the site of the original buildings. You can visit the ruins of the Abbey, which contain tombs of Saxon saints and kings, and a new interpretation centre. There is an entry fee.

The **Canterbury Tales** is a visitor attraction based on Chaucer's literary classic. You walk past life-size reconstructions from the tales, accompanied by a recorded commentary.

Canterbury is only a few miles from the pretty seaside towns of **Whitstable** and **Herne Bay**. The fairy-tale **Leeds Castle** *(☎ 01622-765400)* is also nearby.

VISITOR INFORMATION

Canterbury Visitor Information Centre
34 St. Margaret's Street
Canterbury
Kent CT1 2TG
☎ 01227-766567

GETTING THERE

By train from Victoria Station to Canterbury East. Services run twice an hour and the journey takes 1½ hours.

Frames Rickards' guided coach tour to Leeds Castle and Canterbury (page 241).

REFLECTIONS

'Wel nine and twenty in a companye, / Of sondry folk, by aventure yfalle / In felawship, and pilgrimes were they alle / That toward Caunterbury wolden ryde.' – *The Canterbury Tales*, Geoffrey Chaucer (1387)

Stratford and Warwick Castle

VISITOR INFORMATION

Bridgefoot
Stratford-upon-Avon
Warwickshire
CV37 6GW
☎ 01789-293127

INSIDER'S TIP

There are admission charges to each property or you can buy a combined ticket covering them all.

River Avon

GETTING THERE

By train to Stratford from Paddington station. Services run once every 2 hours and the journey takes 2¼ hours.

By train to Warwick from Marylebone station. Services run once every hour and the journey takes 1¾ hours.

Frames Rickards' guided coach tour to Oxford, Stratford and Warwick Castle (page 243)

Stratford-upon-Avon is the birthplace of William Shakespeare and home of the **Royal Shakespeare Company** (RSC). The RSC has three theatres, which concentrate on the bard's plays, but also show other works.

Shakepeare's birthplace

The Shakespeare Properties are the five historic houses in, or near, Stratford that are connected with the playwright and his family. **Shakespeare's Birthplace** has an exhibition devoted to his 'Life and Background', reconstructed wattle-and-daub walls, plus a traditional English garden. The signatures of several famous visitors are etched in the window panes.

Nash's House, owned by Thomas Nash, who married Shakespeare's granddaughter Elizabeth Hall, has a display of 17th-century furnishings. Outside is **New Place**, the site of the house where Shakespeare lived from 1597 until his death in 1616. **Hall's Croft**, home of Dr. John Hall, who married Shakespeare's daughter Susanna, has an exhibition about Elizabethan/Jacobean medicine.

There are two Shakespeare houses in villages outside Stratford. **Anne Hathaway's Cottage** in Shottery is where Shakespeare came to court his future wife, Anne. A little further from Stratford is **Mary Arden's House**, believed to be the home of Shakespeare's mother, before she married John Shakespeare. The timbered Tudor farmhouse is devoted to agricultural history, with regular displays of falconry.

Warwick Castle

Warwick Castle, eight miles from Stratford, is perhaps Britain's finest medieval castle, with gardens landscaped by 'Capability' Brown. There is an exhibition of medieval life, a dungeon and torture chamber, plus regular battle re-enactments. *(Warwick Castle, ☎ 01926-406600. Mon-Sun: 10am-5pm. Adult £8.95, child (4-16) £5.40, senior £6.40, student £8.95, family £25.)*

Tour 1: London's West End

Adult £20, child £16
London for less discount: 20%
(when booked on ☎ 0171-837-3111)

Mon-Sun:
8.45am-12noon

This guided tour takes you past many of the famous sights of London's West End. You travel along elegant streets and see its Royal Parks and famous buildings.

The day begins with a visit to Westminster Abbey, the setting for state occasions and resting place to many of the country's heroes.

You travel past Downing Street to see the Changing of the Guard at Buckingham Palace. The tour ends in Trafalgar Square.

Trafalgar Square

HIGHLIGHTS

Drive through the
West End
Westminster Abbey
Changing of the Guard

 # Tour 2: City & Tower of London

Adult £29.50, child £25.50
London for less discount: 20%
(when booked on ☎ 0171-837-3111)

Mon-Sun:
1.45pm-5.45pm

On this tour you travel through the City of London, the most ancient part of London and Europe's financial centre.

You see the Bank of England, the Stock Exchange, the Mansion House (home of the Lord Mayor of London) and the Monument to the Great Fire of London.

Visit St. Paul's Cathedral and then the Tower of London, where you see the Crown Jewels and meet the famous Beefeaters, the guardians of the Tower.

Tower of London

HIGHLIGHTS

Drive through the City
St. Paul's Cathedral
Tower of London

 # Tour 3: London Panoramic Tour

Adult £14, child £10
London for less discount: 20%
(when booked on ☎ 0171-837-3111)

Mon-Sun:
8.45am-10.45am

Take a panoramic drive around the City of London and the West End, taking in all of the highlights while listening to a lively commentary.

Starting in the City, you see the Lord Mayor's Mansion House, Tower Bridge, the Tower of London and St. Paul's Cathedral.

You have excellent views over three of London's Bridges and, in the West End, you see Big Ben, Buckingham Palace and all the other big attractions.

Houses of Parliament

HIGHLIGHTS

Guided coach tour
through London

Tour BP: Buckingham Palace

Aug-Sep (only): Mon-Sun:	Mornings £31.50, Afternoons £33.50
Tour BP1: 8.45am-1.15pm	*London for less* discount: 20%
Tour BP2: 1.30pm-5.30pm	(when booked on ☎ 0171-837-3111)

Buckingham Palace is open to the public in August and September. Frames Rickards offers two tours that guarantee admission to this popular attraction.

The morning tour includes a guided coach tour of the West End, followed by a visit to watch the Changing of the Guard. You finish with a tour around the Palace.

The afternoon tour includes a short river cruise, followed by a panoramic tour of the City of London and a visit to the Palace.

Buckingham Palace

HIGHLIGHTS

Guided tour of West End
Changing of the Guard
Palace State Apartments

Tour 7: London River Cruise

Sun (only):	Adult £39, Child £35
8.45am-2.45pm	*London for less* discount: 20%
	(when booked on ☎ 0171-837-3111)

See the sights of London on this guided tour. Drive through the City of London and admire Tower Bridge, St. Paul's Cathedral and the Tower of London.

Listen to the fascinating commentary and stop for photo opportunities in front of famous buildings from London's rich past.

Following the panoramic tour, you take a comfortable all-weather boat, cruise along the Thames and have a three-course lunch (included in the price).

River Thames

HIGHLIGHTS

Panoramic tour of London
Thames boat cruise
Lunch (included)

Tour 27: Elizabethan Banquet

Apr-Oct: Tue, Thu, Fri and Sat:	Adult £44 (Tue-Fri), £46 (Sat)
Nov-Mar: Tue, Fri and Sat:	*London for less* discount: 20%
6.45pm-12midnight	(when booked on ☎ 0171-837-3111)

This tour takes you to the stately home of Hatfield House for an Elizabethan-style evening of feasting and entertainment.

The banquet, which is served by costumed 'serving wenches', consists of five courses of traditional English fare and includes unlimited wine and mead.

A troupe of costumed minstrels and players perform during the banquet. The specially printed menu doubles as a souvenir.

Elizabethan Banquet

HIGHLIGHTS

Elizabethan banquet
Unlimited wine
Costumed entertainers

Tour 28: Ghosts & Taverns

Adult (only): £15
London for less discount: 10%
(when booked on ☎ 0171-837-3111)

Mon, Wed, Fri and Sun
7pm-11pm

You are taken to crooked alleyways, ancient crumbling churchyards and gas-lit courtyards where your guide captures the shadows of times past.

You visit the site of a plague pit where 50,000 victims of the 1348 Black Death were buried in a gigantic mass grave.

Follow the Jack the Ripper trail and visit the sites of selected murders. Hear about the grisly details and the names of the suspects.

Haunted alleys

HIGHLIGHTS

Site of plague pit
Jack the Ripper trail
Visit to two London pubs

Tour 15: Stonehenge & Bath

Adult £47, Child £39
London for less discount: 20%
(when booked on ☎ 0171-837-3111)

Mar-Nov: Mon-Sun:
Dec-Feb: Tue, Thu, Sat and Sun:
8.45am-7pm

This tour starts with a visit to Stonehenge, the majestic circle of Bronze Age stone monoliths that stand in lonely majesty on Salisbury Plain.

Next, you are driven through Salisbury, where you can view the magnificent 13th-century cathedral, which has the tallest spire in England.

Finally to Bath, where you visit the famous Roman Baths and have time to view the rest of the charming city and to go shopping.

Pulteney Bridge

HIGHLIGHTS

Stonehenge
Salisbury
Bath

Tour 14: Leeds Castle and Canterbury

Adult £43, Child £35
London for less discount: 20%
(when booked on ☎ 0171-837-3111)

Apr-Oct: Mon-Sun:
Nov-Mar: Mon, Wed, Fri and Sun:
8.45am-6.30pm

You begin with a visit to Leeds Castle. First built in the 9th century, it is set on two small islands in the middle of a lake.

Next stop is Canterbury, home of England's most important cathedral. There is time for lunch and shopping in the area close to the cathedral.

The tour continues on to Dover, where you view the famous White Cliffs. On the way back to London, you pass through Greenwich.

Canterbury Cathedral

HIGHLIGHTS

Leeds Castle
Canterbury
Dover

Blenheim Palace

HIGHLIGHTS

Oxford
Bladon
Cotswold village
Lunch (included)
Blenheim Palace

Tour 23: Oxford and Blenheim

May-Sep: Tue, Fri and Sun   Adult £42, Child £34
8.45am-6.30pm   *London for less* discount: 20%
                            (when booked on ☎ 0171-837-3111)

First stop is the beautiful historic town of Oxford, home of the famous University. Here, you visit one of the colleges or principal buildings.

You then travel to Bladon, the burial place of Sir Winston Churchill. You have lunch (included in the price) in a beautiful Cotswold village.

Finally, the tour takes you to Blenheim Palace, the ancestral home of the Dukes of Marlborough, where you visit the State Apartments.

Leeds Castle

HIGHLIGHTS

Leeds Castle
Afternoon tea (included)

Tour 39: Leeds Castle

Apr-Oct: Fri and Sat: Adult £31, Child £27
Nov-Mar: Sat only: *London for less* discount: 20%
1pm-6.30pm   (when booked on ☎ 0171-837-3111)

Leeds Castle, England's best-preserved, oldest and most romantic medieval castle, is surrounded by 500 acres of magnificent parkland and gardens.

It was a Royal Palace for 300 years and its famous apartments were created by Henry VIII. It has a superb collection of furnishings, tapestries and art.

Afternoon tea with scones (included in the price) is served in Fairfax Hall, which has a lakeside terrace. The return journey is via Greenwich, over Tower Bridge.

Windsor Castle

HIGHLIGHTS

Windsor Castle
George's Chapel
Runnymede

Tour 5: Windsor & Runnymede

Mon, Wed-Fri and Sun: Adult £25.50, Child £21.50
Apr-Oct: 1pm-6pm   *London for less* discount: 20%
Nov-Mar: 8.45am-1.30pm   (when booked on ☎ 0171-837-3111)

Windsor Castle, the Queen's weekend residence, is the largest inhabited castle in the world. It has been a royal residence since the 11th century.

The tour starts with a guided walk through the Castle precincts, followed by a visit to the State Apartments and St. George's Chapel.

Cross the Long Walk, a three-mile avenue created by Charles II, and drive past the Field of Runnymede, where King John sealed the Magna Carta.

Tour 6: Windsor & Hampton Court

Adult £53, Child £45
London for less discount: 20%
(when booked on ☎ 0171-837-3111)

Apr-Sep: Tue-Thu, Sat and Sun
Oct-Mar: Tue, Thu, Sat and Sun
8.45am-6.30pm

The journey out of London includes a visit to Stoke Poges. Lunch (included in the price) is taken during a cruise on the River Thames to Windsor.

At Windsor Castle, there is a tour that includes the State Apartments, St. George's Chapel and the field of Runnymede, where King John sealed the Magna Carta.

The final stop is Hampton Court Palace, where you visit the State Apartments, the Tudor kitchens, the beautiful gardens and the famous maze.

Windsor Castle

HIGHLIGHTS

Stoke Poges
Windsor
Lunch cruise on
the Thames
Hampton Court

Tour 9: Oxford, Stratford & Warwick

Adult £49, Child £41
London for less discount: 20%
(when booked on ☎ 0171-837-3111)

Mar-Nov: Mon-Sun.
Dec-Feb: Mon, Wed, Fri and Sun.
8.45am-7.15pm

First stop is Oxford, the home of Britain's oldest, most beautiful and most prestigious University. A short visit is made to one of the colleges or principal buildings.

The tour moves on to Stratford-upon-Avon, the home of William Shakespeare. You visit his birthplace and a number of other buildings with which he was associated.

After a stop for lunch (included in the price), there is an opportunity for sightseeing and shopping. The tour is completed with a visit to Warwick Castle.

Christ Church, Oxford

HIGHLIGHTS

Oxford
Stratford-upon-Avon
Lunch (included)
Warwick Castle

Tour F4: English Lakes

Adult £295 (+£55 single supplement)
London for less discount: 10%
(when booked on ☎ 0171-837-3111)

Apr-Oct: Sat (only):
4 day tour
8am-6.30pm

On day 1 you visit Belvoir Castle – home of the Duke of Rutland – and Nottingham Castle. Then there is a drive through Robin Hood country.

Day 2 includes visits to Haworth in Yorkshire, home of the Brontë sisters, and to Dove Cottage, the lakeside home of poet William Wordsworth.

Day 3 is a glorious circular tour of the Lake District which includes a steamer trip. On Day 4 you visit Wedgwood on the way back to London.

The Lake District

HIGHLIGHTS

Belvoir Castle
Nottingham Castle
Lake District

Chester

HIGHLIGHTS

York
Edinburgh
Lake District
Chester
Stratford-upon-Avon

Scotland

HIGHLIGHTS

Edinburgh
Loch Lomond
Scone Palace
Lake District

Eurostar to Paris

HIGHLIGHTS

Eurostar Train
Paris sightseeing tour
Shopping in Paris

Tour F7: A Quick Look at Britain

Apr-Oct: Sat and Tue: Adult £295 (+£50 single supplement)
4 day tour *London for less* discount: 10%
8am-6.30pm (when booked on ☎ 0171-837-3111)

Day 1 takes you to the medieval city of York, where you visit the Minster on your guided walk. Later, you drive through James Herriot country *en route* to Darlington.

On day 2, you visit an Abbey and then travel to Edinburgh, where you have a guided tour of the city and visit the castle.

Day 3 begins with a drive through the Lake District, followed by a visit to Chester. On day 4, you visit Stratford-upon-Avon, before returning to London.

Tour F1: Scottish Interlude

Apr-Oct: Fri (only): Adult £295 (+£45 single supplement)
4 day tour *London for less* discount: 10%
8am-7pm (when booked on ☎ 0171-837-3111)

On day 1, you are driven to the historic town of Edinburgh. Day 2 includes a tour of Edinburgh Castle, the Royal Mile and Holyrood House Park.

On day 3, you travel to beautiful Loch Lomond, tour the hills and lochs of the Trossachs, and visit Scone Palace.

On day 4, you travel through Dumfries and Galloway to England's glorious Lake District. You return to London at approximately 7pm.

Tour 24: Paris & Channel Tunnel

May-Sep: Tue and Sat: Adult £142, Child £132
Apr-Oct: Sat only: *London for less* discount: 10%
7am-10.30pm (when booked on ☎ 0171-837-3111)

If you would like to take a day trip to Paris and experience the magic of the Channel Tunnel at the same time, this is the tour for you.

You are taken by coach to Waterloo Station, where you board a Eurostar Train that takes you in comfort under the English Channel to Paris.

In Paris, you go on a guided panoramic sightseeing tour of the city and go shopping before returning by Eurostar. You may need a Visa – please check.

Visitor Information

Calendar of Events . . .

January

London Parade, floats and aerial display. *(Jan 1. Starts at Westminster Bridge, ☎ 0181-566-8586.)*

Charles 1 Commemoration, procession. *(Jan 26, 1997. Jan 25, 1998. From St. James's Palace to Banqueting House, ☎ 0171-839-8919.)*

February

Chinese New Year celebrations. *(Feb 9, 1997. Feb 1, 1998. Chinatown, ☎ 0171-439-9805.)*

March

Oxford v Cambridge Boat Race *(Mar 29, 1997. Mar 28, 1998. The Thames, Putney to Mortlake, ☎ 0171-379-3234.)*

Chaucer Festival, music and readings. *(Mar 31, 1997. Apr 13, 1998. Southwark Cathedral, ☎ 01227-470379.)*

April

London Marathon *(2nd or 3rd weekend in April Greenwich to Westminster, ☎ 0171-620-4117.)*

Notting Hill Carnival (August)

May

Canalway Cavalcade, boat pageant. *(May 3-5, 1997. May 2-4, 1998. Little Venice, ☎ 0171-586-2556.)*

Chelsea Flower Show *(May 20-23, 1997. May 19-22, 1998. Chelsea Royal Hospital, ☎ 0171-630-7422.)*

FA Cup Final, England's biggest soccer game. *(May 17, 1997. May 16, 1998. Wembley Stadium, ☎ 0181-902-8833.)*

June

Covent Garden Festival of Opera and Musical Arts, two-week festival of opera in shops and bars. *(May 26-Jun 7, 1997. May 25-Jun 6, 1998. ☎ 0171-405-7555.)*

Kenwood Lakeside Concerts, classical concerts with firework displays and laser shows. *(Mid Jun-early Sep: Saturdays (only). Kenwood House, Hampstead Heath, ☎ 0181-348-1286.)* See also page 206.

Trooping the Colour, military pageant to celebrate the Queen's birthday. *(2nd or 3rd week in Jun. Horse Guards Parade, Whitehall, ☎ 0171-414-2479.)*

Wimbledon Lawn Tennis Championships *(Last week of Jun, first week of Jul. All England Tennis Club, Wimbledon, ☎ 0181-946-2244.)*

Royal Ascot Week, famous horse racing week. *(3rd week of Jun. Ascot Racecourse, ☎ 01344-222111.)*

. . . Calendar of Events

The Proms classical concert series *(Jul 18-Sep 13, 1997. Jul 17-Sep 12, 1998. Royal Albert Hall, ☎ 0171-589-8212.)*

September

Royal Tournament, armed forces display. *(Jul 15-27, 1997. Jul 21-Aug 2, 1998. Earl's Court, ☎ 0171-373-8141.)*

Hampton Court Flower Show *(Jul 10-13, 1997. Jul 8-12, 1998. Hampton Court Palace, ☎ 0181-781-9500.)* See pages 212-213.

Riding Horse Parade, equestrian competition. *(Aug 3, 1997. Aug 2, 1998. Rotten Row, Hyde Park.)*

August

Notting Hill Carnival (page 181), live music and a million revellers. *(Aug 24-25, 1997. Aug 30-31, 1998. Notting Hill and Ladbroke Grove area, ☎ 0181-964-0544.)*

London Open House Weekend, hundreds of buildings not normally seen are opened free of charge. *(Sep 20-21, 1997. 3rd or 4th weekend of Sep, 1998. ☎ 0181-347-6007.)*

September

Great River Race, 250 oared boats race from Richmond to the Isle of Dogs. *(12.20pm start. Sep 27, 1997. Sep 5, 1998. ☎ 0181-398-9057.)*

Punch and Judy Festival, traditional English puppeteers. *(Oct 5, 1997. Oct 4, 1998. Covent Garden, ☎ 0171-405-7555.)*

October

Pearly Harvest Festival, 100 Pearly Kings and Queens in costume. *(Oct 5, 1997. Oct 4, 1998. St. Martin-in-the-Fields, Trafalgar Square, ☎ 0171-930-0089.)*

Opening of Parliament, Queen Elizabeth rides in procession to the Houses of Parliament. *(Oct of each year, in-between election years. ☎ 0171-219-4272.)*

Horse of the Year Show *(1st week in Oct. Wembley Arena, ☎ 0181-902-8833.)*

Lord Mayor's Show (November)

Bonfire / Guy Fawkes Night, fireworks displays and bonfires all over London to mark the anniversary of the Gunpowder Plot to blow up Parliament in 1605. *(Nov 5).*

November

London to Brighton Rally, veteran car event. *(Nov 2, 1997. Nov 1, 1998. ☎ 01753-681-736.)*

Lord Mayor's Show, procession through the City to inaugurate new Lord Mayor. *(Nov 8, 1997. Nov 14, 1998. ☎ 0171 332-3456.)*

Remembrance Sunday, royal family attend outdoor service on Whitehall for war dead. *(Nov 9, 1997. Nov 8, 1998. Whitehall, ☎ 0171-730-3488.)*

Children's London . . .

INSIDER'S TIP

Try to avoid school holidays (Christmas, Easter, mid-June to early September) when queues can be horrendous.

London Toy and Model Museum

Rowing on the Serpentine in Hyde Park

Attractions – Many of the attractions in this book are ideal places for keeping children entertained, especially London Zoo (page 193), London Dungeon (not recommended for under eights) (page 155), Madame Tussaud's (pages 168-169), London Planetarium (page 170), the Science Museum (page 115), Natural History Museum (page 116), the Cutty Sark (page 210) and the virtual reality thrills of Segaworld and the other attractions at the Trocadero (page 72).

A wax model at Madame Tussaud's

Children's museums – such as The London Toy and Model Museum (page 182) and Pollock's Toy Museum (page 173) are custom-designed for kids. The Bethnal Green Museum of Childhood *(Bethnal Green tube station, Cambridge Heath Road, ☎ 0181-980-2415)* has an enormous collection of both antique and recent toys. The collection of dolls and dolls houses is worth the trip alone, though there are also displays of soldiers, model trains and planes, and a showcase of children's clothing over the centuries. The Cabaret Mechanical Theatre *(33-34 The Market, Covent Garden Piazza, ☎ 0171-379-7961)* has 100 hand-carved mechanical models operated by pushing buttons. It is especially popular with under fives.

London Planetarium

Parks and Playgrounds – All the big London parks have children's playgrounds, most with modern climbing frames and soft surfaces. There is a large and very popular playground at the northern end of Kensington Gardens. Rowing on the lakes in Regent's Park (page 192) or Hyde Park (page 188) is a traditional English family outing.

Cinemas – Whiteley's (page 184) has an eight-screen cinema, popular with children because of the variety of restaurants and film selections favouring family viewing. Both the Barbican (page 198) and National Film Theatre (page 153) have special children's

. . . Children's London

programmes.

Theatre – The Unicorn Theatre for Children *(6-7 Great Newport Street, ☎ 0171-836-3334)* is the only theatre in the West End especially for young audiences.

Zoos – Apart from London Zoo (page 193), there is a children's zoo in Battersea Park (a five-minute train ride from Victoria to Battersea Park), with pot-bellied pigs, monkeys and plenty of domesticated animals children can touch.

Shopping – Apart from the toy superstore Hamleys (page 89), try Beatties *(202 High Holborn, ☎ 0171-405-6285)* for model railways and radio-controlled toys; the

Early Learning Centre *(225 Kensington High Street, ☎ 0171-937-0419)* for small children; or Warner Bros Studio Store *(178-182 Regent Street, ☎ 0171-434-3334)* with its merchandise and computerised cartoon colouring station.

Restaurants – A great place to have lunch with children at the weekend is at one of the Smollenskys restaurants (pages 88 and 105; discount).

London Zoo

Theme Parks – There are several theme parks on the outskirts of London, each about an hour's journey by public transport. Legoland Windsor, a model town created out of plastic lego building bricks *(☎ 0990-040404)* opened in 1996 and is popular with young children. Thorpe Park *(☎ 01932-562-633)* is a water-fun theme park, where Diana, Princess of Wales, sometimes takes the young princes, has a beach and bathing lake plus thrilling rides like Logger's Leap. Chessington World of Adventures *(☎ 01372-727227)* has nine theme 'lands' and 15 rides including the Vampire roller coaster. Expect long queues.

The **Changing of the Guard** (page 50) at Buckingham Palace never fails to delight children and costs nothing.

Kidsline is a computerised information line with details of children's entertainment. *(☎ 0171-222-8000, term time: Mon-Fri: 4pm-6pm, school holidays: 9am-4pm.)*

Hamleys

Science Museum

Visitor Information . . .

CLIMATE

The weather in Britain can be unpredictable, which makes it a popular topic of conversation. However, it does not rain as much as many foreigners are led to believe. In fact, London has lower annual rainfall than Paris and New York and, in recent years, less than Rome. Brief showers are, however, relatively common and you might want to bring an umbrella with you. See also 'When to Go' page 16.

An umbrella shop

CUSTOMS

Import restrictions on tax/duty-free goods are: **Tobacco**: 200 cigarettes, 50 cigars; **Alcohol**: Two litres of wine, plus one litre of liquor over 22% in proof; **Perfumes**: 60cc perfume, plus 250cc of toilet water; **Other Goods (souvenirs and gifts)**: to the value of £75. There are very strict laws on bringing animals into the country, with a six-month quarantine period compulsory.

ELECTRIC CURRENT

Britain uses 240 volts (50hz) electric current with a unique, large, three-pin plug. North American electrical appliances will need a transformer and an adaptor. Australasian and European appliances will only need an adaptor, which can be bought in London at airport shops and Boots, a chain of pharmacists. British hotel bathrooms nearly always contain an international two-pin electric razor socket.

EMBASSIES / CONSULATES

Australia *(Australia House, The Strand, ☎ 0171 379 4334)*; Canada *(Macdonald House, Grosvenor Square, ☎ 0171 258 6600)*; France *(21 Cromwell Road, ☎ 0171 581 5292)*; Germany *(23 Belgrave Square, ☎ 0171 235 5033)*; Ireland *(17 Grosvenor Place, ☎ 0171 235 2171)*; Japan *(101 Piccadilly, ☎ 0171 465 6500)*; New Zealand *(New Zealand House, 80 Haymarket, ☎ 0171 930 8422)*; Sweden *(11 Montagu Place, ☎ 0171 724 2101)*; United States *(Grosvenor Square, ☎ 0171 499 9000)*; Spain *(39 Chesham Place, ☎ 0171 235 5555)*; Denmark *(55 Sloane Street, ☎ 0171 333 0200)*; Norway *(25 Belgrave Square, ☎ 0171 5915500)*; Italy *(14 Three Kings Yard, ☎ 0171 312 2200)*.

EMERGENCIES

To call for an ambulance, the fire service or the police, dial ☎ 999 from any telephone (it is a free number that operates 24 hours a day).

INSIDER'S TIP

You will find additional visitor information that will be helpful before you go to London, when you arrive, and when planning your itinerary on pages 16-21.

... Visitor Information ...

Hospitals (with 24-hour casualty services) – St. Mary's Hospital *(Praed Street, Paddington, ☎ 0171-725-6666)*; University College Hospital *(Gower Street, entrance on Grafton Way, Bloomsbury, ☎ 0171-387-9300)*; Chelsea and Westminster Hospital *(369 Fulham Road, Chelsea, ☎ 0181-746-8000)*; Guys Hospital *(St. Thomas Street, entrance on Weston Street, South of the Thames, ☎ 0171-955-5000)*; St. Thomas's Hospital *(Lambeth Palace Road, South of the Thames, ☎ 0171-928-9292)*.

Chelsea & Westminster Hospital

ETIQUETTE

Smoking is now forbidden in many public places in London. You cannot smoke anywhere on the tube, on buses, in theatres nor in most cinemas. However, the majority of restaurants still have smoking sections and very few pubs have restrictions.

St. Mary's Hospital, Paddington

Londoners are renowned for their willingness to queue quietly and to apologise profusely for bumping into you in public places. A less accurate popular perception is that the British are cold and reserved. In fact, modern Londoners are friendly and easy going, particularly with foreigners. The best way to start a conversation is undoubtedly with a comment about the weather.

HEALTH AND SAFETY

Citizens of all EU countries are entitled to free National Health Service treatment. Citizens of other countries get free on-the-spot treatment at accident and emergency units at NHS hospitals, but must pay for all other medical services, including any admission to hospital wards. Health insurance is, therefore, advisable for visitors. Pharmacists can only dispense a limited range of drugs without a doctor's prescription.

London policeman

London has a well-deserved reputation as a safe city. Most police do not carry guns and violent crime is rare. However, as in any other large city, you should take care of your valuables and watch out for pickpockets, particularly in crowded areas. The London police headquarters is New Scotland Yard *(☎ 0171-230-1212)*.

Report all thefts to the police (your insurance company will probably require this) and call to cancel all credit cards (see 'Useful Numbers', page 259).

LOST PROPERTY

If you lose something on a bus or tube train, try the London Transport Lost Property Office *(200 Baker Street, ☎ 0171-486-2496. Mon-Fri: 9.30am-2pm.)*. In a

. . . Visitor Information . . .

taxi: Black Cab Lost Property Office *(15 Penton Street,* ☎ *0171-833-0996. Mon-Fri: 9am-4pm.).* For other lost property, try your nearest police station.

LUGGAGE STORAGE

Major London train stations have left luggage facilities: Charing Cross *(Mon-Sun: 6.30am-10.30pm)*; Euston *(Mon-Sun: 24 hour)*, Paddington *(Mon-Sun: 7am-midnight)*, Victoria *(Mon-Sun: 7.15am-10pm)* and Waterloo *(Mon-Sat: 6.30am-11pm. Sun: closed).*

MARKETS

London's markets are famous both for their atmosphere and the bargains you can find. The three most famous markets are:

A post box

Portobello Market (page 183) – London's renowned antiques market. Second-hand clothes and all kinds of bizarre goods are sold from a mile-long stretch of stalls. *(Portobello Road. Notting Hill Gate or Ladbroke Grove tube stations. Sat: 8am-5pm.)*

Camden Market – A huge market selling clothes, crafts, books, records, antiques and many other items. *(Camden High Street. Camden Town tube station. Sat-Sun: 8am-6pm.)*

Petticoat Lane Market – Cheap fashion goods, odds and ends. *(Middlesex Street. Liverpool Street tube station. Sun: 9am-2pm.)*

MAIL / POST

You can purchase stamps from post offices and from most newsagents. Letters and cards can be mailed at post offices or post boxes (painted red). Post offices are generally open Mon-Fri: 9am-5.30pm, Sat: 9am-12.30pm.

MEDIA

Listings – The best way to find out what's happening in London is to buy *Time Out*, a magazine that comes out on Wednesdays. It contains full listings for all London cinemas, theatres, clubs and many other forms of entertainment. *The Evening Standard* newspaper (Mon-Fri) prints listings, but they are less comprehensive.

Main post office close to Trafalgar Square

Newspapers – A higher percentage of people reads a daily newspaper in the UK than in any other country. Newspapers are either tabloids, which are small in size and often frivolous, or broadsheets, like *The Daily Telegraph* and *The Times*, which are larger and more

... Visitor Information ...

serious.

Radio - London has many radio stations catering for

different tastes. The main ones are Capital Radio and BBC Greater London Radio (GLR). There are several national stations, including Radio 1 for pop music, Radio 2 for easy listening, Radio 3 for classical music, Radio 4 for current affairs, Radio 5 for sport and news and Classic FM for popular classical music.

A newspaper seller

Television – There are five national terrestrial channels: BBC1, BBC2, ITV, Channel Four and Channel 5. Many hotels have cable TV with dedicated sports and movie channels.

MONEY

Currency – The British currency is the pound sterling (£). There are 100 pence (p) in one pound. Coins come in denominations of 1p, 2p, 5p, 10p, 20p, 50p, £1 and, from November 1997, £2. Notes are in denominations of £5, £10, £20 and £50. You may find £50 notes hard to change and they will always be checked for forgery.

Money changing – You can change money at banks or at bureaux de change. Although bureaux de change stay open longer hours, they sometimes charge much higher commissions (transaction fees). With the *London for less* vouchers on page 283, you pay no transaction fee at Travelex/Mutual of Omaha outlets listed in the margin.

NATIONAL HOLIDAYS

Known as Bank Holidays, because the banks are closed, most shops and attractions remain open except on Christmas Day and Boxing Day. If in doubt, please check.

New Year's Day	*Jan 1*
Good Friday	*Mar 28 (1997) / Apr 10 (1998)*
Easter Monday	*Mar 31 (1997) / Apr 13 (1998)*
May Day Holiday	*May 5 (1997) / May 4 (1998)*
Spring Bank Holiday	*May 26 (1997) / May 25 (1998)*
Summer Bank Holiday	*Aug 25 (1997) / Aug 31 (1998)*
Christmas Day	*Dec 25*
Boxing Day	*Dec 26 (1997) / Dec 28 (1998)*

TRAVELEX / MUTUAL OF OMAHA LOCATIONS

US airports:
Atlanta, Baltimore, Boston, Cleveland, Columbus, Detroit, Fort Lauderdale, Indianapolis, JFK (all terminals), La Guardia, Las Vegas, Los Angeles (all terminals), Memphis, Minneapolis, New Orleans, Newark, Norfolk (Virginia), Omaha, Ontario (California), Palm Springs, Pittsburgh, Portland (Oregon), San Diego, San Francisco, Tampa.

Heathrow:
Terminal 2 - airside arrivals (baggage reclaim), arrivals, departures.
Terminal 3 - airside arrivals (baggage reclaim), arrivals, departures, airside departures.
Terminal 4 - airside arrivals, arrivals, departures, airside departures.

Gatwick:
South terminal - airside arrivals, arrivals, departures.
North terminal - arrivals, The Avenue shopping arcade, airside departures.

Central London:
142 Southampton Row. 9 Russell Square. Royal National Hotel, Bedford Way. Imperial President Hotel, Russell Square. Tower of London.

. . . Visitor Information . . .

OPENING HOURS

Banks – Opening times vary. Generally, banks are open Mon-Fri: 9.30am-3.30pm, but a few stay open until 4.30pm. Some branches are open on Saturday mornings. Most banks have 24-hour cash machines, from which money can be withdrawn using credit or debit cards.

A traditional London pub

Bars, pubs and restaurants – The establishments offering discounts in this guide have their opening hours stated. The law requires a special licence for the sale of alcohol after 11pm (see page 200 for late-night bars and night clubs).

Shops – The establishments offering discounts in this guide have their opening hours stated in their entry. In general, shops are open Mon-Sat: 10am-6pm. Some shops also open on Sundays.

Sundays – Traditionally, Sunday is the day that London rests. Many Londoners leave the city at the weekend and some areas (notably the City) are almost totally deserted. However, most of the big attractions open as normal on Sundays and, although many shops close, markets such as Camden (page 252) are very busy. West End Theatres are closed on Sunday evenings.

St. Paul's Cathedral

PUB LUNCHES

Many London pubs serve cheap and cheerful lunches, usually offering traditional dishes such as Shepherd's Pie, Steak and Kidney Pie and Rhubarb Crumble. The typical pub lunch is served from 12noon to 2pm and costs about £5.

RELIGIOUS SERVICES

To find a religious service close to you, ring the relevant contact listed below.

Westminster Cathedral

Baptist *(London Baptist Association, 1 Merchant Street, ☎ 0181-980-6818)*; Buddhist *(The Buddhist Society, 58 Eccleston Square, ☎ 0171-834-5858)*; Church of England (Anglican) *(St. Paul's Cathedral, ☎ 0171-248-2705)*; Jewish *(Liberal Jewish Synagogue, 28 St. John's Wood Road, ☎ 0171-286-5181, or United Synagogue (orthodox), Woburn House, Tavistock Square, ☎ 0171-387-4300)*; Moslem *(Islamic Cultural Centre, 146 Park Road, ☎ 0171-724-3363)*; Roman Catholic *(Westminster Cathedral, Victoria Street, ☎ 0171-798-9055)*.

SPECIAL TRAVELLERS

Disabled – Many London museums, restaurants and

. . . Visitor Information . . .

hotels have wheelchair ramps. Artsline (☎ 0171-388-2227) provides information about access to arts and events for the disabled.

Elderly – Concessions are usually available for senior citizens (women 60-plus and men 65-plus), but they may not always be advertised, so be sure to ask. You can obtain *London for less* discounts, on top of senior discounts, at most major attractions.

Westminster Cathedral

Students – An International Student Identity Card is needed to obtain student concessions. For the cheapest accommodation, join the International Youth Hostel Federation. STA Travel *(86 Old Brompton Road, ☎ 0171-361-6161 for European flights, ☎ 0171-361-6262 for worldwide flights)* specialises in discount fares for those under the age of 26 and students. Council Travel *(28A Poland Street, ☎ 0171-287-3337)* is America's largest student/youth travel group, with a London office near Oxford Circus. You can obtain *London for less* discounts, on top of student discounts, at most major attractions.

Lord's Cricket Ground

Gay – The Lesbian and Gay Switchboard (☎ 0171-837-6768) is a 24-hour helpline providing information on gay-related activities in London.

SPORT

Soccer or football is the most popular spectator sport in England, though cricket, rugby, golf, athletics and tennis events also attract huge crowds.

American Football – The London Monarchs (☎ 0171-629-1300) play teams from the US and Europe at Wembley (☎ 0891-888-777) in March and April. Two top US teams compete in the NFL Bowl at Wembley in August.

Wembley Stadium

Athletics – There are usually a couple of major meetings every year at Crystal Palace stadium in south London (☎ 0181-778-0131). Athletes can train free at West London Stadium and Regent's Park.

Cricket – International matches are played in summer at two London grounds, Lord's (☎ 0171-289-8979) and the Oval (☎ 0171-582-6660).

Football – The season runs from Aug-May. The main London clubs are Arsenal and Tottenham (north London), Chelsea and Queen's Park Rangers (west London), Crystal Palace and Wimbledon (south London) and West Ham (east London). Tickets are available on the day for most matches.

Oval Cricket Ground

. . . Visitor Information . . .

Golf – Greater London has dozens of golf courses, though you will have to travel a few miles out of the centre of the city. There are popular public courses at Hounslow Heath (☎ *0181-570-5271*) and Richmond Park (☎ *0181-876-3205*).

Rugby – International matches are played during the season (Sep-Apr) at Twickenham (☎ *0181-979-2427*).

Wimbledon

Swimming – There are dozens of pools in London, with good ones at Chelsea Sports Centre (☎ *0171-352-6985*) and Porchester Baths (☎ *0171-792-2919*). For hardy, outdoor swimmers, there are lakes on Hampstead Heath and in Hyde Park that you can swim in.

Tennis – London has hundreds of tennis courts in public parks, including Holland Park and Parliament Hill. The Wimbledon Lawn Tennis Championships are held in late June/early July *(All England Lawn Tennis Association,* ☎ *0181-946-2244)*.

Working Out – Most sports centres and large hotels have multi-gyms.

TAXES

Value Added Tax (VAT) is a sales tax of 17.5% levied on most goods (exceptions include books, food and children's clothes). VAT is included in the marked price so you will not notice that you are paying it.

Afternoon tea at the Dorchester

If you are resident outside the European Union (EU) and are staying in Britain less than three months, you can reclaim VAT on any goods that you take home with you. To do so, you must take your passport when you go shopping and complete a form in the store. When you leave the country you must give a copy to customs at the airport. Usually they will ask to see the goods so you should pack them in your hand luggage. The tax refund is later returned to you, usually either by cheque or by credit card refund. If you have the goods shipped home, the VAT should be deducted before you pay. Most major London stores, such as Harrods, Harvey Nichols and Liberty, are used to dealing with customers requiring VAT-exemption.

TEA (AFTERNOON TEA)

Many visitors to Britain will be disappointed to learn that the English now drink more coffee than tea. Nevertheless, the tradition of afternoon tea is alive and well. The best place to take afternoon tea is in one of the large, luxury hotels or department stores, most of which are located in Mayfair. Here is a selection of

. . . Visitor Information . . .

recommended places, most of which require
reservations and will refuse admission if you are
wearing jeans or sports shoes:

Claridges *(Brook Street, ☎ 0171-629-8860. Mon-Sun:
3pm-5.30pm. £16.50.)*; **Fortnum and Mason** *(181
Piccadilly, ☎ 0171-734-8040. Mon-Sat: 3pm-5.15pm.
Sun: closed. Reservations not accepted*; **Ritz** *(Piccadilly,
☎ 0171-493-8181. Mon-Sun: 2pm-5.30pm. £21.00.)*;
Waldorf *(Aldwych, ☎ 0171-836-2400. Mon-Fri: 3.30pm-
6pm. £15-18. Tea dances Sat-Sun: 3.30pm-6pm. £22-25.)*

The Ritz Hotel

TELEPHONES

Your *London for less* card gives you instant access to
an inexpensive telephone service. It can be used for
both international and domestic calls from any
telephone box or hotel phone (page 8).

For calls made without *London for less*, dial 100 to
reach the operator, 155 for the international
operator. For directory inquiries dial 192. Within
London, there are two codes: 0171 for inner London,
0181 for outer London.

TIPPING

Restaurants – Many restaurants include a service
charge in the bill. When this is included, you are not
expected to tip. When a service charge is not
included, it is normal to tip 10-15%. We recommend
you consider tipping 15-20% on any *London for less*
discounted meal price, to ensure that the tip is not
discounted too.

Relaxing in a London pub

Pubs / bars – It is not normal to tip in London pubs,
although the habit is creeping in at certain
fashionable bars.

Taxis and hairdressers – The standard tip is 10-15%.

Porters – Tip 50p-£1 per suitcase, depending on size
and how far it is carried.

TOILETS

Public toilets may be marked as 'Public
Conveniences', 'WCs' or 'Lavatories'. Most charge 10p
or 20p. When sightseeing, museums, hotels,
department stores and restaurants are your best bet. If
you require directions, you should ask for the toilets.
In England, 'bathrooms' are places where people have
baths and the term 'restroom' might not be
understood.

*Victoria Tourist
Information Centre*

TOURIST INFORMATION

The two largest Tourist Information Centres (TICs) are

. . . Visitor Information . . .

*Regent Street Tourist
Information Centre*

the London TIC, in the forecourt of Victoria Railway Station, and the British Travel Centre on Lower Regent Street (just south of Piccadilly Circus). Smaller TICs can be found at Heathrow Airport (Terminals 1,2,3) and Liverpool Street Station.

TRAVELLING IN LONDON

Public transportation – The easiest way to get around London is on the **Tube** (subway/underground train), with trains every 3-10 minutes depending on the time of day. **Buses**, especially the upper decks of double-deckers, are a good way of seeing famous buildings and landmarks but take longer and get caught in London's infamous traffic snarl-ups.

Daily or weekly Travelcards offer unlimited travel on tubes, buses and trains and can be bought at any tube station. The daily card covering zones 1 and 2 (a large

The London Underground (the 'Tube')

area around the centre) costs £3, is ideal for the short stay visitor but is not valid before 9.30am. The weekend Travelcard, covering Saturday and Sunday, costs £4.50 for zones 1 and 2 and is valid all day, including before 9.30am. For information on bus and tube routes, times and possible delays, call the Travel Information line ☎ 0171-222-1234 (24hrs).

Taxi – London's metered Black Cabs, with their famous bowler-hat style shape, are clean and reliable though rather expensive. Expect to pay at least £5 for a short ride. You can hail these cabs, which display illuminated 'For Hire' roof signs when they are available. Minicabs, which must be booked by telephone, are less reliable than black cabs but are generally cheaper.

Car – Driving in central London is not recommended. Even if you know the route to your destination, prepare for heavy traffic. Parking can be even more of a problem. Cars left on yellow lines or in residents' permit areas will be swiftly clamped or impounded, with £50-150 release charges. Parking meters and car parks are difficult to find and expensive.

TRAVELLING OUTSIDE LONDON

See 'Beyond London', pages 220-221.

TRAVELLING TO THE REST OF EUROPE

Crossing the channel to France is quick and easy. You have a choice of around 20 ferry and hovercraft routes, in addition to the Channel Tunnel rail link.

INSIDER'S TIP

For more information about getting around in London see page 19.

. . . Visitor Information . . .

There are ports all along the south coast of England, but the shortest crossing is at Dover. All the main ports are linked by rail to either London Victoria or London Waterloo.

Eurostar (☎ 0345-303030) runs trains from Waterloo International Station through the Channel Tunnel to Paris and Brussels. Motorists can take cars on **Le Shuttle** (☎ 0990-353535) trains departing from the Channel Tunnel entrance at Folkestone.

Frames Rickards offers cheap day trips to Paris on Eurostar trains (page 244).

USEFUL TELEPHONE NUMBERS

Emergencies – Dial ☎ 999 for ambulance, fire or police.

Eurostar to Paris

Artsline – Information about access to arts events for disabled people (☎ 0171-388-2227).

Railway information – (☎ 0345-484-950).

Capital Radio Helpline – General advice on London life (☎ 0171-484-4000).

Lost credit cards – American Express (☎ 01273-696-933); Visa (☎ 01604-230-230); Mastercard (☎ 01702-362-988); Diners Club (☎ 01252-516-261).

Emergency Dental Care – (☎ 0171-937-3951).

English Heritage – Information about the many historic buildings they look after (☎ 0171-973-3000).

London Transport – 24-hour information line (☎ 0171-222-1234).

National Car Parks – Information about car parks in your area (☎ 0171-499-7050).

National Trust – Information about its historic properties and gardens in London (☎ 0171-222-9251).

Sportsline – Information about sporting activities (☎ 0171-222-8000).

Time – Dial ☎ 123 for the 24-hour speaking clock.

WEIGHTS, MEASURES & CLOTHING SIZES

Britain uses both the imperial and the metric system.

Clothing sizes – In London, some clothes and shoes are sold in UK sizes and others in European sizes. To convert American women's clothing sizes to British, add 2 (e.g. an American size 8 is a British 10), for shoes, subtract 2 (e.g. an American 8 is a British 6). Men's suit and shirt sizes are the same in Britain and America, but shoes are ½ size bigger in America (e.g. an American 10 is a British 9½).

INSIDER'S TIP

To convert from Celsius to Fahrenheit, multiply the number by 9, divide by 5 and add 32.

To convert from Fahrenheit to Celsius, subtract 32, multiply by 5 and divide by 9.

Index of Discounters . . .

ART GALLERIES, ATTRACTIONS AND MUSEUMS

Apsley House	189	RP
Bankside Gallery	157-158	SR
Banqueting House	58	WM
Bramah Tea and Coffee Museum	156	SR
Britain at War Experience	156	SR
British Museum	166-167	BL
Cabinet War Rooms	59	WM
Chiswick House	218	GL
Cutty Sark	210	GL
Dickens House	172	BL
Dr. Johnson's House	143-144	CY
Dulwich Picture Gallery	218	GL
Florence Nightingale Museum	158	SR
Freud Museum	217	GL
Guards Museum	62	WM
Hampton Court Palace	212-213	GL
House of Detention	143	CY
Institute of Contemporary Arts (ICA)	63	WM
Jewel Tower	61	WM
Jewish Museum	217	GL
Kensington Palace	191	RP
Kew Gardens	216	GL
London Brass Rubbing Centre	80	WE
London Dungeon	155	SR
London Planetarium	170	BL
London Toy & Model Museum	182	BA
London Zoo	193	RP
Madame Tussaud's	168-169	BL
National Portrait Gallery	78-79	WE
Pollock's Toy Museum	173-174	BL
Ranger's House	217	GL
Shakespeare's Globe Theatre	154	SR
Showscan's Emaginator	72	WE
St. Paul's Cathedral	136-137	CY
Tate Gallery	56-57	WM
Theatre Museum	77-78	WE
Tower Bridge Experience	141	CY
Tower Hill Pageant	140	CY
Tower of London	138-139	CY
Westminster Abbey Chapter House	53	WM
Wimbledon Tennis Museum	218	GL

PERFORMING ARTS

Almeida	203	Theatre
BBC Symphony Orchestra	204	Orchestra
English National Opera	202	Opera
London Philharmonic	204	Orchestra
Philharmonia	204	Orchestra
Royal Ballet	203	Ballet
Royal Court Theatre	203	Theatre
Royal Opera	203	Opera
Royal Shakespeare Company	202	Theatre
West End Shows	202	Theatre

. . . Index of Discounters . . .

HOTELS

Adelphi Hotel ★★★	35	£££	SK
Airways Hotel ★★	33	££	WM
Albany Hotel ★★★	34	£££	SK
Amber Hotel ★★	36	£££	SK
Bailey's Hotel ★★★★	35	£££££	SK
Barkston Gardens Hotel ★★★	36	£££	SK
Beaver Hotel ★★	39	££	SK
Blakemore Hotel ★★★	46	£££	BA
Bonnington ★★★	40	£££	BL
Burns Park Hotel ★★★	37	£££	SK
Cranley ★★★	39	££££	SK
Eden Park Hotel ★★★	45	£££	BA
Euston Plaza Hotel ★★★	41	££££	BL
Flora Hotel International ★★	34	££	SK
Generator	41	£	BL
Gloucester ★★★★	38	£££££	SK
Harrington Hall Hotel ★★★	36	££££	SK
Henley House Hotel ★★★	37	£££	SK
Henry VIII Hotel ★★★	43	£££	BA
Hillgate Hotel ★★★	45	£££	BA
Holiday Inn Garden Court ★★★	41	££££	BL
Holiday Inn Kensington ★★★★	38	£££££	SK
Hotel Plaza Continental ★★★	40	££	SK
Kensington Plaza Hotel ★★★	35	£££	SK
Langham Court Hotel ★★★★	42	££££	BL
London Tourist Hotel ★★	38	££	SK
Mandeville Hotel ★★★	42	££££	BL
New Linden Hotel ★★	43	£££	BA
Norfolk Towers Hotel ★★★	46	£££	BA
Paragon Hotel ★★★	37	£££	SK
Park International Hotel ★★★	39	£££	SK
Pavilion Hotel ★★★	43	£££	BA
Prince William Hotel ★★	44	££	BA
Quality Hotel Heathrow ★★★	46	£££	GL
Queen's Park ★★★	44	£££	BA
Queensway Hotel ★★	44	££	BA
Rochester Hotel ★★★★	33	£££££	WM
Rubens Hotel ★★★	33	££££	WM
Strathmore Hotel ★★★	34	££££	SK
Town House ★★★	40	££	SK
Westminster Hotel ★★★	45	£££	BA
White Hall Hotel ★★★	42	£££££	BL

KEY TO ABBREVIATIONS

BA = Bayswater and Notting Hill
BL = Bloomsbury and Marylebone
CY = City of London
GL = Greater London
MA = Mayfair and St. James's
RP = Royal Parks

SK = South Kensington and Chelsea
SR = South of the River
WE = West End
WM = Westminster
★ = Hotel rating category (see page 32)
£ = Hotel price category (see page 32)

... Index of Discounters ...

SHOPS

... Index of Discounters ...

RESTAURANTS

. . . Index of Discounters

RESTAURANTS (CONTINUED)

Modern British	The Clivedon Room	176	BL
Modern British / Wine Bar	Carriages	65	WM
Modern British / Wine Bar	Ebury Wine Bar	64	WM
Pancake House	My Old Dutch	82	WE
Pancake House	My Old Dutch	125	SK
Pizza	Pizza Chelsea	126	SK
Pizza	Pizza Pizza	85	WE
Polish	Wodka	124	SK
Russian	Borshtch 'n' Tears	122	SK
Seafood	Wheeler's	85	WE
Tex / Mex	Chi-Chi's	185	BA
Tex / Mex	Chi-Chi's	88	WE
Tex / Mex	Los Locos	84	WE
Thai	Thai Terrace	122	SK
Traditional English	Vic Naylor's	150	CY
Wine Bar / Modern British	Carriages	65	WM
Wine Bar / Modern British	Ebury Wine Bar	64	WM

TOURS

PHOTO CREDITS

The Publishers would like to thank the following people and organizations for permission to reproduce their photographs over which they retain copyright. Any omission from this list is unintentional and every effort will be made to include these in the next edition of this publication. Debra Sweeney (principal photography), National Portrait Gallery (Andrew Putler), Westminster Cathedral 1995 Centenary Trust, Science Museum, Odeon Cinemas, Museum of the Moving Image, Stoll Moss Theatres, Royal Academy Of Arts (Martin Charles), Leighton House Museum, Golden Hinde Educational Museum, Selfridges, Tate Gallery Publishing Limited, Tate Gallery (John Webb)(Marcus Leith), *Beata Beatrix* by Dante Gabriel Rossetti, presented to the Tate Gallery by Georgiana, Baroness Mount-Temple in memory of her husband, Francis, Baron Mount-Temple 1889, *Ophelia* by John Everett Millais, present to the Tate Gallery by Sir Henry Tate 1894, Museum of London (Andy Chopping), MoLAS, Ministry of Sound, Hippodrome, National Postal Museum, London Transport Museum, National Maritime Museum, Greenwich, Café de Paris, Parliamentary Copyright, House of Commons Education Unit, Segaworld, Harrods, Hamleys of London, The Comedy Store (Jez Coulson of Insight Photography), Ronnie Scott's (David Redfern), Hard Rock Café (ID Publicity), The Savoy Group, The Dorchester Hotel, Lloyd's of London, Liberty Retail Limited, The Ritz Hotel (Ann Scott Associates), Tony Stone Worldwide, Tower Hill Pageant, The Waldorf Meridien Hotel, Victoria & Albert Museum, HMS *Belfast* (Imperial War Museum), National Army Museum, The Natural History Museum (Neal Potter Associates), London Tourist Board, Gatwick Express Limited, Eurostar (U.K.) Limited, operators of the U.K. arm of Eurostar, international high speed passenger service to Europe, Royal Collection Enterprises/Her Majesty Queen Elizabeth II, The National Gallery, Commonwealth Galleries Barbican Centre (J.P. Stankowski), South Bank Centre, Courtauld Institute Galleries, The Wallace Collection, Joe Cornish Photographer, Imperial War Museum, English Heritage, London General House, Virgin Atlantic Airways Limited, Museum of Mankind, London Docklands Development Corporation, Warner Village Cinema, London Regional Transport, Salisbury District Council (Steve Day), Southern Tourist Board (Peter Titmuss), Bath Tourism Bureau, Canterbury City Council, Warwick Castle Warwick "The finest mediaeval Castle in England", Stratford On Avon District Council, Cambridge Tourist Information, Blenheim Palace (Chris Andrews), York Tourism Bureau, Edinburgh & Lothians Tourist Board.

Customer Response Card

We would like to hear your comments about *London for less*
so that we can improve the book. Please complete
the information below and mail this card.
No stamp is required, either in Britain or overseas.

1) Name:...

2) Address:...

3) Telephone no:..

4) Where did you purchase your book?...

5) What is the reason you chose *London for less*?.......................

....

....

6) How many days were you in London?.......................................

7) Please circle discounts used:
      Attractions ~ Performing Arts ~ Tours ~ Hotels ~ Shops ~
   Restaurants ~ Nightclubs ~ Currency Exchange ~ Telephone Calls

8) What was the total of the discounts that you received? £..........

9) On a scale of 1 to 5 (where 5 is the best) how would you rate
   London for less?
            1   *2*   *3*   *4*   *5*

10) What did you like most about the book?.................................

....

....

11) What would you like to see improved?...................................

....

....

12) Any other comments...

....

....

....

....

By air mail
Par avion

IBRS/CCRI NUMBER: PHQ-D/2560/W

NE PAS AFFRANCHIR

NO STAMP REQUIRED

RESPONSE PAYEE
GRANDE-BRETAGNE

Metropolis International (UK) Limited
222 Kensal Road
LONDON
GREAT BRITAIN
W10 5BR